infants
their social environments

edited by Bernice Weissbourd, Family Focus
        Judith S. Musick, Thresholds Mothers'
        Project

National Association for the Education of Young Children
Washington, D.C.

Photographs:
Faith Bowlus, 12, 170
Jan Brown, 164, 199
Lynne Bruna, 69
Ellen Levine Ebert, 7, 23, 138, 177
Manolo Guevara, Jr., 78
University of Washington Media Services, 89
Diana S. Palting, 155
Joan Silvern, 190
Michael D. Sullivan, 96
Bob Taylor, 48, 117
Barbara Young, 104, 131

Cover design: Rebecca Miller

National Association for the Education of Young Children
1834 Connecticut Ave., N.W.
Washington, DC 20009

Library of Congress Catalog Card Number: 81-82289
ISBN Catalog Number: #0-912674-76-8
NAEYC #319

Printed in the United States of America.

Contents

List of Contributors

Rose Bromwich
Department of Educational
  Psychology
California State University,
  Northridge
Northridge, California

Ellen Khokha
Dorli Burge
Eleanor Baxter
Wallie Kass
Suzanne Fust
c/o Rose Bromwich

Roseanne Clark
Thresholds Mothers' Project
Chicago, Illinois

Bertram Cohler
Department of Social Sciences
Committee on Human
  Development
University of Chicago
Chicago, Illinois

Laura Dittmann
Garrett Park, Maryland

Magda Gerber
Resources for Infant Educarers
Los Angeles, California

Mary Giffin
The Irene Josselyn Clinic
Northfield, Illinois

Alice Sterling Honig
College for Human
  Development
Syracuse University
Syracuse, New York

Judith S. Musick
Thresholds Mothers' Project
Chicago, Illinois

Craig T. Ramey
Frank Porter Graham
  Child Development Center
University of North Carolina at
  Chapel Hill
Chapel Hill, North Carolina

Douglas B. Sawin
Department of Psychology
University of Texas at Austin
Austin, Texas

Diana T. Slaughter
School of Education
Northwestern University
Evanston, Illinois

Romayne Sternad
Belmont, California

Bernice Weissbourd
Family Focus, Inc.
Evanston, Illinois

Introduction

A growing interest by early childhood educators in children under the age of three has been developing, as reflected in annual conference sessions of the National Association for the Education of Young Children. This interest was, in part, the result of research which indicated that even the very young infant was far more competent than had previously been realized (Brazelton 1973; Condon and Sander 1974; Bower 1966, 1974; Stern 1974). Along with the interest sparked by this research evidence, there was an ever-increasing need and demand for quality child care services for these children. Finally, as educators and psychologists began to focus more closely on early learning and the development of competency, they saw a need to provide primary prevention/intervention programs for children as early as possible. This was part of a growing awareness that differences in early intellectual competence and academic achievement were due less to formal schooling functions than to a child's general background of preschool experience and personal characteristics developed within the family during the early years of life (Kohlberg 1968). "The earlier the better" became a rule of remediation, and infant intervention programs proliferated throughout the country. Initially the target populations for these programs were most often infants living in poverty areas where it was felt the greatest risks to developmental progress existed. These programs have since become more divergent in scope, encompassing a variety of areas of developmental risk. Some have been successful, others have not.

These mixed results are partially due to a somewhat simplistic view of the role of early developmental experience. We probably need to reexamine the attitude that a single, traumatic event or brief early experience will cause permanent damage. Infants are resilient, and because many of the major developmental functions common to our species are under maturational control, there is a strong tendency to get back on track after deflection from a developmental pathway (Emde 1981). This means that many of the predictions made by intervention program developers were incorrect. Some children just got better by themselves, whereas others possessed certain vulnerabilities that interacted with the environment to make them relatively impervious to intervention efforts.

As we have come to see infants as active participants in their own development, we can better understand the "bidirectionality of effects" (Clarke-Stewart 1977). That is, rather than formless children being molded or shaped by their social and caregiving environments, there is increasing evidence that infants' own innate temperamental and other characteristics will have important effects in determining their immediate interpersonal environment and the influence of that environment on their development (Escalona 1968; Thomas and Chess 1980). Human infants are organized for social interaction from the beginning of life and participate in mutual exchanges. Thus we cannot regard individual infants as unchanging targets of caregiving behaviors. As infants change their social reality they change, and some continuities from infancy to later stages may be more a function of environmental continuities than of enduring traits in the child. Thus when the effects of abnormal early experience endure, we should consider the environment as well as the individual child. Transactions in the family and other caregiving environments have a role in influencing what opportunities prevail and what early experiences endure.

Although we do not yet know the long-range effects of intervention and early enrichment efforts or if there is developmental continuity from infancy to later years (Clarke and Clarke 1976; Kagan, Kearsley, and Zelazo 1978), we do know that there are certain qualities of the social and caregiving environments that are nurturing and others that fail to promote optimum development. Even when we take into account the differences in patterns of socialization and childrearing found among the many ethnic and cultural groups within the United States, there still remain some core and critical needs that must be met in order for children to develop in healthy and adaptive ways.

The editors of this book assume that the abilities of the human being to establish social relations and to develop the skills necessary for communicating with others are acquired early in the parent-child relationship. Infants come to understand themselves as one person in a world of other persons as their early personality and sense of self takes form within the family. Efficacy, competence, and knowledge of the world are powerfully influenced by the quality of the early social and caregiving environments. Indeed, children's adaptive abilities appear to be an outgrowth of experiences with empathic, consistent, and contingently responsive caregivers who help children understand and structure experiences as they internalize the adults' caring.

Important lessons will be learned within the family. Social, personality, and even intellectual characteristics emerge slowly as an outgrowth of the relationships children form with others in interaction with their own biological organization and propensities. Babies are, in a sense, *pre*social beings because they have the potentiality but require development within a social world to become fully social (Richards 1974). For most infants the primary social world is the family, but, increasingly, child care settings outside the home are serving that function for a portion of the day. Just as biologically endowed infants shape and modify their social world, so they are, in a sense, structured by it, and their biology is modified and given direction. Infants require more than simple nurturance of inborn qualities to become competent, functional members of society. They require positive guidance and direction within a caring and responsive interpersonal environment. The fact of biology requires that we grow up in a family or reasonable substitute for it, not only for protection and nurturance but in order to become an integrated person who has assimilated the knowledge, techniques, and roles required for adaptation.

It is within the family, and particularly within that special subsystem of the family, the mother-child relationship, that children develop language and thought as well as basic social and personality attributes. Although the mother-child relationship is only one aspect of the larger family system, for infants and young children it is the matrix from which they extract their first understanding of themselves and the world, receiving their earliest and most critical lessons in becoming a thinking and social being. Fathers and other significant caregivers are taking on greater and greater significance in the infant's life. Nevertheless, the psychological needs of infants remain the same if they are to realize their potential as fully functioning human beings. As social conditions change, children and families undergo changes that influence development. Family processes in the Depression differed from those in the affluent 1970s; changing roles for parents and the availability of day care will continue to alter the development of infants and children in the future. Researchers are observing these changes in order to understand how they may influence children's development. These trends should also be a major concern of those involved in making social policy. We will need to look closely at the ways in which childrearing is modified by these shifts and ascertain how these modifications affect children's social-emotional and cognitive development.

This book reflects the ever-closer connection between research and application of research findings. For example, research such as that of Ainsworth and her colleagues (Ainsworth 1979) has influenced the development of guidelines for foster care, adoption, and day care. Research on children in alternative care settings (Kagan, Kearsley, and Zelazo 1978) has helped to revise our theories of what constitutes the optimal early environment for infants and young children. As our understanding of early development increases so too should our ability and desire to help our youngest citizens to develop to their fullest potential. However, there is still a considerable gap between our knowledge and what is being done in terms of social policy and program development. Our hope is that the considerable knowledge generated by leaders in this field, many of whom are represented in this book, will assist policy makers in designing programs that provide appropriate social and caregiving environments for infants and young children. While more mothers work, we must continue to affirm children's need of, indeed their right to, an environment that provides consistent caring and responsive nurturance.

References

Ainsworth, M.D.S. "Infant-Mother Attachment." *American Psychologist* 34, no. 10 (1979): 932-937.

Bower, T.G.R. *Development in Infancy.* San Francisco: Freeman, 1974.

Bower, T.G.R. "The Visual World of Infants." *Scientific American* 215 (1966): 80-92.

Brazelton, T.B. *Neonatal Behavioral Assessment Scale.* National Spastics Society Monograph. Philadelphia: Lippincott, 1973.

Clarke, A.M., and Clarke, A.D. *Early Experience: Myth and Evidence.* London: Open Books, 1976.

Clarke-Stewart, K.A. *Child Care in the Family: A Review of Research and Some Propositions for Policy.* New York: Academic Press, 1977.

Condon, W., and Sander, L. "Neonate Movement is Synchronized with Adult Speech: Interactional Participation and Language Acquisition." *Science* 183 (1974): 99-101.

Emde, R.N. "Changing Models of Infancy and the Nature of Early Development: Remodeling the Foundation." *Journal of American Psychoanalytic Association* 29 (1981): 179-219.

Escalona, S. *The Roots of Individuality: Normal Patterns of Development in Infancy.* Chicago: Aldine, 1968.

Kagan, J.; Kearsley, R.; and Zelazo, P. *Infancy: Its Place in Human Development.* Cambridge, Mass.: Harvard University Press, 1978.

Kohlberg, L. "Early Education: A Cognitive-Developmental View." *Child Development* 39 (1968): 1014-1062.

Richards, M.P.M. "First Steps in Becoming Social." In *The Integration of a Child into a Social World,* ed. M.P.M. Richards. London: Cambridge University Press, 1974.

Stern, D. "Mother and Infant at Play: The Dyadic Interaction Involving Facial, Vocal and Gaze Behaviors." In *The Effect of the Infant on Its Caregiver,* ed. M. Lewis and L. Rosenblum. New York: Wiley, 1974.

Thomas, A., and Chess, S. *The Dynamics of Psychological Development.* New York: Brunner/Mazel, 1980.

Judith S. Musick
Bernice Weissbourd

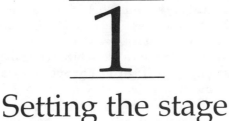

Setting the stage

This book examines many critical issues of a broad and developing field. Thus it is appropriate to begin with a broad overview of recent research findings on infancy. Honig's chapter addresses issues most relevant to the assessment of infants and their caregiving environments and to the design and implementation of programs for infants and toddlers. Her picture of the infant as a complex and competent interactive being gives us a sense of the importance of viewing infants and their social environment as a dynamic unity. Even when dealing with the more purely cognitive or intellective functions, we must remember that it is through the social world that the child is introduced to the worlds of language and thought. Adults engage in verbal and nonverbal dialogue with babies; they introduce objects to the infant's view, and they help to direct and sustain the infant's attention to the relevant aspects of the material environment.

We move from Honig's review of research to an examination of a variety of ways of looking at, assessing, and programming for infants and their caregivers. Giffin discusses the developmental needs of the child; offers techniques for assessing whether these needs are being met; and finally suggests the design and implementation of appropriate settings for infants and toddlers. Giffin's psychoanalytic perspective makes her especially sensitive to what the child requires for healthy ego development, and much emphasis is placed on assisting caregivers to detect early signs of pathology in both mother and child.

Giffin notes that it is frequently the children at high risk who are cared for in group settings. The chapter by Ramey focuses on low-income children within a specially designed day care setting. The children of poverty have frequently been characterized as being at high risk because of poor school achievement and later behavior difficulties. The

issues surrounding the relationship between poverty and risk are complex and not fully understood at present. Nevertheless, one can assume
that all infants, regardless of background, require stimulating, responsive environments that are appropriate to the needs of each individual.

Like other researchers such as Caldwell, Honig, Kagan, Keister, and
Clarke-Stewart, Ramey concludes that very young children can be cared
for in group care settings without adversely affecting their development,
providing these settings are of high quality. Such programs currently are
scarce. The cost of maintaining excellent infant care facilities is often so
prohibitive that one might question (as do researchers Bowlby, Fraiberg,
the Robertsons, and Winnicott) the value of supporting such group care
programs. The issues are complex, covering the spectrum of the needs of
families from infants whose parents are unable for a variety of reasons to
care for them adequately to infants whose parents are both employed full
time.

The chapters by Gerber and Sternad deal with goals and approaches
to infants based on the authors' theoretical and philosophical beliefs
about infant development. Although Gerber speaks of normally developing and handicapped infants, much of her approach is derived
from her work as a child therapist. Sternad's experience is with developmentally delayed children. In both chapters, the role of parents
and other caregivers is examined, and suggestions are made for implementing techniques of intervention. It is important to note that when
one looks beyond the different terminology, the underlying concepts of
what constitutes an appropriate environment and the emphasis on the
role of adults in interaction with the infant is very much the same in these
two chapters. However, the degree of intrusiveness necessary differs in
designing programs for delayed as opposed to normal children. Both the
kind and the amount of stimulation offered the infants will vary with the
abilities of the children to process that which is received. When children
do not naturally reach out to the world of objects and people, special
efforts will need to be made to bring that world to those children.

Infancy researchers have recently looked beyond infant and parent
behaviors to an in-depth study of the dyad as an interactive unit. What is
the "feel" of this relationship? Are the caregiver and child in synchrony
with one another? Is there mutuality, joint action and attention, and a
sense of reciprocity? In addition to observations and measurements of
the dyadic interaction, efforts are currently being made to enhance and
enrich the parents' capacity to effectively interact with their children. An
excellent example of this sort of effort can be found in the work of
Bromwich, Khokha, Burge, Baxter, Kass, and Fust. Bromwich et al.

recognize that infants bring much to early mother-child interactions and are not merely passive recipients of stimulation. Indeed, the infants' own characteristics in interacting with those of their mothers will to a great degree determine the ease and flow of their early relationship. Assisting mothers to understand their reactions to the behavior and personality of their infants can be helpful in relieving both anxiety and guilt. Bromwich et al.'s Parent Behavior Progression is designed to aid the professional not only in assessing the developing relationship but also in evaluating intervention efforts.

The Thresholds Mothers' Project described in the chapter by Musick, Clark, and Cohler is an intensive intervention program aimed at high-risk families based on clinical and research data. Theory and research from the fields of psychoanalysis and developmental psychology are integrated in a model program designed to foster a bond between parent and child where one has previously not existed. Efforts are aimed at strengthening the ties between mothers who find it difficult to parent and children who have developed maladaptive patterns of coping. The knowledge gained from the study of disturbed patterns of interaction is useful for understanding other parents. When the mother-child relationship gets off to a bad start, or goes awry, elements necessary for establishing a good relationship become strikingly apparent. The therapeutic nursery that provides a structured, stimulating, and responsive environment to ameliorate the problems of these children at risk intensifies the basic principles of a quality group setting.

Research and program planning for mothers and infants are occurring in a rapidly changing social environment. The stresses inherent in our society significantly affect parents and subsequently their young and dependent children. The changing roles and attitudes of parents are reflected in the chapters by Dittmann, Sawin, Weissbourd, and Slaughter. What will be the effect on children of greater participation in childrearing by fathers and other caregivers? What will be the effect of the greater ambivalence and difficulty in parenting experienced by so many parents? To what extent will day care for infants proliferate, and in what ways will its impact be felt?

The varied environments of infancy include those internal to children, such as temperamental and biological factors, as they interact with the multiple external environments found in the social and caregiving world. Dittmann presents a case for viewing the systems of society in ways that will enhance children's opportunities for optimal growth and development, whether this takes place within the group care setting or within the family.

Sawin's research on fathers examines the position that more traditional views may need to be exchanged for models that deal with the totality of infants' social ecology. The significant impact of fathers is deeply intertwined with all of the social relationships involving infants including the family system.

Weissbourd looks at parents as developing people whose own experiences affect their ability to respond and react to their children. Parenthood represents a stage in the life cycle with interpersonal issues that must be negotiated and are strongly influenced by the community and society. These forces are addressed by Slaughter in the final chapter on social policy.

The gap between research knowledge and applied program planning is still considerable and is further a reflection of the low priority currently given to the health and welfare of our nation's children. It appears that there is the greatest lack where there is the greatest need for careful thought and appropriate support.

Alice Sterling Honig

2

Recent infancy research

Reasons for renewed interest in infancy research

The upsurge of interest in research on children from birth to three years of age has been sparked by the increasing numbers of parents in the labor force who need quality care for their very young children. If we are to provide quality care for infants, we need to know a great deal about infant development and about infants in relation to their caregivers, those special people who help facilitate babies' growth and development.

Another push for good infant research has come from developmentalists who have begun to realize that, as Piaget theorized, the roots of preoperational and intellectual behaviors lie in sensorimotor experiences and strivings for competency during the infancy period.

Research in the field of infancy has also been fueled by society's concern for increased at-birth risks to infants born to teenage mothers (Walters 1975). One out of every five infants born today is born to a teenage mother. The numbers of babies born to very young teenage mothers has risen sharply. "The rates are rising fastest for girls least able to care for a baby" (Baldwin 1976, p. 5). Research efforts in the last decade have focused on pediatrics, infant nutrition, and child development.

Part of the enthusiasm for research also comes from a new conception of infants. Infants are not just big, inert dolls. They are competent. Babies are able to protect their biological and psychological integrity against assaults from sensory stimulation. They can turn away to avoid strong odors, shut their eyes against bright lights, or yell loudly when hungry. Their engaging smiles are offered to any adult who has tendered to their needs. Researchers want to map the parameters of these competencies and learn just how responsive and efficacious babies can be,

5

given the many sensory abilities babies have.

Cross-cultural workers have contributed to renewed interest in which human characteristics are due to nature or nurture. Do babies grow the same across cultures? How do childrearing methods for the socialization of early toileting behaviors, aggression behaviors, or dependency behaviors differ?

Parents are once again being viewed as crucial people in young children's lives. During the Fifties and Sixties we concentrated so on intervention strategies, on creating quality programs for the child, that we overlooked the importance of parenting. We now realize that no matter how terrific we are as programmers for very young children, we must become interested in parents, the first teachers, the most important adults in young children's lives.

Another reason why there has been an upsurge of interest in infancy research has been the ongoing inquiry into the extent and consequences of sex discrimination and sex differences in growth and development. What are the differentiations of sex roles in males and females? Do they begin in infancy? Are they biological? Are they nurtured by different caregiving styles? What are the contributions of adult caregivers to patterns of sex role differences appearing among young boys and girls?

Another source of research has been renewed attention to fathers (Lamb 1976). May the next decade prove even more fruitful in examining the ways of fathers with their young ones!

The following survey of infant research is divided into ten categories: competence; biology of the infancy period; the importance of bonding and attachment; infant language; the at-risk infant; infant environments; sex role differentiation; fathers and infants; intervention models with infants; and theory in relation to infant development, findings, and research. Previous and current research in these areas are included to preserve a sense of ongoing efforts to understand infants and work in their behalf.

Competence

The findings on infant competence are fascinating. In the United States today, over 70 percent of new mothers think that infants are blind at birth. Yet infants recently have been found to be far more competent than anyone realized. One of the researchers who has contributed to our knowledge is Fantz (1963). He slid a basket with a six-day-old baby into a small chamber with a plastic dome. The experimenter could see whether

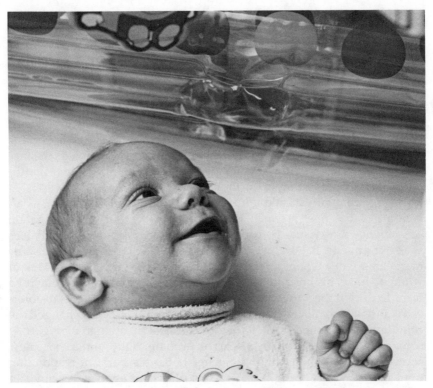

Perhaps as we develop more experimental ingenuity in modifying modest body responses such as head turns or sucks, we will begin to see more competence in infants, more of their ability to discover contingencies in their environment, and more pleasure as they learn how to control the environment.

the baby was looking at a bull's-eye pattern, a blank piece of paper, or a checkerboard design just by watching the reflections of the pattern on the baby's eyeballs. Fantz and other researchers have found that babies have definite preferences for looking at more interesting patterns.

Fagan (1976) found seven-month-olds were very competent when looking at photos of different men's faces—fatter men, skinnier men, funnier looking men, handsome men, and faces in different poses. If they had seen a man's face several times, they tended to want to choose a different man's face to look at. The infants were quite capable of discriminating not only one man's face from another but one pose of the same face from another pose. If the babies had seen a face in full view, they preferred to switch and look at it in a side view because the new one was novel and interesting. During the first year of life babies do much more than eat and have their diapers changed!

Kagan's work and Lewis's research have also demonstrated competencies in infant visual discrimination. Lewis (1977a) had either a mother or a stranger stand in front of the baby and speak under one of two conditions. Sometimes the voice came out from where the face was, and sometimes Lewis displaced the voice with a loudspeaker to the side of the baby. That is very disconcerting, even for a grownup, to listen to! But infants as young as one month old made exploratory responses when there was a violation of the usual integrated pattern of audiovisual stimulation. After all, even in those first weeks of life, babies become accustomed to hearing a voice come out of the same location as the face at which they are looking. If you violate this expectancy in one-month-olds, they search around as if they know that a face and a voice that belongs to that face should not be coming from different places.

Some of the new research reveals infants' auditory discrimination competence and visual perceptual discrimination competence. Babies seek out novelty. Babies love learning. Papoušek (1961) has done some marvelous work where a few-months-old baby gets a light to look at when he turns his head to the left. Once the baby has learned that if he turns to the left the light will come on, after a while he becomes disinterested and will not turn to the left anymore. Then, Papoušek changed the conditions. He turned the light on only for head turning to the *right*. At some point, then, if the baby's head turns to the right, under these new contingency conditions, the researcher obtains a burst of responding until the baby has "caught on" to this new contingency. A baby can competently respond even if required to carry out a complicated pattern such as turn left-right-left-right in order to turn on the light. Babies can create and test hypotheses and babies can solve problems. They will work with vigor and pleasure to discover the contingencies in such laboratory experiments. Bower (1974) has remarked that such "problem solving is the true motivation for human infants in a learning situation" (p. 8).

Perhaps until now researchers have not been ingenious enough. While newborn babies have no myelinization of the great motor neurons yet (myelin is the fatty sheath that permits the emergence of voluntary motor control), they have sensory competence within the first few days. Papoušek's work capitalized on this fact in an effort to find out how competent babies really are.

Perhaps the most amazing demonstration of early competence was provided by an experiment of Siqueland and Lipsitt (1966) that was carried out with one-day-old infants. These researchers were able to establish a head turning response to one side when a buzzer was sounded and to the other side when a bell was sounded. When this discrimination had been learned, the presentations were reversed and all of the babies learned the discrimination reversal quite easily!

Bruner has done beautiful work to demonstrate contingency learning (1973, p. 289). A special nipple is placed in the baby's mouth. The harder the baby sucks, the more a motion picture figure will come into sharp focus on the screen directly in front of the baby. Or, to reverse this procedure, the picture is in focus and the more strongly an infant sucks, the more effectively will she drive the picture out of focus. Those babies work hard to bring or keep the picture in focus! Lewis (1977b) once remarked, "Now that we know how competent infants are, I can see the day when we'll put a nipple with a transducer in the baby's mouth, and he will be in a little train car, and the more he sucks the more he can give himself a ride around the living room floor, while daddy and mommy are busy cooking dinner or doing something else!"

The "violation of expectancy" research done by Charlesworth (1969) on infant surprise was also important in understanding infant competence. Babies watched a toy going behind a screen and saw it come out the other end several times, and then the toy did not reappear. The infants' faces registered surprise. Although babies do not have object permanence in a Piagetian sense yet, they are surprised because their expectancies have been violated. Infants as young as eight weeks of age will anticipate the reappearance of an object that has gone behind a screen (Bower, Broughton, and Moore 1971).

McGraw (1935) is a marvelous researcher who did the earliest work we know in infant competence. She taught one- and two-year-old children swimming, roller skating, jumping from 70-inch towers (straight leaps into her arms), and clambering up enormous numbers of blocks that went up to the ceiling of a room. McGraw was honored at the 1977 meetings of the Society for Research in Child Development. She showed films of Johnny and Jimmy (twins featured in her 1935 book) when they were in their twenties. The twins came to her home, and she filmed their motoric behaviors. For example, she put a ladder up along the side of her house. You could tell instantly that the young man climbing the ladder with aplomb had had all that infant motor training. You could tell also from trampoline jumping and other exercises just which twin had been trained and which twin had not so many years ago.

The last bit of competence research I would like to mention involves the promotion of competence in handicapped infants. Bower (1977) describes work with a blind eight-week-old baby. An auditory mobile was installed in the crib—a mobile that made sounds rather than presenting visual stimuli. By kicking his legs and setting the mobile in motion, the blind baby could produce a change in sound. The baby had never smiled in eight weeks of life. But when he learned to kick and produce a change of sound, he smiled and cooed. The smiles were vigorous and forceful. The wonderful implications are that *pleasure in problem solving will help a child grow in sensorimotor and intellectual competence and also promote emotional happiness expressed in smiling and cooing*.

Competence is one of the really rich areas of infancy research. Perhaps as we develop more experimental ingenuity in modifying modest body responses such as head turns or sucks, we will begin to see more compentence in infants, more of their ability to discover the consequences of actions on their environment, more pleasure as they learn how to control the environment. These research results give us some food for thought. If you are a baby who cries for food and who cannot control the environment, and if nobody comes to relieve your hunger pangs, nobody comes to change that uncomfortable wet diaper, what are you learning about your competence to make changes in your environment? The world seems a disorderly, inconsistent, and discouraging place for such a baby. Hopefully, the initial, *positive* causality learning of a baby is: "If I'm distressed, someone comes to comfort me." This first syllogistic reasoning in figuring out what to expect of the world and in developing trusting attitudes toward people occurs at "gut" level.

Biological research

One of the most impressive things about biological research in infancy in the last decade has been the finding of so many factors that place a fetus or an infant at risk developmentally. When I was in graduate training, we were taught that few events happening to the mother while the baby was in the uterus would affect the baby. For example, a mother might not ingest enough calcium or iron, but the baby would take what she or he needed. The mother might lose her teeth, but the baby would be just fine, sloshing around in that cozy amniotic sac. We have, of course, known that some maternal diseases (such as German measles contracted during early pregnancy) and some conditions (such as incompatibility of Rh blood factors between mother and infant) have serious deleterious consequences (Hardy 1969).

A lot of the biological research of the last decade has shown that the picture is far more complex. So many factors are known now that can seriously compromise the chances for optimal status at birth. That is one of my concerns for this country now in terms of a public policy. Are we actively ensuring every chance for each baby to be born biologically at the peak point it should be born?

Smoking

Some of the research findings that have led to an increasing concern for biologically optimal births came from large-scale research studies in Great Britain. Davie et al. (1972), for example, reported that smoking by pregnant mothers was correlated with a decrease in reading scores later on in public school. Mothers who smoke during pregnancy are more likely to have an undersized baby. Nicotine causes the blood vessels of the placenta to narrow and diminish the supply of food and oxygen to the unborn baby. One cause of retarded growth in the womb is carbon monoxide, one of the gases in cigarette smoke. Studies have shown more carbon monoxide in the blood of the unborn baby than in the blood of the smoking mother (American Cancer Society 1976). The widespread increase in smoking among teenage girls in this country, coupled with the increasing rates of teenage pregnancy, should alert us to potential dangers for babies as yet unborn.

Stress and alcohol

Severe stress of the pregnant mother may be associated with complications of pregnancy and with temperament difficulties of the baby (Ferreira 1965). If the parents are screaming and fighting, there is a flow of adrenaline through the placenta, making jumpier babies for months after birth.

Alcohol can have serious teratogenic consequences. Moderate drinkers often have babies with lower than expected birth weights (Streissguth et al. 1980). Low birth weight is often a warning signal of developmental difficulties. Babies of heavy drinkers have been born with facial bone abnormalities and brain damage. Distinctive features of the fetal alcohol syndrome in babies include small heads, abnormal eyes, and retarded growth.

Drug effects

We have learned more now about drug addicted mothers. There has been a special effort to study heroin addiction and angel dust withdrawal symptoms in the neonatal period. Heroin affected babies have more rapid eye movements, greater variability in heart rates, and no truly quiet sleep (Schulman 1969). Babies born to heroin or methadone ad-

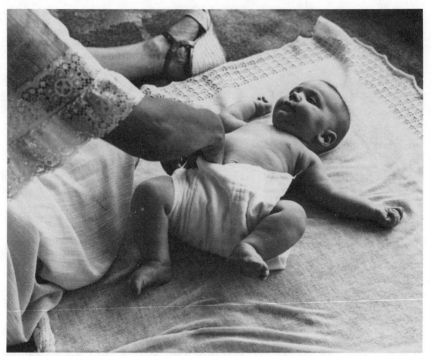

Unless babies' dependency needs are met early, they are likely to become more *rather than less dependent and flexible.*

dicted mothers are born addicted, are irritable, hard to comfort, and are twice as likely to die within days after birth (Ostrea and Chavez 1979).

We have also learned about the effects of drugging the mother at the time of birth in terms of infant motor sluggishness. Analgesia and anesthesia during labor and delivery have been shown to have a depressing effect on sensorimotor functioning for at least the first four weeks (Bowes et al. 1970). What does this imply in terms of the mother-infant bonding process if a mother does not have a very alert baby?

Nutrition

Nutritional work has advanced a good deal in the last decade in exploring the factors that go into nourishing the fetus. Women who ate very poorly as teenagers have uteruses that are not as competent as possible at feeding their infants even though the obstetrician puts them on the best diet during pregnancy in their twenties. Optimal biological development of a baby begins when the female body is growing up.

Some nutrition studies have centered on the effects on infant development of iron deficiency anemia (Honig and Oski 1978). Iron deficiency anemia, according to HEW reports, involved about 18 to 20 percent of the children in the United States. We found irritability, lowered attention span, and lowered IQ scores in babies with iron deficiency anemia. When one-half of the babies were randomly given intramuscular iron therapy, their developmental scores improved significantly one week later.

Will mothers with babies who are irritable, throwing toys, and screaming want to take care of them with the same loving care as mothers who have calmer babies? My concern is not just for the symptomatology, biologically, that nutrition or drug conditions create in the infant; it is for the reciprocal relationship that is then affected by these biological situations. We need to be much more alert in pediatric practice, especially in hospitals where low-income patients come in to well-baby clinics. Examination for iron depletion and iron deficiency anemia should be added as a routine checkup.

Biological state

Wolff (1966) has studied six different sleeping and waking states of infants. Infants' responses to stimulation depend on their state and the stimulus. One can increase neurological alertness by bringing babies to the shoulder—they widen their eyes and become more alert visually.

Perception

Gibson and Walk (1960) have done pioneer work on depth perception in infants. Creeping babies placed on a glass table see either an oilcloth pattern directly under the piece of glass or an oilcloth four feet down under the glass. If the babies perceive the oilcloth far below, it looks as if there is a drop off. They will not creep on that table surface area even if their mothers try to lure them or call to them from across that perceptual barrier. Gibson's visual cliff work indeed adds to our growing awareness of infant competencies.

Biological research on competencies has been helpful in suggesting ways we can help handicapped infants by using sensory, perceptual, or motor competencies that babies actually do have rather than by concentrating on areas in which they have deficits. Another result of biological research in the last decade lies in our increasing awareness that there is a tremendous interaction of biological and social factors in influencing infant growth and development.

Temperament

Other pioneer research is the work of Thomas et al. (1963) on the different kinds of neonatal temperaments and on individual stability in activity levels over the first two years of life. Thomas has shown that original characteristics of temperament tend to persist over the years and that there are three major biological temperament groups. Some babies are easier to parent than others. One type of temperament is characterized by *positiveness* in mood, regularity in bodily function, moderate to low intensity of reactions, adaptability, and positive approach to new situations. Would it be easier or more difficult to get such a baby to sleep through the night or to adapt such a baby to a family's habits?

Another constellation of characteristics describes *difficult* children who are irregular in body functioning and unusually intense in their reactions. Such babies may be irritable in response to changes in the environment and struggle or withdraw in the face of new stimuli. Some babies are very suspicious of new foods, while others will eat even spiced mushrooms, for example. Babies seem to be very different in terms of being willing to reach out and try new experiences in food, places, or people.

The third type of temperament these researchers called *slow to warm up* biologically. Such infants typically have a low activity level, tend to withdraw on first exposure to new stimuli, are slow to adapt, are somewhat negative, and have low-intensity reactions.

How do different parenting styles mesh with different infant temperament styles? Perhaps if caregivers are aware of and act sensitively in response to these differences, babies will thrive better.

Bonding

A new emphasis on the fundamental importance of maternal-infant bonding and attachment has been given by recent research, particularly that of Klaus and Kennell (1976). The importance of bonding in the animal kingdom has been well known. If a baby goat is taken away from its mother at birth, that mother will butt it away and not take care of it when the baby is returned a few hours later. Hospital procedures for women giving birth frequently fail to consider that the strength of attachments and affections may be affected by an enforced lack of contact of the mother with the newborn baby. In some studies, babies are put to the breast within ten minutes after birth. These tiny new beings, very ineffective in the beginning, lick at the nipple. This licking starts contractions of the uterus, even though the babies cannot suck with the expertise they will gain with nursing practice in the early weeks. This early body contact is important for the mother's system and also promotes deep feelings of tenderness and attachment to the new baby.

Early pioneers in this field were Spitz and Ribble and Bowlby. Bowlby's (1958) ethological theory implies that bonding of baby and mother is a way to ensure the highest quality caregiving and thus increase chances for infant survival.

Recent research has helped us to understand the importance of bonding using split-screen television techniques. A mother and newborn are observed talking with each other. Two television cameras are used to obtain a separate film of the baby and of the mother. Then the two pictures are shown together, so that the two participants are seen at the same time, side by side. The body responses and nuances of the dyadic interaction can easily be followed. Some of this work has been done by Stern (1973) and some by Brazelton and his colleagues at Harvard (1973). Stern, using the split-screen technique, has watched "The interaction game." Mothers will change their facial expressions, wiggle their ears, their eyes, their mouths, make crazy wide-open, pop-eye faces, and do things that you would not expect of any sane human being. All for the sake of getting a baby to respond.

Brazelton et al. (1973) have reported, in analyzing his split-screen experiments, that babies are marvelous regulators of their own homeostatic level of sensory stimulation. If mothers eye-gaze too long, the babies turn away, and only cue back in when they are ready for a new cycle of mutual gazing and interaction. Brazelton has observed lengthy, fixed eye-gazing by new mothers. *Never* in adult life does one find a woman gazing continuously into someone's eyes unless she is ready to fight him or make love with him. But with babies, mothers will continuous-gaze for enormous periods, letting baby drift in and out, controlling the sensory stimulation so they do not get overloaded or irritable. Brazelton believes that babies given this kind of bonding experience are in cyclical synchrony with their mothers. "An infant who is constantly bombarded by an insensitive mother will quickly establish a pattern of prolonged non-attention and brief periods of attention. . . . Failure to meet the infant's needs for synchrony violates the rules for interaction, rules which are vital not only to his development but for his very survival" (Brazelton 1975, pp. 52-53).

Klaus and Kennell (1976) have focused on long-range social effects of these synchronous dyadic interactions. Some of their studies have been done with premature infants. One group of mothers with premature babies were allowed to enter the nursery and touch their preemies in the very first few days. Another group was not permitted tactile contact until after 21 days. When tested at 42 months, children in the early contact group obtained significantly higher Stanford-Binet intelligence scores—99 vs. 85 for the babies who were touched by mothers only after 3 weeks.

The delicate responsive nuances that keep mothers and babies in harmony, in sensitive interactive contact, were explored in a further study of newborns (Lozoff et al. 1977). If crying newborns were attended to within 90 seconds, the infants were soothed in 5 seconds. If mothers took longer than one-and-one-half minutes to attend to their babies, then the babies would not be soothed for at least 50 seconds.

In another study Kennell (1975, p. 40) describes a group of mothers given extended contact with babies beginning one hour after delivery. The control group had routine care from birth on in the baby nursery of the hospital, with 20-minute feeding visits permitted every 4 hours. Mothers in the experimental group showed significantly different maternal behavior. At one month, they stayed closer to their infants. They showed more attempts to soothe their babies during the pediatrician's physical exam of the baby. They offered much more eye contact and fondling during feeding situations filmed in the home after the mothers came home from the hospital. At one year these differences persisted. At two years the early-contact mothers had much more positive linguistic behavior with their toddlers. These mothers asked twice as many questions in talking with their two-year-olds. They used more adjectives and fewer commands.

The quality of the early bond seems to have an effect very far into the early years of life. If the mother is separated from her baby in a neonatal care unit in a hospital, are we training pediatric nurses to give appropriate body and eye and voice contact? Are expectant mothers aware of how important it is to establish and sustain early body contacts with their babies?

Classic research by Ainsworth and her colleagues has also helped us to see how important close attachment and close physical contact are between the parent and infant. Bell and Ainsworth's (1972) work on infant crying has shown that if parents have close physical contact with the infant and promptly respond to crying in the early part of the first year of life, babies will use crying less frequently toward the end of the first year as a means to get their needs met. They may call for something or smile or coo or thrash around, but they will not use crying as communication as frequently. This discounts the old wives' tale that if you don't let them cry, you are spoiling them.

Maternal responsiveness to signals fosters the development of communication skills. Babies come to feel that they are competent communicators. As you see now, some of our areas of research begin to overlap. This kind of responsiveness of mothers, according to Ainsworth, gives children confidence in their increasing competence to get their needs met and encourages them in means/ends relationships. If the baby cries and somebody comes, the baby feels efficacious.

Some of the recent work in bonding and attachment has been carried out by Sroufe and Waters (1977), who feel that securely attached infants should be able to do very much what Harlow's (1958) infant monkeys did when they had the cloth mother. If you recall, the wire mother had the nipple and the cloth mother had huggability. Babies clambered up the wire mothers only when they needed to eat, but they went to the cloth mothers when they needed contact comfort. If the monkey who had become attached to the cloth mother was left alone in a big empty room and given a scary pull toy, the infant became terribly upset, shrieked away to a corner, sucked his thumb, rocked, and masturbated. But if the cloth mother was in the room, the monkey climbed up on her, hugged her, then climbed down and courageously explored that staring monster toy. Sroufe has found that the same process occurs with mothers who are well attached and give a secure base to their babies—the babies can go farther afield to explore the unknown. And the quality of these babies' play will be richer. *They are more likely to try novel settings and materials because they have a secure attachment and a base to which they can go back for comfort.*

Remember the Greek myth of Antaeus, son of Gaea, Goddess of the Earth? If Antaeus could touch Mother Earth now and again during a battle, his strength would increase and he could fight on unbeatably. Hercules only conquered Antaeus when he held him so he could not get down and touch Mother Earth. It is strange how this ancient myth relates to the information we are learning about ourselves as humans in our infancy.

Sroufe believes that attachment is very important as an organizational construct. We need to understand the extent to which an attachment relationship is an asset to infants. Infants can pursue constructive exploratory goals because they have this bonding. Bonding is an asset for an infant not just because we think it is good for mothers and fathers and babies to love one another but because it also increases the infant's ability to pursue constructive social and exploratory goals.

Matas et al. (1978) assigned attachment classifications to 50 infants at the age of one year. The researcher then followed these babies in terms of their ability and their competence in tool-using problems at age two. Some of the problems were very difficult for those two-year-olds, but the well-attached babies were less easily frustrated. "At 24 months, the competent toddler still maintains the positively toned reciprocal relationship with its caregiver; confronts problems enthusiastically; and persistently finds pleasure in mastery" (Arend, Gore, and Sroufe 1979). Insecurely bonded infants showed strikingly poor adaptation to tool-using situations a year later. They were less able to use the caregiver for assistance, more negativistic, and gave up more quickly.

Children who were not securely attached a year earlier exhibited more tantrum behavior and more dependence behavior at age two. Thus, the attachment research shows that unless a baby's dependency needs are met early (no matter how much we want children to be on their own and toilet trained and taking care of themselves early!), they are likely to be *more* rather than less dependent and flexible. Stayton et al. (1971) found that children who were securely and positively attached to mothers early in the first year were more compliant to mothers in the second year of life. They continued to be more ego-resilient and curious when followed through the kindergarten years. We must meet an infant's early needs for nurturance to ensure optimal development later on. Of course, Erikson's epigenetic theory (1963) predicted this many years ago.

The security of attachments early in infancy predicts competence and autonomous explorations later on. Lewis has suggested that "it may be the case that all relationships in which significant learning takes place are characterized by information exchange within a socio-emotional context" (1977a, p. 283).

Language development

As interest emerged in the development of language competence and production in young children, delightful research on toddlers was published in the early 1960s (Bellugi and Brown 1964; Bloom 1970). It is no easy task to sit in a home with a baby with emerging language development and to try to elucidate the toddler's repertoire. Bellugi and Brown tried decorous experimental techniques, such as, "Which is right Adam? I have two foot or two feets or two feet?" "Pop goes the weasel," Adam burst out in cheerful response. Doing language research with toddlers can be a somewhat frustrating experience for the researcher!

Some of the particularly interesting language research examines social class differences in adult speech with toddlers. Schachter's work (1979) focused on differences in the kind of language directed to toddlers by low-socioeconomic status (SES) mothers compared with higher SES Black mothers and White mothers. Schachter found no race differences at all. She did find marked social class differences. Higher SES mothers spoke to their children twice as much and reacted with three times as much responsive talk to their toddlers. The low SES mothers used "don't" about one in every 4 utterances and the higher SES mothers about one in every 12 utterances. When higher SES mothers said "don't" they tended more often to explain. When they refused the child, they provided substitutes or alternatives. Low SES mothers often ignored their child's initiatives.

When the higher SES mothers responded to their infants, they responded in-kind. When their child expressed a desire, they responded to it. If the child garbled her or his speech, they made a correction. The speech of higher SES mothers was more relevant to the child's vocalizations and needs. When low SES mothers used responsive speech with toddlers, they were more likely to use control categories or to ignore the child's requests, desires, or initiatives. These findings reveal clear social class differences in language experiences of the two-year-old. Such social class differences have been found as early as 12 weeks (Lewis and Wilson 1972). Middle-class mothers were more likely to vocalize *contingently* in response to their infants' vocalizations. Lower-class mothers with equal amounts of vocalization were more likely to touch but not talk to their vocalizing babies.

Elardo, Bradley, and Caldwell (1975) found that the level of emotional and verbal responsibility of working class Black or White mothers during their children's infancy correlated more than other aspects of the home environment with preschool language subscale scores on the Illinois Test of Psycholinguistic Ability. Such findings lend emphasis to the important role parents can play as language facilitators in the earliest years. Fowler and Swenson (1975) worked with mothers of three infants to design at-home interactions to see how early children could learn to talk. The babies began to imitate words at 5½ months, speak words at 7 months, and put words together at 12 months. Babies have more potential language competence than psycholinguistic norms would lead us to believe.

In toddlerhood, children are just beginning to integrate many emerging skills. Sometimes they cannot even walk and bend over to pick up a toy without a sudden sit down. They may toddle around a corner and knock right into the wall. They have great will, but not quite enough ability to carry out budding initiatives smoothly. If a toddler's parent can phrase questions, requests, or controls in positive or clarifying ways, perhaps both parent and toddler can get through this period more easily with the child's self-esteem and the parent's good will more intact. Honig and Wittmar (1981) have found that low-income male toddlers in day care are far more likely to respond to or comply with their caregivers when choice questions or open-ended questions are asked rather than convergent questions that require a specific single answer.

The roots of language development lie in the sensorimotor period of infancy. Hunt (1977) remarked that he believes the basis of language development depends particularly on object permanence development. If we provide enough peek-a-boo, hide-a-toy, and other object permanence games with babies, we may be helping not only to provide the foundations for the concept of the permanence of objects but also for the understanding and use of words that denote and describe objects, people, and events.

I have found in working in an infant nursery, for example, that I could not teach a baby to use a word like *cup* correctly if the baby did not know enough about a cup to pick it up and make appropriate drinking motions. Meaning is learned not in words at first, but at the sensorimotor level, the level of body understandings and communications. As MacNamara has explained, infants learn their language "by first determining, independent of language, the meaning which a speaker intends to convey. The infant uses meaning as a clue to language" (1972, p. 1). The ELAS Scale (Honig and Caldwell 1965) was developed at the Syracuse University Children's Center to assess both early words babies can use and the early gestures that indicate babies are decoding the meanings of familiar experiences and people. Friedlander (1970) has summarized research in infancy in the underinvestigated field of receptive language development.

Moerk (1974) has looked at the ways in which mothers and infants change the kinds and complexity of language they use with each other during the first years of life. For example, during the first two years he found parents use many prods. The parent helps baby find the right words or corrects the baby; "Man come," reports baby. "Yes, the mail carrier came," mother responds. "Want dat," points baby. "Oh, you want your Teddy Bear," says father. Prompt and directive feedback by parents decreases toward the end of infancy as do baby imitations of mother and baby labeling of pictures for mother. On the other hand, from then on there is an increase, both for parents and children, in questions and answers and descriptions of the environment and of what they were doing. Moerk has provided a history of the peaks and declines in language functions of babies and parents during the early years. His work (1976) reveals how readily middle-class mothers can adapt their language developmentally to infant language abilities. Maternal length of utterance, as well as type of verbal interchange, varies with the child's age.

Snow (1972) has also done research that shows how mothers modify their speech to their children in the first and second years. Mothers use shorter phrases and easier words. Even nonmothering adults simplified and shortened their speech for two-year-olds as compared to their speech with ten-year-olds.

Work by Tizard et al. (1972) in residential nurseries in England has important implications for infant language encouragement in group care settings. Tizard used a time-sampling technique to study language development in two- to five-year-olds living in residential nurseries. In one nursery there were 50 caregivers per week. The director tried to discourage any building of attachment because she felt that staff morale declined if nurses became attached to babies who grew into children available for adoption. Nevertheless, in these residential nurseries there was usually a good staff to child ratio, lots of storybooks, and lots of toys. Tizard, using the Reynall Developmental Language Scales, found that where the staff talked more with the children and where the staff was trained more, the children were doing better in language development. But, she also found that the staff tended to talk less to the younger babies. In centers that have infants and older preschoolers, it is crucial that the staff is comfortable about communicating verbally with infants as much as they are with older children. (See Honig et al. 1973 for a description of an infant day care setting in which infants and preschoolers received equal language input from caregivers.) Tizard also found that child language comprehension scores were highest when staff stability was higher, staff was more experienced, and the staff-child ratio was better.

Most of the recent infant language research, then, gives us a better sense of the importance of sensitive, responsive, rich early language interactions with caregivers in a baby's life to ensure an optimal language learning environment. Even more basically, the establishment of referential, communicative, turn-taking joint interactions between loving caregivers and their tiny infants may be essential to prime the baby for language learning later (Bruner 1977).

At-risk and premature babies

More premature babies are now being saved by incubator care and fine neonatal unit care in hospitals in large cities (Goldstein et al. 1976; Parmelee and Haber 1973). But what are the effects of the quality of the human interactions on babies who have been left in incubators, untalked to, uncuddled, unhandled? If we are going to save many more premature and at-risk babies, what kinds of activities should the neonatal nursery staff be doing to optimize development? Also, what kinds of subtle interactions characterize infants of differing neonatal status? Can we pinpoint where disturbances occur? Field (1977) reports on interactions at three-and-one-half months of mothers with preterm, post-term, and full-term infants. Using a split-screen videotape, Field found that the salient features of a disturbed infant-mother interaction are an overactive mother and a more fussy, gaze-averting baby.

Minde and his colleagues' (1975) research in Toronto's nurseries reveal that the lowest interaction and the least frequent visits were made by mothers with no support systems. The fathers were abusive, or had abandoned the family, or the parents were in the process of separation. These mothers had very few friends to share griefs or concerns with, and they visited, touched, and were concerned with the infant least. Therefore, if premature babies are to flourish, we must consider the *social support systems* for mothers who have preemie babies. (See Hough and Stevens 1981.) What are the societal supports that are relevant? In Minde's study mothers who visited their babies the most often had husbands and the husbands visited the babies with them. These mothers also had lots of good friends apparently with whom they could talk about events and allay their fears about the baby. The visited babies were held more and had their eyes open more.

The Kauai pregnancy study (Werner et al. 1971) in Hawaii examined 3,000 pediatric clinical ratings. When infant IQ was under 80 at 20 months, there was high stability of low IQ (<80) at 10 years of age. In this longitudinal study, researchers found twice the frequency of IQs under 85 on Cattell tests in infancy for the more severe cases of perinatal stress. It is striking that in the Kauai study only 56 percent of the babies were born free of any perinatal or prenatal complications. What does this say about preparation for pregnancy and the care of the pregnant mother? More attention needs to be given to prenatal and perinatal stress and risk factors.

Willerman, Broman, and Fiedler's research (1970) also points out that there is very high continuity with later mental abilities for babies who are

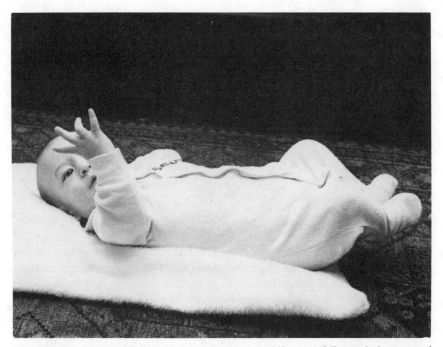

If you can detect a skill or interest just as it is emerging, and if you carefully watch the process of how the baby explores and learns, you will be able to encourage new skills and understandings more sensitively.

born at-risk and have poor developmental scores neonatally. There is practically zero prediction for full-term, well-developed babies from infancy scores to later scores. But if there is an at-risk factor such as prematurity, then there is much better predictability from low developmental scores in infancy to low scores at later ages. At-risk infants who performed poorly in the first year showed practically no residue of certain perinatal complications (unless physical handicap was involved) when the babies were reared in higher SES families.

Cohen (1977) has investigated preterm infants and their parents. She provided many reciprocal positive interaction games for parents to play with their premature babies. Reciprocal positive interactions correlated well ($r = .61$) with Bayley developmental scores at age two. The regression equations were not changed by reexamining the predictions separately for social class. This research points to the importance of specific caregiver playful interactions, vocalizations, and games for later competence among preterm infants regardless of social class.

Perinatal research by Littman (1977) has shown that infants with a

greater number of medical problems beyond the neonatal period performed less well on all developmental tests at age two. This research
suggests that preterm and at-risk infants need to be followed up. Babies
should be brought back to check on perinatal complications and to assist
parents in learning responsive appropriate ways to stimulate their babies
(Scarr-Salapatek and Williams 1973). Some hospital personnel have
counted success with at-risk infants simply as the number of babies kept
alive and able to leave the hospital. Such an attitude would seem to
neglect the necessity of checking on developmental progress and of
helping parents learn skills for coping with and optimizing the development of at-risk infants.

Infant environment

Yarrow and his coresearchers (1972) have done a great service by
evaluating the environments in which infants live. The variety of toys
offered and the responsiveness of the toys that the baby has to play with
is important. There is a difference between having a big wooden horse to
roll back and forth and having a toy that runs when you turn on the
batteries. Always look for toys that will be responsive to an infant's
playful explorations. Such toys also facilitate the baby's motivation to
play longer with toys and to explore problem-solving toys. Yarrow has
conceptualized not only dimensions of the inanimate environment but
also of the personal environment of babies. He characterizes the personal environment as having levels and variety of social stimulation,
amount of positive affect, positive contingent responses to infant vocalization, and contingent responses to distress calls by the infant. Such
personal aspects of the infant's environment correlated positively with
developmental scores and with goal-directed behaviors of babies.

It is intriguing that these findings corroborate Ainsworth and Bell's
research (1973) in which six maternal variables were examined: maternal
sensitivity vs. insensitivity to infant signals, acceptance vs. rejection,
cooperation vs. interference, frequency of verbal commands, frequency
of physical interventions, and giving of floor freedom to babies during
their waking hours. A stepwise multiple regression using these six
maternal variables with IQ as the criterion variable resulted in a multiple
R of .70. That is, mothers who both were sensitive to infant signals and
permitted their babies floor freedom to explore the world tended to have
babies with higher developmental scores. Mothers who were insensitive
to signals and restrictive of opportunities for babies to interact with their
environment tended to have babies with lower developmental scores.

My favorite study on dimensions of the environment that are good for babies is Carew's study (1976) at Harvard. Carew and her colleagues did naturalistic observations of middle and low SES home environments of infants from one year to three years of age. At three years of age, Carew took independent measures of the competence of the infants. She used not just psychometric tests but problem-solving tasks in the child's own home. Then she went back to all those years of observation to see what kinds of family interactions were associated with competence or lack of competence at the end of the infancy period. The following is a summary of some of those findings.

1. When babies were the most competent, the mother was a good organizer, arranger, and shaper of infant experiences and routines.

2. Homes of competent infants had toys that were typical of a nursery school—crayons, paper, scissors, and such.

3. Competent children were allowed to help a lot with household chores—dusting, hammering, raking leaves, helping to sort laundry.

4. Fathers in the families of the competent babies spent more positive interaction time with their children. (All the families were two-parent families.)

5. Competent children were allowed access to what we would call more messy and perhaps even slightly dangerous items. There were blunt scissors in the homes for these children. Parents allowed their toddlers to help wash dishes even though a puddle might have to be sponged up from the kitchen floor. There is no one more enthusiastic at helping wash dishes than a two-year-old with soapsuds up to the shoulders!

6. Parents read to infants daily. Reading (with expression, interest, change of voice tone, and conversing about the story) correlates positively with later intellectual achievements in this and many other studies.

7. In the most competent children's homes, TV was severely limited and supervised. The children could watch one hour of a program such as "Sesame Street." In the least competent infants' homes, children watched six hours a day if they wanted and viewed any program.

8. Parents of competent children *modeled* appropriate activities for them. If the parents wanted a child to do something, they showed her or him how.

9. Mothers of competent children were good *observers*. They kept an eye out to see where their child was developmentally and what the child was doing in which part of the house. The mother gauged her responses and activities according to her observations of the child's interests, abilities, and temperament.

10. When the mother was highly restrictive and punitive, the child's competence was severely damaged. Mothers of competent infants often *participated* with the child during activities—praising, encouraging, suggesting, permitting, and facilitating.

11. Competent children's parents had firm, consistent household rules, and provided reasons for their rules.

12. The mothers of competent infants behaved as *teachers*. The mothers conversed, posed questions, transmitted information, and helped their children to solve problems. They helped their children to understand the unfamiliar. Smilansky (1968) observed that few low-income parents see themselves as teachers, and, of course, parents are the first and most precious teachers of all.

13. Mothers of competent infants engaged in dramatic play. For example, one day the researcher arrived and found a mother with her 16-month-old in the kitchen. Both had toy badminton rackets in their hands and were playing pretend badminton. Did you ever play fantasy train trip with young children? Did you ever see your child hiding in your closet among your clothes and say, "Where's Joan? I've lost Joan! What will Daddy say when he comes home? Where can Joan be?" All the while Joan, in full visibility in the closet, is entranced with joy at this pretend game. Role-playing games help promote cognitive competence. Other games and entertainments of these parents often had intellectual content. Entertainment by parents of less competent infants often involved just physical, rough-and-tumble play.

Interactive effects of environmental variables

Some of the research on optimal child growth environments looks at interactions between various aspects of the environment. Some research examines interactions between biological variables and environmental variables. For example, Beckwith (1971) found that Cattell Developmental Quotients of ten-month-old adopted infants correlated positively with both the extent to which a mother talked to and touched the baby and the extent to which the infant was given an opportunity to explore the home. Thus, positive personal interactions plus opportunities to explore and learn on one's own contribute to higher developmental scores. The teaching caregiver provides a loving, secure atmosphere and materials that allow the infant safely to discover through personal interactions and persistent explorations the physics and chemistry principles of how solids and liquids work.

Drillien (1964) in some of the early research on at-risk infants found that if a baby was premature and also raised in a low-income family, then the baby was eight times as likely to be in the lowest IQ quartile at four years of age (mean IQ = 63). Yet, by four years, low birth weight infants reared in middle-income homes had a normal mean IQ of 97. Thus, it seems that adverse intellectual consequences of low birth weight can be attenuated by favorable economic and home circumstances.

Davie (1972), in the National Child Development Study in England, also found this dual-risk situation. Low birth weight combined with rearing in lower-SES families led to delayed progress in school by age seven.

Golden, Birns, and Bridger (1973) examined changes in cognitive development during the critical infant period from 18 to 36 months. This is a transitional period from the sensorimotor to the symbolic (early preoperational) level of intelligence. Intelligence scores of Black males were strongly related to educational and economic conditions of the home by three years of age. The gap between middle SES and welfare children was greater than 20 IQ points.

Ricciuti (1975) examined the potential interactions between SES and biological influences on psychological development. He reported studies in which children had been severely malnourished in infancy and lived in low-income homes. When these infants were released (after hospitalization) to an adoptive family, their growth five years later was much superior to those children returned to the parental home. This was particularly true if the parental home was crowded as well as impoverished, where parents had fewer than five years of schooling, and where there was a common-law rather than formal marriage. In Lima, Ricciuti found that mothers of tall infants had two-and-one-half years vs. one grade of school, had fewer liaisons or marriages, and fewer pregnancies than mothers of shorter children. Tallness was associated with better developmental scores.

Elardo, Bradley, and Caldwell (1975) looked at differentiated aspects of the home environment. Particular aspects of the home environment at both 12 months and 24 months correlated significantly with 36-month Stanford-Binet IQ scores. As can be seen in table 2.1, the variables "maternal involvement with child" and "provision of appropriate play materials" prove particularly significant in relation to Binet performance at 36 months. When these correlations were reexamined at 54 months (Bradley and Caldwell 1976), the three home environment variables that correlated highest with Stanford-Binet IQ scores were still "provision of appropriate play materials" ($r = .56$), "maternal involvement with child" ($r = .55$), and "emotional and verbal responsivity of mother" ($r = .50$).

Infancy research of the past decade has helped to focus more specific-

Table 2.1

Correlations between inventory of home stimulation score at
12 months and at 24 months with mental test scores at 36 months

Home environment variables	12 months	24 months
Emotional and verbal responsivity of mother	.387**	.495**
Avoidance of restriction and punishment	.241*	.406**
Organization of physical and temporal environment	.389**	.413**
Provision of appropriate play materials	.561**	.635**
Maternal involvement with child	.468**	.545**
Opportunities for variety in daily stimulation	.283*	.499**
Total score	.551**	.695*
Multiple correlation	.588**	.718*

*p < .05
**p < .01

ally on parameters of an infant's rearing environment that can help a baby flourish developmentally. Other research has increased awareness of the variation in rearing environments for babies in different cultures around the world (Honig 1979; Whiting 1967).

Sex role differentiation

Recent sex role research has provoked a lot of rethinking about the bases for sex role differences that have been previously documented. To give you an idea of how difficult it will be to untangle nature from nurture in the determinations of sex roles attributes, let me describe a recent study (Will, Self, and Dafan 1976). A six-month-old baby was sometimes dressed in pink and called Beth, and adults played with her; sometimes the baby was dressed in blue and called Adam, and adults played with him. Each of the adults who played with the baby said, of course, they *knew* it was a little girl or little boy from the way it behaved: Look how sweet and feminine she had been, or look how vigorous and sturdy he had been! We will have a difficult time understanding the interaction of biological and environmental determinants of sex differences until we do a great deal more work in this area in which our awareness and our research are just beginning to grow.

Recent researchers have tried to assess the effects of labeling on socially mediated sex differences in infancy. Condry and Condry (1976) were interested in how parents and other adults shape boylike and girllike behaviors. Hundreds of adults were asked to rate the emotional responses of an infant (observed on videotape) presented with a variety of stimuli. The same infant in a particular situation was seen as displaying different emotions and different levels of emotional arousal depending on the sex attributed to the infant and on the sex of the rater.

Kagan (1972) and Birns (1976) have elucidated how very early sex differences seem to emerge. Moss (1974) found that during the first three weeks of life, mothers stimulated and attended to boy infants more but imitated the vocalizations of females more frequently.

Even earlier sex typing behavior by caregivers has been reported in a Tufts University research project (cited in Rogers 1977, p. 270). Thirty first-time parents rated day-old babies who did not differ in weight, length, or Apgar scores. Daughters were rated as softer, finer featured, and smaller. Sons were more often described at one day as hardy and well coordinated.

Lyberger-Ficek and Sternglanz (1975) observed that nurses in the hospital attended more to newborn males than females. This held true under all conditions observed, including crying, fussing, vocalizing, or quiet states.

Fagot (1974) examined reactions of both parents as a function of sex of toddler during an observed play situation in the home. Male toddlers played more with blocks, handled toys more, and played with transportation toys. Girls played more often with soft toys and dolls; they danced, asked for help, and dressed up more often than male toddlers. Male infants were punished for feminine behaviors significantly more than girls for masculine characteristics.

Thus, despite the admirable work done by Maccoby and Jacklin (1974) in coordinating research on sex differences, we still have a long way to go before we can understand the mechanisms by which caregivers nurture typical sex roles or attribute sex stereotyped characteristics to male or female infants.

Fathers and infants

It is a real pleasure to report that the father, long neglected as an important figure in an infant's life, has recently begun to receive active research attention (Honig 1977).

Historically, this acknowledgment of a critical role for fathers of infants has come in a roundabout way. Bowlby (1958) defined the child's relationship with his mother as the most important, especially during the early years. Bowlby stated:

> In the young child's eyes, father plays second fiddle and his value increases only as the child's vulnerability to deprivation decreases. Nevertheless, . . . fathers have their uses even in infancy. Not only . . . [can] they provide for their wives to enable them to devote themselves to the care of the infant and toddler, but, by providing love and companionship, they support her emotionally and help her maintain that harmonious contented mood in the aura of which the infant thrives. (p. 363)

In general, research has shown that fathers spend little time with their infants. Investigators (Kotelchuck 1976; Lamb 1976; Spelke, Zelazo, Kagan, and Kotelchuck 1973) have studied infants' attachment behaviors to their mothers and fathers. Infants 12 to 21 months of age did not register any preference for either parent, when separation protest, vocalizing, and smiling were the measures used. Lamb's (1976) research suggests that there are important differences between mothers and fathers in the areas of play and physical contact. Fathers engaged in more rough-and-tumble play, while mothers held the infant more, usually for caregiving or for curtailing of infant's activities. Mothers initiated more play with daughters than sons. Boy babies were held longer than girl babies by their fathers. Lamb observed, "When both parents are present, fathers are more salient persons than mothers. They are more likely to engage in unusual and more enjoyable types of play and, hence, appear to maintain the infant's attention more than the mothers do" (p. 324). Kotelchuck (1976) found that fathers spent 37 percent of their time in "enjoyable play activities" with baby compared to 26 percent of mother's time. Fathers played different kinds of games with infants, more vigorous games. Fathers seem to be more fun for babies! In Kotelchuck's study, those few infants who did not relate well to father (i.e., spent at least 15 seconds in his proximity on his arrival) came from families with the lowest amount of father caregiving.

In the split-screen experimental work at Harvard Medical School ("Infants Respond to Differing Behaviors of Mother, Father" 1977), infants were paired with mother, father, or stranger. Very different responses were observed in each dyadic interaction for babies from ten days to six months old. Typically, mother and infant would play reciprocal vocalization games. The infant's movements tended to be smooth and rounded. In contrast, the infant-father interaction typically consisted of short intense vocalizations, with reciprocity. Fathers showed short bursts of a tapping kind of touch to baby's body. Babies showed more abrupt body movements in dyadic interaction with fathers.

Some very provocative research on mother-father-infant relations was reported by Clarke-Stewart (1977). The higher the child's intelligence at 15 months, the more likely it was that the father would play with the baby at 30 months. And the chain of interaction seemed to proceed thus: Mother was really adept at eliciting reactions from and responding to the baby. A very alert, responsive baby developed. The father perceived this and then became more interested in interacting with the baby.

Some of the new research on fathering is beginning to explore the linkages between parent, infant, and spouse relationships (Pederson 1975). Pederson suggests that the father's warmth and affection may help support the mother and make her more effective. Parke and O'Leary's work (1975) suggests that the father's interest in the baby is likely to enhance the mother's interest in the baby. Parke's work suggests that mothers and fathers seem to touch male babies significantly more than female babies, and that fathers can be just as good as mothers in terms of holding infants and taking care of them. With increasing numbers of working mothers of infants, it is likely that we will become even more aware of the role of the father in nurturing infant development, both at a primary level and as a support for the mothering one.

Intervention models with infants

Infancy intervention research is not receiving the governmental support that funded so many brave, vigorous, and creative projects a decade ago. Our knowledge about caregiver training in infant care settings, about appropriate toys and curricula, staff ratios, and ecology was boosted significantly by those earlier projects.

Infant group care

You probably know about some of the classic and pioneer projects: Keister's program (1970) in Greensboro, North Carolina, or Caldwell's Children's Center in Syracuse and Kramer School Project in Little Rock

(Elardo and Caldwell 1974). The Parent-Child Centers, and especially the Parent-Child Development Centers in Birmingham, Houston, and New Orleans, were model programs for working with infants and their families (see Johnson et al. 1975, for a description of the Houston PCDC). Lally's Family Development Research Program in Syracuse provided enriched group care for infants and home visits with mothers (Lally and Honig 1977).

One of the crucial questions asked of these projects that provided enriched group care for infants was whether or not such day care was detrimental to infant emotional or cognitive development. The answer seems to be no if the caregivers are nurturant, responsive adults, and the quality of care is exemplary.

For example, Fowler and Kahn (1976) found continuing high ratings on IQ tests and on measures of socioemotional development for infants from a range of socioeconomic groups who had participated earlier in enriched group care. Caldwell et al. (1970) found no dilution of emotional attachment between mothers and infants, whether middle- or low-SES, as a function of day care for two years. Some investigators (such as Kagan et al. 1976) would add the further caution that detrimental effects may not be found if the children come from supportive families. Kagan studied Asian and Caucasian babies in day care from 3 to 30 months of age in comparison to matched home-reared controls.

The New York City Infant Day Care Study describes a five-year investigation of the effects of day care on the child and family. These results, which do not indicate deficits for day care children, are particularly interesting because they represent research into programs not designed specifically with research components or to provide showcase optimal child care environments ("Average Day Care: Harmful or Beneficial?" 1977).

Home teaching

Some infant intervention programs have focused on home teaching with mothers and infants (Lambie, Bond, and Weikart 1974). Gordon pioneered this concept (1971). Some parent programs have varied the kind of curriculum offered to determine which efforts with mothers might, for example, promote more language competence (Kessen and Fein 1976). They found that, regardless of SES, families with extensive kin relations were far more likely to be responsive to the programs. Thus, the ecology of infant intervention efforts is important. Children from families with an extended network of close family relations were more likely to show sustained problem solving. (See Hough and Stevens

1981.) Therefore, a supportive family network for parents may be a crucial variable in an intervention program to optimize an infant's functioning. Lally's program found similarly that the supports provided to the family were an important factor in the success of implementation of a home visitation program for helping families enhance the lives of their infants (Lally and Honig 1975).

Other intervention projects such as the BEEP project (Whitesides 1977) have tried to provide a variety of supports, including medical services and childrearing information, for mothers of infants.

Another question that has been raised frequently is whether or not infant intervention can increase cognitive competence. Heber's work (Heber and Garber 1973) particularly, and that of the quality research programs already referenced, suggest that while infants are in programs, cognitive gains are achieved. Lazar et al. (1977) have recently followed up children from many longitudinal intervention projects to see if there were any long-term effects of participation. A typical finding was that experimental children showed advances compared to controls years later. For example, Palmer (1978), in the Harlem Infant Study, had given two- and three-year-old boys two hours of tutoring weekly for eight months. By fifth grade, experimental children were reading three months ahead of the control group. Only 22 percent of the experimental children compared to 45 percent of the control children had repeated one or more grades. It appears that infant intervention may indeed show sustained effects of enrichment during elementary school years.

Intervention with high-risk infants

Infant intervention projects with high-risk infants have received particular attention in recent years (Caldwell and Stedman 1977; Goldstein et al. 1976; Ramey et al. 1979; Tjossem 1976).

Parent groups

Some projects have involved low-income teenage mothers with their infants (Field et al. 1980). Badger (1981) used group sessions to teach and motivate young unwed mothers to carry out appropriate behaviors and learning games with their babies.

Materials

Curricular guides for infant care and stimulation are a creative outcome of many of these infant intervention projects (Greenfield and Tronick 1980; Honig 1973, 1981; McDiarmid et al. 1975; Sparling and Lewis 1979). The Syracuse project also produced a detailed manual for training caregivers (Honig and Lally 1981). It is heartening to know of the wealth of information now available on how to help create optimal loving and learning and living experiences for babies (White 1975; Willis and Ricciuti 1975). The infancy intervention research projects have provided a great deal of practical information. They have increased our sensitivity to issues of tempo, ecology, rhythms of days, styles and processes of interaction, developmental appropriateness of toys, and the importance of integrating learning into routine daily experiences.

Since research evidence for the effects of infant day care is still fairly sparse, people often ask "Is it OK to leave babies in day care for a long day?" The answer, of course, is "It depends." What is happening at home? Is a mother bashing the child's head against the wall? Or feeling like doing it? Is she a wonderful mother who loves to stay home and take care of baby, or is he a wonderful father who is an active caregiver? What is the quality of care in the day care setting? Are the caregivers well-trained, patient, responsive adults with physical energy and a sense of humor to cope with the rigors of providing long hours of quality care?

Stone's (1974) three films on infant group care in Israel are jewels for describing quality infant group care. When you see Hannah's (the metapelet, or caregiver, in the film) ability to work serenely at the tempo of an infant and toddler, to be responsive, to be eliciting of language and provocative of language, rewarding of language, the way in which she structures the rhythms of the day, and her developmental match with the infant's learning style and competence level, it is so fantastic you would not mind leaving an infant there eight hours a day! And to top it off, the caregiver maintains a supportive positive relation with the parents so that the baby feels secure—his mother and his metapelet are friends. These films portray an ideal care situation.

On the other hand, I have seen custodial care in a fine physical setting—beautiful walls and furnishings, but bottles propped up at three months, and no talking or eye contact while babies were being diapered or held. So I feel that research evidence is not yet strong enough to answer the question about the long day care day for infants. Is it good or bad? It depends on who the caregivers are and the quality of care offered. Brazelton (1977) has also suggested that it depends not only on the quality of the caregiver's relation with the infant but also on the quality of the caregiver's positive emotional support for the mother. Otherwise a mother may feel the caregiver is better at the job. This could lead the mother to withdraw self-protectively from her intense positive emotional bond with her baby.

Intervention research with abused infants

The intervention experiments have shown us that we know how to give quality care. There are many films and written materials to use. There are also some excellent resources for those working with abusive mothers and infants (Bromwich 1981; Fraiberg 1980). Fraiberg uses a therapeutic intervention method to reach the abusive mother of an infant, the mother who alternately neglects the baby and beats on it. Fraiberg has found that only as one deeply reaches into the personal experiences of the mother, into the past parenting that the young woman herself went through—*her* rage, *her* grief, *her* pain—will one help her feel with and for her baby. A mother may say "I hated it when my mom took the strap to me." But does the mother *feel* or just say it? When the therapist gets to the feeling part, Fraiberg reports something that sounds quite miraculous. As the young woman reaches through to these deep buried feelings in herself of pain and rage and hatred, all of a sudden she hears that her baby has been screaming for 20 minutes. She runs and picks it up and catches the baby to her breast.

Stephenson (1975) has also reported some innovative attempts to work with very high-risk toddlers, siblings, and their neglecting and abusing parents. The seriousness of parental abuse whether neglect, emotional indifference, hostility, physical hurt, or combinations thereof have been documented dramatically. "Although most children in the maltreatment groups were functioning at the normal developmental level at nine months, they appeared relatively retarded at 24 months" (Egeland and Sroufe 1981). Maltreatment patterns had negative consequences despite variability in resilience of some infants.

Theory in relation to infant development

This last category will focus on research that has been carried out in a particular theoretical framework or that has tried to elucidate experimentally the process or behaviors predicted by a given theory. Many of the studies referred to earlier have been theoretically based. For example, Ainsworth's work has been very influenced by Bowlby's ethological theories of infant attachment and development.

A stimulus-response behavioral analysis theoretical framework has been used by the Gewirtzes in analyzing infant-caregiver interactions in the Israeli kibbutz. Gewirtz (1971) has also used the S-R paradigm to analyze imitation learning in young children. Many of the experiments that demonstrate neonatal perceptual learning or sensory competence or discriminative control have been based on reinforcement (operant conditioning) models.

Psychoanalytic theory profoundly influenced the form and process of the experimental therapy designed by Fraiberg for helping adolescents disturbed in their mothering patterns in her research reported in the previous section.

Some recent research has been predicated on Eriksonian theory that the development of basic trust versus mistrust is the foundation of later socioemotional development. The infant who emerges from the first year of life such that his first nuclear conflict has been decided more in favor of basic trust than mistrust will be in a better position for coping with the developmental crises of succeeding life stages. Beller and his colleagues (Gordon et al. 1973) have carried out collaborative research to delineate the behaviors and interactive processes that define trust between a toddler and an adult. This study tried to identify the characteristics of trust as displayed with the mother and with a strange play-lady under a variety of problem-solving or game situations.

Piagetian theory has accounted for an impressive amount of theory-oriented research with infants in the past decade. First, several investigators have been active in establishing infant assessment scales based on Piaget's ordinal steps in sensorimotor development. As behaviors emerge and become consolidated and integrated into the baby's total behavior pattern, the consistency of progression through the six stages of the sensorimotor period has been demonstrated and replicated by researchers.

Babies do not solve a three-screen hiding problem before they can play a single-screen game and find a hidden toy (Piaget 1952). There is lawfulness and predictability to the way development proceeds. Uzgiris and Hunt (1975) have been working for a decade on ordinal Piagetian scales of infant development. They have found that there is a very complicated grid pattern of relationships. There are complex dependencies between the development of one sensorimotor domain such as object permanence and another domain such as the development of means/ends relationships, or spatial understandings, or causality relations. It looks as if spatial understanding can only arise when some concept of object permanence has been attained. But the relations among all these different areas of infant development are still a little obscure.

Gratch (1976) has done a lot of work on a particular stage of object permanence—Stage Four. When one has been hiding a toy under

Screen A over and over and the baby keeps finding it, and then, right in full view of the baby one hides the toy under a new screen (B), where does the Stage Four baby look? Under Screen A. Gratch tries to elucidate the developmental significance of typical infant responses at a particular stage in learning object permanence.

McCall (1974) in his monograph on infant play and exploration was likewise struck by the dovetailing of his research findings with Piagetian theory. His felicitous summary of the evidence easily serves as a guidepost with strong methodological implications for optimizing the environments in which infants are reared.

> Both the animal and human data suggest that the early opportunity to explore a variety of animate and inanimate objects is related to the speed, vigor, and amount of manipulative exploration of novel and/or complex objects in the environment. These results suggest a developmental principle in which exploration of the environment provides the child with learned experience about his world which in turn modifies what stimulus events will next recruit his exploratory attention. Presumably, objects and events which represent moderate departures from his remembered experiences or accustomed level of environmental complexity will be explored most. (p. 7)

The implications for caregivers from this Piagetian equilibration principle is that if you can detect a skill or interest just as it is emerging, and if you carefully watch the process of how the baby explores and learns, you will be able to encourage new skills and understandings more sensitively.

Some research has been done to see whether Piagetian sensorimotor development could be advanced through specific games and activities carried out with babies from low-income families (Honig and Brill 1970; Paraskevopoulos and Hunt 1971). The first study suggests that in ordinary households babies usually get ample sensorimotor involvement with their environment so that sensorimotor learnings cannot markedly be advanced, although object permanence development did seem to be more susceptible to enrichment. When institutional babies were compared with enriched low-income babies (in the Hunt study), marked advances in certain sensorimotor competencies were found for the stimulated infants. Thus, although research has confirmed the orderly progression of Piaget's stages and processes of sensorimotor development, we are not yet sure of the minimal stimulation and opportunities necessary for normal development of sensorimotor competencies during the first years.

Other researchers have used other cognitive models, such as a generalized expectancy model, to account for the importance of mother-infant interactions for facilitating later development. For example, Lee-Painter and Lewis (1974) have noted:

> We believe that contingency is an important feature of the mother-infant interactional system not only as reinforcement but for its motivational effect. While the contingency of a maternal response does reinforce a particular infant behavior, at the same time it facilitates the development of a general cognitive expectation that the infant's action can influence its environment. . . . This pattern of generalized expectancy can be used as an explanation of the fact that the infant whose cries are reinforced [by early adult response] during the first half-year of life is the infant who shows not more crying, but more verbal communication of all kinds at the end of the first year. (p. 2)

Further on in their paper, Lee-Painter and Lewis go on to propose:

> that the social competence of the infant is of great importance to its development of a world view. For example, let us look at a period of interaction between a mother and her infant: The infant cries and the mother looks over and says, "Don't cry, baby." The infant pauses and then continues to cry. The mother then picks up the baby and pats its back. The infant stops crying. The mother says, "Your diaper is wet." The infant smiles as she changes the diaper. The mother starts singing a song to her baby. How can we describe this interaction? Certainly we must agree that within this structure social and emotional elements exist. But is it not reasonable to call some elements of this interaction cognitive? Infant and mother have each transmitted messages which were received by the other. The behavior of one influences and modifies the behavior of the other. The infant's ability to sustain this chain of interaction facilitates his learning and his actions affect his environment. Thus, the very nature of the interaction is cognitive, and it is this type of cognitive structure which we must explore if we are to understand the process of development. (p. 8)

Thus the importance of reciprocal, mutually responsive chains of interactions between mother and infant have been proposed by a wide variety of theorists, such as Piaget, Erikson, and Sears and Lewis, as facilitators not only of socioemotional functioning but also as facilitators of the development of cognitive structures.

Research on prosocial behaviors is challenging Piagetian theory that egocentric behavior predominates during the infant and preschool years. Yarrow et al. (1973) have found that the capacity for altruism, empathy, and nurturant actions toward others can be found in some infants under two years of age and two-thirds of these baby altruists continued to behave more socially when looked at five years later.

Conclusions

Research evidence to date appears remarkably compatible with at least two implications from Piaget's theory of development: the importance of a variety of appropriate environmental experiences for the process of equilibration, and the basic and crucial role of the equilibration process in the establishment of new and differentiated cognitive structures and competencies. Yet research evidence also suggests strongly that the emergence of these cognitive structures is facilitated within loving social-emotional relationships. Perhaps the most salient finding of the past decade's infancy research is that *loving and learning are intrinsic and intertwined for infant flourishing.* Erikson and Piaget together can provide a theoretical matrix from which one can draw implications for programs to optimize experiences for infants.

Theory and research have added much to our understanding of how to make life better for babies. Let us all use these understandings to go forth and make life better for babies!

References

Ainsworth, M.D.S., and Bell, S.M. "Mother-Infant Interaction and the De-velopment of Competence." In *The Growth of Competence,* ed. K.S. Connoly and J.S. Bruner. New York: Academic Press, 1973.

American Cancer Society. "When a Woman Smokes." December 1976.

Arend, R.; Gore, F.L.; and Sroufe, L.A. "Continuity of Individual Adaptation from Infancy to Kindergarten: A Predictive Study of Ego-Resiliency and Curiosity in Preschoolers." *Child Development* 50 (1979): 950-959.

"Average Day Care: Harmful or Beneficial?" *Carnegie Quarterly* 25, no. 3 (Summer 1977).

Badger, E.D. "Effects of Parent Education on Teenage Mothers and Their Off-spring." In *Teenage Parents and Their Offspring,* ed. K.G. Scott, T. Field, and E. Robertson. New York: Grune & Stratton, 1981.

Baldwin, W.H. "Adolescent Pregnancy and Childbearing: Growing Concerns for Americans." *Population Bulletin* 31, no. 2 (1976).

Beckwith, L. "Relationships Between Attributes of Mothers and Their Infants' IQ Scores." *Child Development* 42, no. 4 (1971): 1083-1097.

Bell, S., and Ainsworth, M.D.S. "Infant Crying and Maternal Responsiveness." *Child Development* 43 (1972): 1171-1190.

Bellugi, U., and Brown, R. "The Acquisition of Language." *Monographs of the Society for Research in Child Development* 29, no. 92 (1964).

Birns, B. "The Emergence and Socialization of Sex Differences in the Earliest Years." *Merrill-Palmer Quarterly* 22 (1976): 229-254.

Bloom. L. *Language Development: Form and Function in Emerging Grammars.* Cambridge, Mass.: MIT Press, 1970.

Bower, T.G.R. *Development in Infancy.* San Francisco: W.H. Freeman, 1976.

Bower, T.G.R. *A Primer of Infant Development.* San Francisco: W.H. Freeman, 1977.

Bower, T.G.R.; Broughton, J.M.; and Moore, M.K. "The Development of the Object Concept as Manifested by Changes in the Tracking Behavior of Infants Between 7 and 20 Weeks of Age." *Journal of Experimental Psychology* 11, no. 2 (1971).

Bowes, W.A.; Brackbill, Y.; Conway, E.; and Steinschneider, A. "Effects of Obstetrical Medication on Fetus and Infant." *Monographs of the Society for Research in Child Development* 35, no. 4 (1970).

Bowlby, J. "The Nature of the Child's Tie to His Mother." *International Journal of Psychoanalysis* 39 (1958): 350-373.

Bradley, R.H., and Caldwell, B.M. "The Relation of Infant's Home Environments to Mental Test Performance at Fifty-Four Months: A Follow-Up Study." *Child Development* 47 (1976): 1172-1174.

Brazelton, T.B. "Mother-Infant Reciprocity." In *Maternal Attachment and Mothering Disorders,* ed. M.H. Klaus, T. Leger, and M.A. Trause. Sausalito, Calif.: Johnson Baby Products Co., 1975.

Brazelton, T.B. "What Must We Think about a Passive Model for Infancy?" Paper presented at the annual conference of the National Association for the Education of Young Children, Chicago, November 1977.

Brazelton, T.B.; Koslowski, B.; and Main, M. "The Origins of Reciprocity: The Early Mother-Infant Interaction." In *The Effect of the Infant on Its Caregiver,* ed. M. Lewis and L. Rosenblum. New York: Wiley, 1973.

Bromwich, R. *Working with Parents and Infants: An Interactional Approach.* Baltimore: University Park Press, 1981.

Bruner, J.S. "Organization of Early Skilled Action." *Child Development* 44 (1973): 1-11.

Bruner, J.S. *Beyond the Information Given: Studies in the Psychology of Knowing.* New York: Norton, 1973.

Bruner, J.S. "Early Social Interaction and Language Acquisition." In *Studies in Mother-Infant Interactions,* ed. H.R. Schaffer. London: Academic Press, 1977.

Caldwell, B.M., and Stedman, D.J., eds. *Infants' Education: A Guide for Helping Handicapped Children in the First Three Years.* New York: Walker, 1977.

Caldwell, B.M.; Wright, C.; Honig, A.S.; and Tannenbaum, J. "Infant Day Care and Attachment." *American Journal of Orthopsychiatry* 40, no. 37 (1970): 397-412.

Carew, J.V.; Chan, I.; and Halfar, C. *Observing Intelligence in Young Children.* Englewood Cliffs, N.J.: Prentice-Hall, 1976.

Casati, I., and Lezine, I. *The Stages of Sensory Motor Intelligence in the Child from Birth to Two Years.* Paris: Center of Applied Psychology, 1968.

Charlesworth, W.R. "The Role of Surprise in Cognitive Development." In *Studies in Cognitive Development,* ed. D. Elkind and J. H. Flavell. New York: Oxford Press, 1969.

Clarke-Stewart, K.A. "And Daddy Makes Three: The Father's Impact on Mother and Young Child." *Child Development* 49 (1978): 466-478.

Cohen, S.E. "Caregiver-Child Interaction and Competence in Preterm Children." Paper presented at the biennial meeting of the Society for Research in Child Development, New Orleans, March 1977.

Condry, J., and Condry, S. "Sex Differences: A Study of the Eye of the Beholder." *Child Development* 47 (1976): 812-819.

Cornell, E.H., and Gottfried, A.W. "Intervention with Premature Human Infants." *Child Development* 47 (1976): 32-39.

Davie, R.; Butler, N.; and Goldstein, H. *From Birth to Seven: A Report of the National Child Development Study.* London: Longman, 1972.

Drillien, C.M. *The Growth and Development of the Prematurely Born Infant.* Baltimore: Williams & Wilkins, 1964.

Egeland, B., and Sroufe, A. "Developmental Sequelae of Maltreatment in Infancy." In *New Directions for Child Development*, 1981.

Elardo, P.T., and Caldwell, B.M. "The Kramer Adventure: A School for the Future?" *Childhood Education* 50, no. 3 (January 1974): 143-152.

Elardo, R.; Bradley, R.; and Caldwell, B.M. "The Relation of Infants' Home Environments to Mental Test Performance from Six to Thirty-Six Months: A Longitudinal Analysis." *Child Development* 46 (1975): 71-76.

Erikson, E. *Childhood and Society.* New York: Norton, 1963.

Fagan, J.F. "Infants' Recognition of Invariant Features of Faces." *Child Development* 47 (1976): 627-638.

Fagot, B.I. "Sex-Determined Parental Reinforcing Contingencies in Toddler Children." Paper presented at the biennial meeting of the Society for Research in Child Development, New Orleans, March 1977.

Fagot, B.I. "Sex-Related Stereotyping of Toddlers' Behavior and Parental Reaction." *Developmental Psychology* 10 (1974): 554-558.

Fantz, R.L. "Pattern Vision in Newborn Infants." *Science* 140 (1963): 296-297.

Fein, G.G. "The Social Context of Mother-Infant Relations: A Study of Home-Based Education." Paper presented at the biennial meeting of the Society for Research in Child Development, New Orleans, March 1977.

Ferreira, A.J. "Emotional Factors in Prenatal Environment: A Review." *Journal of Nervous and Mental Disease* 141 (1965): 108-118.

Field, T. "Effects of Early Separation, Interactive Deficits, and Experimental Manipulations on Mother-Infant Interaction." Paper presented at the biennial meeting of the Society for Research in Child Development, New Orleans, March 1977.

Field, T.M.; Widmayer, S.M.; Stringer, S.; and Ignatoff, E. "Teenage, Lower Class, Black Mothers and Their Preterm Infants: An Intervention and Developmental Follow-Up." *Child Development* 51 (1980): 426-436.

Fowler, W., and Khan, N. *A Follow-Up Investigation of the Later Development of Infants in Enriched Group Care.* Document No. ED 093 506. Urbana, Ill.: ERIC Clearinghouse on Early Childhood Education, 1976.

Fowler, W., and Swenson, A. "The Influence of Early Stimulation on Language Development." Paper presented at the biennial meeting of the Society for Research in Child Development, Denver 1975.

Fraiberg, S. *Clinical Studies in Infant Mental Health: The First Year of Life.* New York: Basic Books, 1980.

Friedlander, B.Z. "Receptive Language Development in Infancy." *Merrill-Palmer Quarterly* 16 (1970): 7-52.

Gewirtz, J.L. "Conditional Responding As a Paradigm for Observational Imitative Learning and Vicarious Reinforcements." In *Advances in Child Development and Behavior, Vol. 6,* ed. H.W. Reese. New York: Academic Press, 1971.

Gibson, E.J., and Walk, R.D. "The Visual Cliff." *Scientific American* 202 (1960): 64-71.

Golden, M., and Birns, B. "Social Class and Cognitive Style in Infancy." *Child Development* 42 (1971): 2114-2116.

Golden, M.; Birns, B.; and Bridger, W. "Review and Overview: Social Class and Cognitive Development." Paper presented at the biennial meeting of the Society for Research in Child Development, Philadelphia, April 1973.

Goldstein, K.M.; Caputo, D.V.; and Taub, H.B. "The Effects of Prenatal and Perinatal Complications on Development at One Year of Age." *Child Development* 47 (1976): 613-621.

Gordon, I.J. *Early Child Stimulation Through Parent Education: Final Report.* Gainesville, Fla.: University of Florida, Institute for Development of Human Resources, 1971.

Gordon, I.; Beller, E.K.; Lally, J.R.; Yarrow, L.; Moreno, P.; Rand, C.; and Freiberg, K. *Studies in Socioemotional Development in Infancy: A Collaborative Study.* Washington, D.C.: Office of Child Development, 1973.

Gratch, G. "On Levels of Awareness of Objects in Infants and Students Thereof." *Merrill-Palmer Quarterly* 22 (1976): 157-176.

Greenfield, P., and Tronick, P.M. *Infant Curriculum: The Bromley Health Guide to the Care of Infants in Groups.* Rev. ed. Santa Monica, Calif.: Goodyear, 1980.

Hardy, J.B. "Rubella and Its Aftermath." *Children* 16, no. 3 (1969): 91-96.

Harlow, H. "The Nature of Love." *The American Psychologist* 13 (1958): 673-685.

Heber, R., and Garber, H. *The Milwaukee Project: Early Intervention as a Technique to Prevent Mental Retardation.* Storrs, Conn.: National Leadership Institute Teacher Education/Early Childhood, March 1973.

Honig, A.S. *Fathering: A Bibliography.* (Catalog #164). Urbana, Ill.: ERIC Clearinghouse on Early Childhood Education, 1977.

Honig, A.S. "Child-Rearing Practices of Urban Poor Mothers of Infants and Three-Year-Olds in Five Cultures." Paper presented at the biennial meeting of the Society for Research in Child Development, San Francisco, March 1979.

Honig, A.S. *Infant Education and Stimulation (Birth to 3 Years.) A Bibliography.* (Catalog #1300-48). Urbana, Ill.: ERIC Clearinghouse on Early Childhood Education, 1973.

Honig, A.S. "What Are the Needs of Infants?" *Young Children,* in press.

Honig, A.S., and Brill, S. "A Comparative Analysis of the Piagetian Development of Twelve-Month-Old Disadvantaged Infants in an Enrichment Center with Others Not in Such a Center." Paper presented at the annual meeting of the American Psychological Association, Miami, September 1970.

Honig, A.S., and Caldwell, B.M. "The Early Language Assessment Scale (ELAS)." Unpublished manuscript, Syracuse University Children's Center, 1965.

Honig, A.S.; Caldwell, B.M.; and Tannenbaum, J. "Patterns of Information Processing Used by and With Young Children in a Nursery School Setting." *Child Psychiatry and Human Development* 3, no. 4 (1973): 216-230.

Honig, A.S., and Lally, J.R. *Infant Caregiving: A Design for Training.* 2nd ed. Syracuse, N.Y.: Syracuse University Press, 1981.

Honig, A.S., and Oski, F. "Developmental Scores of Iron Deficient Infants and Effects of Therapy." *Infant Behavior and Development* 1 (1978): 168-176.

Honig, A.S., and Wittmer, D.S. "An Inquiry into Questions Asked by Teachers of Children from Low Income Families in Day Care Settings." In Proceedings of the Tenth Annual Conference on Piaget and the Helping Professions, Los Angeles: University of Southern California Press, 1981.

Hough, R.A., and Stevens, J.H., Jr. "Research in Review. Social Networks as Supports for Parenting." *Young Children* 36, no. 3 (March 1981): 50-60.

Hunt, J. McV., 1977: personal communication.

"Infants Respond to Differing Behavior of Mothers, Fathers." *Clinical Psychiatry News* 5, no. 2 (February 1977).

Johnson, D.L.; Leler, H.; Kahn, A.J.; Hines, R.P.; Torres, M.; and Sanchez, P. Progress Report: Houston Parent-Child Development Center. University of Houston, Texas, May 1975.

Kagan, J. "The Emergence of Sex Differences." *School Review* 80, no. 2 (1972): 217-227.

Kagan, J.; Kearsley, R.B.; and Zelazo, P. "The Effects of Infant Day Care on Psychological Development." *ERIC Newsletter* 10, no. 2 (1976).

Keister, M.E. *"The Good Life" for Infants and Toddlers.* Washington, D.C.: National Association for the Education of Young Children, 1970.

Kennell, J. "Evidence for a Sensitive Period in the Human Mother." In *Maternal Attachment and Mothering Disorders,* ed. M.H. Klaus, T. Leger, and M.A. Trause. Sausalito, Calif.: Johnson Baby Products, 1975.

Kessen, W., and Fein, G.G. *Home-Based Infant Education: Language, Play, and Social Development.* Document No. ED 118 233. Urbana, Ill.: ERIC Clearinghouse on Early Childhood Education, 1976.

Klaus, M.H., and Kennell, J.H. *Maternal-Infant Bonding.* St. Louis: Mosby, 1976

Kotelchuck, M. "The Infant's Relationship to the Father: Experimental Evidence." In *The Role of the Father in Child Development,* ed. M.E. Lamb. New York: Wiley, 1976.

Lally, J.R., and Honig, A.S. "Education of Infants and Toddlers from Low-Income and Low-Education Backgrounds." In *Infant Assessment and Intervention,* ed. B. Friedlander, G. Kirk, and G. Sterritt. New York: Brunner/Mazel, 1975.

Lally, J.R., and Honig, A.S. *Final Report, Family Development Research Program.* ERIC Document No. ED 143 458. Syracuse, N.Y.: Syracuse University Children's Center, July 1977.

Lamb, M.E. "Interactions Between Eight-Month-Old Children and Their Fathers and Mothers." In *The Role of the Father in Child Development,* ed. M.E. Lamb. New York: Wiley, 1976.

Lambie, D.Z.; Bond, J.T.; and Weikart, D.P. *Home Teaching with Mothers and Infants.* Ypsilanti, Mich.: High/Scope, 1974.

Lazar, I.; Hubbell, V.R.; Murray, H.; Rosche, M.; and Royce, J. *The Persistence of Preschool Effects: A Long-Term Follow-Up of Fourteen Infant and Preschool Experiments.* Washington, D.C.: Office of Human Development Services, 1977.

Lee-Painter, S., and Lewis, M. "Mother-Infant Interaction and Cognitive Development." Paper presented at the annual meetings of the Eastern Psychological Association, Philadelphia, April 1974.

Lewis, M. "Early Sex Differences in the Human: Studies of Socioemotional

Development." *Archives of Sexual Behavior* 4, no. 4 (1975):329-335.

Lewis, M. "Early Socioemotional Development and Its Relevance for Curriculum." *Merrill-Palmer Quarterly* 23, no. 4 (1977a): 279-286.

Lewis, M., 1977b: personal communication.

Lewis, M., and Wilson, C.D. "Infant Development in Lower-Class American Families." *Human Development* 15 (1972): 112-127.

Littman, B. "Precursors and Correlates of Two-Year-Old Competence in Preterm Children." Paper presented at the biennial meeting of the Society for Research in Child Development, New Orleans, March 1977.

Lozoff, B.; Brillenham, G.; Trause, M.A.; Kennell, J.H.; and Klaus, M.H. "The Mother-Newborn Relationship: Limits of Adaptability." *Journal of Pediatrics* 91 (July 1977).

Lyberger-Ficek, S., and Sternglanz, S.H. "Innate Sex Differences in Neonatal Crying: Myth or Reality." Paper presented at the biennial meeting of the Society for Research in Child Development, Denver, April 1975.

MacNamara, J. "Cognitive Basis of Language Learning in Infants." *Psychological Review* 79, no. 1 (1972): 1-13.

Maccoby, E.E., and Jacklin, C.N. *The Psychology of Sex Differences*. Stanford, Calif.: Stanford University Press, 1974.

Matas, L.; Arend, R.A.; and Sroufe, L.A. "Continuity of Adaptation in the Second Year: The Relationship Between Quality of Attachment and Later Competence." *Child Development* 49 (1978): 547-556.

McCall, R.B. "Exploratory Manipulation and Play in the Human Infant." *Monographs of the Society for Research in Child Development* 39, no. 155 (1974).

McDiarmid, N.J.; Peterson, M.A.; and Sutherland, J.R. *Loving and Learning: Interacting with Your Child from Birth to Three*. New York: Harcourt, Brace, Jovanovich, 1975.

McGraw, M.B. *Growth: A Study of Johnny and Jimmy*. New York: Appleton-Century, 935.

Minde, K.; Ford, L.; Celhoffer, L.; and Boukydis, C. "Interactions of Mothers and Nurses with Premature Infants." *Canadian Medical Association Journal* 113 (1975): 741-745.

Moerk, E. "Changes in Verbal Child-Mother Interactions with Increasing Language Skills of the Child." *Journal of Psycholinguistic Research* 3, no. 2 (1972): 229-258.

Moerk, E. "Principles of Interaction in Language Learning." *Merrill-Palmer Quarterly* 18 (1972): 229-258.

Moerk, E. "Processes of Language Teaching and Training in the Interactions of Mother-Child Dyads." *Child Development* 47, no. 4 (December 1976): 1064-1078.

Moss, H.A. "Early Sex Differences and Mother-Infant Interaction." In *Sex Differences in Behavior*, ed. R.C. Friedman, R.M. Richart, and R.L. Vande Wille. New York: Wiley, 1974.

Ostrea, E.M., Jr., and Chavez, C.L. "Perinatal Problems (Including Neonate Withdrawal) in Maternal Drug Addiction: A Study of 230 Cases." *The Journal of Pediatrics* 94 (1979): 292-295.

Palmer, F.H. "The Effects of Early Childhood Intervention." Paper presented at the annual meeting of the American Association for the Advancement of Science. Denver, 1977. (ERIC Document No. ED 143 427, 1978)

Papoušek, H. "Conditioned Head Rotation Reflexes in Infants in the First

Months of Life." *Acta Pediatrica* 50 (1961): 565-576.

Paraskevopoulos, J., and Hunt, J. McV. "Object Construction and Imitation under Differing Conditions of Rearing." *Journal of Genetic Psychology* 119 (1971): 301-321.

Parke, R.D., and O'Leary, S. "Father-Mother-Infant Interaction in the Newborn Period: Some Findings, Some Observations, and Some Unresolved Issues." In *The Developing Individual in a Changing World, Vol. 2. Social and Environmental Issues*, ed. K. Riegel and J. Meacham. The Hauge: Mouton, 1975.

Parmelee, A.H., and Haber, A. "Who Is the 'Risk Infant'?" *Clinical Obstetrics and Gynecology* 16 (1973): 346-387.

Pederson, F.A. "Mother, Father, and Infant As an Interactive System." Paper presented at the symposium "Fathers and 'Infants' "at the meetings of the American Psychological Association, Chicago, August 1975.

Piaget, J. *The Origins of Intelligence in Children*. New York: International University sities Press, 1952.

Ramey, C.T.; Favian, D.C.; and Campbell, F.A. "Predicting IQ from Mother Infant Interactions." *Child Development* 50 (1979): 804-814.

Rheingold, H. "Independent Behavior of the Human Infant." In *Minnesota Symposium on Child Development*, Vol. 7, ed. A.D. Pick. Minneapolis: University of Minnesota Press, 1973.

Ricciuti, H.N. "Interaction of Adverse Socio-Environmental, Nutritional, and Health Conditions Influencing Early Development: A Review of Recent Research." Paper presented at the Conference of the International Society for the Study of Behavioral Development, University of Surrey, Guildford, England, July 1975.

Rogers, D. *Child Psychology*. 2nd ed. Monterey, Calif.: Brooks/Cole, 1977.

Scarr-Salapatek, S., and Williams, M.L. "The Effects of Early Stimulation on Low Birth-Weight Infants." *Child Development* 44 (1973): 94-101.

Schulman, C.A. "Sleep Patterns in Newborn Infants As a Function of Suspected Neurological Impairment of Maternal Heroin Addiction." Paper presented at the meeting of the Society for Research in Child Development, Santa Monica, California, March 1969.

Schachter, F.F. *Everyday Mother Talk to Toddlers*. New York: Academic Press, 1979.

Siqueland, E.R., and Lipsitt, L.P. "Conditioned Head-Turning Behavior in Newborns." *Journal of Experimental Child Psychiatry* 3 (1966): 356-376.

Smilansky, S. *The Effects of Sociodramatic Play on Disadvantaged Pre-School Children*. New York: Wiley, 1968.

Snow, C.E. "Mothers' Speech to Children Learning Language." *Child Development* 43 (1972): 549-565.

Sparling, J., and Lewis, I. *Learningames for the First Three Years*. New York: Walker, 1979.

Spelke, E.; Zelazo, P.; Kagan, J.; and Kotelchuck, M. "Father Interaction and Separation Protest." *Developmental Psychology* 9 (1973): 83-90.

Sroufe, L.A., and Waters, E. "Attachment As an Organizational Construct." *Child Development* 48 (1977): 1194-1199.

Stayton, D.J.; Hogan, R.; and Ainsworth, M.D.S. "Infant Obedience and Maternal Behavior: The Origins of Socialization Reconsidered." *Child Development* 42 (1971): 1057-1069.

Stephenson, P.S. *Project Toddler: Interim Report*. Division of Child Psychiatry,

University of British Columbia, Canada, September 1975.

Stern, D. "Mother and Infant at Play: The Dyadic Interaction Involving Facial, Vocal, and Gaze Behaviors." In *The Effect of the Infant on Its Caregiver,* ed. M. Lewis and L. Rosenblum. New York: Wiley, 1973.

Stone, J. *Infant Development in the Kibbutz. Rearing Kibbutz Babies. Day Care for a Kibbutz Toddler. Study Guide for Three Films on Kibbutz Infancy.* New York: Institute for Child Mental Health, 1974.

Streissguth, A.P.; Landesman-Dwyer, S.; Martin, J.C.; and Smith, D.W. "Teratogenic Effects of Alcohol in Humans and Laboratory Animals." *Science* 209 (1980): 353-361.

Thomas, A.; Chess, S.; Birch, H.G.; and Hertzig, M.E. *Behavioral Individuality in Early Childhood.* New York: New York University Press, 1963.

Tizard, B.; Cooperman, O.; Joseph, A.; and Tizard, J. "Environmental Effects on Language Development: A Study of Young Children in Long-Stay Residential Nurseries." *Child Development* 4 (1972): 337-358.

Tjossem, T.D., ed. *Intervention Strategies for High Risk Infants and Young Children.* Baltimore: University Park Press, 1976.

Uzgiris, I., and Hunt, J. McV. *Toward Ordinal Scales of Psychological Development in Infancy.* Urbana, Ill.: University of Illinois Press, 1975.

Walters, J. "Birth Defects and Adolescent Pregnancies." *Journal of Home Economics* 62 (November 1975): 23-29.

Werner, E.E.; Bierman, J.M.; and French, R.E. *The Children of Kauai: A Longitudinal Study from the Prenatal Period to Age Ten.* Honolulu: University of Hawaii Press, 1971.

White, B. *The First Three Years of Life.* Englewood Cliffs, N.J.: Prentice-Hall, 1975.

Whitesides, B. "The Brookline Early Education Project." *Young Children* 33, no. 1 (November 1977): 64-68.

Willerman, L.; Broman, S.H.; and Fiedler, M. "Infant Development, Preschool IQ, and Social Class." *Child Development* 41, no. 1 (1970): 70-77.

Whiting, B., ed. *Six Cultures: Studies of Child Rearing.* New York: Wiley, 1967.

Will, J.A.; Self, P.A.; and Dafan, N. "Maternal Behavior and Perceived Sex of Infant." *American Journal of Orthopsychiatry* 46 (1976): 135-139.

Willis, A., and Ricciuti, H. *A Good Beginning for Babies: Guidelines for Group Care.* Washington, D.C.: National Association for the Education of Young Children, 1975.

Wolff, P. "The Causes, Controls, and Organization of Behavior in the Neonate." *Psychological Issues* 5, no. 17 (1965).

Yarrow, L.J.; Rubenstein, J.L.; Pederson, F.A.; and Jankowski, J.J. "Dimensions of Early Stimulation and Their Differential Effects on Infant Development." *Merrill-Palmer Quarterly* 18 (1972): 205-218.

Yarrow, M.R.; Scott, P.; and Zahn-Waxler, C. "Learning Concern for Others." *Developmental Psychology* 8 (1973): 240-260.

Mary Giffin, M.D.

3

Assessing infant and toddler development

To be an infant is to be at risk, regardless of the wealth of nurturing and the quality of the supportive environment and personnel. The research of Thomas, Chess, and Birch (1970) has confirmed that 15 percent of infants are "difficult." This primary dysfunction is undoubtedly a psychobiologic condition. Even for the 85 percent of infants who are not described as difficult, there are two major factors that must be stabilized if healthy development is to become possible: the movement from physiologic disequilibrium to homeostasis, and the development of mutual cuing between the mother and infant. All infants are, in some sense, at risk. The children of young mothers, children of poverty, children with poor nutrition, these are children at *high risk*. It is frequently the children at high risk who are the infants in group settings. Rather than debating the advantages and disadvantages of the varying types of group settings, it seems more important to focus on detection of children at high risk with a view toward appropriate intervention. Indeed, while the debate continues over advantages of caring for infants in the varying kinds of groups, babies who are showing unmistakable evidence of pathological symptoms are growing into toddlers.

Child development issues

Neonates are totally egocentric beings. They react with their whole body—passionately despairing when hungry or in pain, blissfully relaxed when satisfied. Gradually, around the end of the first month of life, they begin to associate a tone of voice and a firm set of hands with being fed or made comfortable, and they quiet down when these reassuring sounds or sensations are perceived. This is the beginning of the de-

47

The teacher's own observation and intuitive reading of mother and child are the most reliable diagnostic tools.

velopment of the crucial capacity to tolerate the delay of gratification. The sensitive mother or caregiver helps the baby gradually increase this tolerance. Feeding the baby too quickly robs the baby of the chance to learn to wait. Feeding after too great a delay leads to a state of overwhelming tension. Inappropriate timing of this early stage can have lasting consequences.

By about three months of age, the fleeting smiles of neonates become social smiles in response to their smiling mother. This interplay helps babies toward a growing awareness that there is someone out there who feeds, soothes, plays, and relieves their unpleasant tensions. As babies explore their toes, fingers, faces, the faces of their mothers, as well as objects in cribs, they are making a map of the boundaries of their bodies. They learn that all does not begin and end with oneself.

Somewhere between six and eight months, their cognitive faculties have developed to the point where the "someone out there" is a specific person whom they need desperately. Whereas before any comforting adult would do, now only mother will do. As babies perceive their separate, helpless state, strangers intensify their need for mother. If there has been multiple or indifferent mothering, a baby will not show this typical "stranger anxiety" and may not be developing a necessary sense of self (and others). Again, the sensitive mother will help her child learn to tolerate the anxiety about separateness by supporting without smothering, by accepting rather than rejecting dependence on her. In this way the anxiety becomes more manageable, and as babies begin to creep or walk, they practice leaving mother and exploring the world. Their curiosity is stimulated to explore further if that world is safe and interesting and mother is never too far away. As they make these strides for independence and autonomy, they frequently check back to make sure that mother is available and that, therefore, the world is secure. New mothers may be puzzled and at times irritated by the alternating progression and regression of their child's behavior. Mothers might be more tolerant and flexible if the child care worker reassures them that this pushing ahead and pulling back is normal and necessary and will occur repeatedly throughout childhood.

One of the ways in which children increase their capacity to cope on their own is to invest a favorite toy or blanket with the loving and comforting qualities of mother. The presence of this transitional object signals a decrease in the child's total reliance on mother. While Linus has made the security blanket something to be tolerated with a smile, mothers should know that it is evidence of a healthy and important stage in the emerging personality.

The crucial task of the first year is the development of a sense of self. Learning to trust in the essential reliability and consistency of others forms the bedrock for trust in one's self. Thus equipped, toddlers use their boundless energies to learn about the world of objects and people. They experiment endlessly with what they can do with their bodies in that world. Climbing, walking, running, they explore with gusto the ups and downs and the ins and outs of their environment. It is important for the child care worker to assess both the quality of the toddler's activity and the quality of the mother's response to it. It is during this period that the overanxious mother can squelch healthy curiosity and bind the child to her with dependency based on fear. Conversely, the studiedly casual or pathologically negligent mother will fail to protect her child adequately. Thus, both the child who appears anxious and constricted and the child who has an unusual number of injuries or who repeatedly ingests harmful substances should alert the child care worker to inquire closely into what is happening at home. If the mother is clearly adequate, the possibility of an organically damaged child should be investigated. When the degree of overprotection or of indifference and neglect exceed the bounds of normality, a referral of mother to a mental health worker would be appropriate.

The back and forth pattern of personality growth is particularly evident during this second year of life. Exuberant independence alternates rapidly with whining and clinging. Each new accomplishment may be preceded and followed by brief periods of fussing and general crankiness. The child care worker's patience with parental complaints and sympathetic support can do much to help parents weather this difficult period. Without such support, parents may be too frustrated and overwhelmed to cope with the power struggles that typically mark the end of the second year of life.

As the two-year-olds learn the power of the word "no," they wield it at every opportunity, flaunting their increasing autonomy. Again, the sensitive parent needs to gauge how much pressure is *just enough* for compliance in matters that cannot be compromised. Too little pressure (or protection) may result in anxious, driven, intrusive behavior. Too much pressure may result in hostile withholding and constriction. Such behavior would be clearly observable during the day care program.

During the third year of life, the quality of the child's language becomes a significant diagnostic index. The child care worker will be engaged with the child directly in conversation during which she or he can check for linguistic competence. Any noticeable limitation in the verbal capacity of the child warrants concern and careful inquiry as to what has been happening in the child's life. While it is common for children to develop fears and problems with eating and sleeping during the third year of life, these are usually transitory and of short duration. Finally, if the child shows evidence of weight loss or frailness or excessive fatigue, the child care worker should seek every opportunity to meet with the parent to pursue the symptoms of insomnia or eating problems. Intervention is most effective at this age.

Assessing early personality development

During the past eight years the staff of the Irene Josselyn Clinic, where I am Medical Director, have been developing an assessment chart that has proved valuable in alerting clinicians to the early signs of pathology (see table 3.1). This chart represents an attempt to highlight crucial developmental landmarks in the emerging personality of the child from birth to age three. Its value is enhanced if these maturational levels are viewed in conjunction with the clinical observations of the developmental process during the first three years.

Since Spitz (1965) published his studies on institutionalized babies, we have known that babies need much more than food and physical care. If crucial factors such as attachments are either lacking or inappropriate, children not only may develop serious emotional difficulties but also may fail to thrive or even survive. In our clinic we see many children whose difficulties stem from very early, often subtle, disturbances in the mother-infant relationship, rather than from either clear-cut demonstrable trauma or severe pathology within the home environment.

Pediatricians, child care workers, day care teachers, and other professionals are in the best position to recognize early signs of these emotional difficulties in baby and mother and can intervene effectively to prevent the development of serious problems. Teachers in day care centers may well be in a unique position to respond to the needs of high-risk children. Observations made by professional day care staff may lead to interventions which could interrupt a potential and lethal pattern of behavior.

We have attempted to extract observable behavior, attitudes, and physical states in both mother and child that should alert the professional. For example, we would expect a physician to inquire in detail as to the baby's diet and food intake if there were inadequate weight gain. So too, we would expect caregivers of young children to be concerned and inquiring if by four or five months the baby had never smiled or the mother consistently looked depressed or harassed.

Table 3.1 Early signs of pathology in personality development

Age of child	Observed in mother	Observed in child	Areas of concern for inquiry	Trial intervention
Birth to 3 months	More than normally anxious Exhausted Disinterested Frozen appearance: unsmiling stiff flattened affect Unusually awkward in holding or dressing baby	Failure to thrive unexplained by physical causes Inability to be comforted by mother No smiling in response to professional's efforts to elicit Extremes in body tone when held: rigid flaccid	Be alert to discrepancies between reports and observations Are eating, sucking, sleeping, cuddling, and elimination gratifying to mother and child? Does mother recognize need for environmental stimulation, especially by the age of 6 to 12 weeks? Is mother enjoying baby? Is mother getting time off?	Take enough time to: praise reassure give specific directions Evaluate mother's response to above *Continue to use these interventions throughout the 36 months*

Age of child	Observed in mother	Observed in child	Areas of concern for inquiry	Trial intervention
3 to 6 months	Continuance of earlier behaviors (if pattern is unchanged be concerned by 3 months and refer mother to mental health care by 6 months)	Continuance of earlier behaviors, especially lack of smiling response and extremes in body tone	Continuance of earlier behaviors, and appearance of new problems	Depending on assessment of parents' ability to cope: provide more support, encourage parent to be more independent
	Inappropriate timing of response to child	Lack of playfulness and joy	Is child beginning to amuse self?	Encourage mother to allow child to experience some frustration
	Unable to make sensible, independent judgment, and/or overreliance on professional	Excessive crying and irritability	Does child have increased capacity to delay gratification?	Determine whether child is neurologically damaged
		Inability to be soothed or to soothe self		
	Too clinging or too casual with baby	Lack of or overresponse to environmental stimuli	Is mother becoming sensitive to the baby's cues: need for food, sleep, play?	
	Unaware of or unconcerned about safety precautions	Inability to bite or chew		
		Absence of cooing and babbling		

Table 3.1 Early signs of pathology in personality development (Continued)

Age of child	Observed in mother	Observed in child	Areas of concern for inquiry	Trial intervention
6 to 9 months	Too intense or too casual about infant's increased mobility	If earlier behaviors continue, check out visual or auditory problems	Is there purposeful mobility: beginning separations at child's initiative?	Neutralize stranger anxiety by mode of relationship
	Inability to accept and foster infant's capacity to soothe self	Lack of joyful interaction between mother and infant	Can the infant soothe self, including use of transitional objects?	Explain that stranger anxiety is a natural indication of the child's growing awareness of self and others
	Inability to accept child's stranger anxiety and unwillingness to accommodate reasonably to it	Lack of stranger anxiety	What is the quality of communication between mother and infant?	
		Lack of response to mother's efforts at soothing	Is there stranger anxiety?	
			Can mother let others care for infant?	

Age of child	Observed in mother	Observed in child	Areas of concern for inquiry	Trial intervention
9 to 18 months	Insensitive to or lacking in accommodation to child's increased need for exploratory behavior	No signs of beginning to walk	Is there increased exploratory behavior on child's part?	Support mother's physical and emotional attempts to cope with the demands of her child
		Lack of curious exploration of environment		
	Inability to expect and support child's temporary regressions such as: clinging demands for attention decrease in ability to entertain self general irritability	Tense child in constant motion	Is there increasing unpredictability as a sign of normal growth? clinging demands for attention less ability to entertain self food fads sleep disturbances separation problems	Advise against separations of long duration at this age
		No babbling or evidence of beginning acquisition of words		Support child's use of transitional object
				Encourage appropriate limit-setting
			What is the quality and quantity of language development?	

Table 3.1 Early signs of pathology in personality development (Continued)

Age of child	Observed in mother	Observed in child	Areas of concern for inquiry	Trial intervention
18 to 24 months	Mother tuned out to child's activities	Impulse ridden	Can child use toys and amuse self?	Encourage mother to remain flexible in face of changing needs of child; don't base expectations on timetables and books!
	More than usual amount of frustration with her blossoming toddler: overly restrictive or too casual with play and exploration, lack of verbal interaction or overtalking to child	Lack of response to playful cooperation with child care worker	Is child curious and free to explore?	
		General inhibition: lack of physical exploration of surroundings, no curiosity, unable to separate from mother	Does child understand speech?	Refer mother for help if: her limit-setting seems pathological the child exhibits no babbling or responsiveness to language
			Does child communicate verbally with mother?	
	Infantalization of specific developmental areas: overindulgence with bottle overly concerned about eating	No babbling or responsiveness to verbal communications	Does mother provide help when needed, but allow increasing independence?	
		Unable to calm self after distressing event	Is mother accommodating to changes in eating and sleeping patterns?	
			How is she handling weaning? cont'd.	

Age of child	Observed in mother	Observed in child	Areas of concern for inquiry	Trial intervention
cont'd.			Is she setting appropriate limits?	
			Is child accident prone?	
			Is the home child-proofed for safety?	
			Is there evidence of child abuse?	

Table 3.1 Early signs of pathology in personality development (Continued)

Age of child	Observed in mother	Observed in child	Areas of concern for inquiry	Trial intervention
24 to 36 months	Inability to accept child's thrust for independence and initiative	Excessive difficulty in separating from mother	Is mother supporting surge for independence?	Determine if child understands meaningful verbal communication
	Inability to set appropriate limits	Inhibition of exploration	Are there eating or sleeping problems?	Note mother's attitude and disparities between staff observations and her reports
	Pressuring for precocious development and achievements, e.g., early reading	Needs constant permission from mother	Are there any phobias?	
		Impulse ridden, unable to respond to limits	What is mother doing about toilet training?	If excessive and persistent fears or unusual and prolonged regressions occur, schedule additional appointments and maintain close contact
		Robotlike	Does child seek out others as playmates?	
		Language development: little or no speech excessive talking lack of comprehension	How is TV used in this family? For this child?	
		Accident prone	What kinds of toys and activities are provided for this child?	If, after above, fears or regressions continue, refer for special help

We recognize that it takes time to attempt to tune in and to deal with the psychological state of mother and baby, but we are convinced that this extra time, especially in the first year of life, is well spent. It may serve to prevent the development of serious problems and seems little enough to do for the infants who have a rightful claim on their own healthy maturation.

Observing as a diagnostic tool

The underlying premise for the design of the chart is that the teacher's own observation and intuitive reading of mother and child is the most reliable diagnostic tool. Many parents, especially those with a first child, are reluctant to ask questions or are unable to observe and report data that would be most relevant. They may say everything is fine when, in fact, it is not, or they may ask many different questions but fail to report a crucial piece of information. They have no base line against which to measure their own reactions or their baby's. Thus, the child care worker must at all times be alert to discrepancies between what is reported (or omitted) and what is observed.

In the early months of the child's life, the mother's physical and mental state is often the first signal that things are not going well. Thus, the first column of the developmental assessment chart deals with behavior that can be observed in the mother or concerns that she may bring. The second column highlights observations that can be made of the child in the day care setting. These observations will give the teacher firsthand data. In column three we have described those areas of inquiry of particular significance to the child's psychosocial development that go beyond physical well-being. This inquiry is crucial when the child care worker's concern has been aroused by something observed in mother and/or child. Any discrepancies between what is reported by the mother and what is observed should be investigated. Active inquiry can be the first step in the intervention process described in column four. Here we suggest a number of trial interventions that may alleviate the problem. Our emphasis is on extra time. The anxious, harassed, or withdrawn mother needs more than the usual amount of encouragement, praise, and support. The baby who seems in some way not to be developing as expected needs to be played with, handled, talked with, and engaged in activities. It may seem unreasonable to ask for extra time in view of the pressures of a day care center, but as a preventive measure the extra investment of time is essential.

We have indicated the importance of an appropriate referral if supportive measures fail. Suitable resources for diagnosis and treatment vary widely from one part of the country to another or may not be available at all. However, when such resources do exist at universities, hospitals, mental health clinics, through Head Start programs, or therapeutic nursery schools, day care staff should avail themselves of them and refer mother and/or child earlier rather than later. Given the closeness of the mother-child unit in the first three years of life, it would be hard to imagine a problem in the mother that would not in some way reverberate in the child and vice versa. Thus, any problem should be of concern to the teacher whether it appears in the parent or the child. If a problem is spotted in the child and the mother is unperturbed, careful inquiry of the mother is indicated with the intervention suggested in the chart. If a problem is spotted in the mother, the day care staff may feel reluctant to intercede. However, careful and supportive inquiry with the mother will usually reflect her awareness of the problem; she will be relieved to have the day care staff make explicit the problem of which she has been aware. If some difficulty is observed in both mother and child, active intervention with perhaps referral to a child development center is indicated.

Using the assessment chart

Evaluation of the growing potential of the child is of great practical import. All human beings willing to care for infants are positively motivated in their behalf regardless of other factors that may lead to their professional involvement. If such caregivers can be helped to become diagnosticians in behalf of the infants in their settings, young children may be helped to get the evaluations and interventions they need.

When the infants are first observed in the day care setting, they can be evaluated for their ability to be comforted, for extremes in body tone, or for their capacity to smile on stimulation. If they show no capacity to be comforted, if the extremes of body tone when being held are great, or if no smiling response is noted, day care workers may wish to think in terms of intervention. Teachers will first need to inquire of the mother about her own gratification in meeting the infant's needs. Are the infant's cuddling, sleeping, eating gratifying to her? Also, does the mother recognize the need for environmental stimulation, especially by the ages of 6 to 12 weeks? This may be the time when additional mother-caregiver contact can be helpful, provided each has time and energy for the interchange that will give help and reassurance to the mother. If such efforts cannot be used by the mother, then referral to a child development specialist may seem indicated.

Similarly, the mother of a three- to six-month-old infant might be too clinging or, conversely, too casual with the baby. Perhaps one might observe her inappropriate or poorly timed responses to the child as well. Looking at the child, we may find little or no smiling response or extremes of body tone. At this point there should be concern for the mother-child dyad. Additionally, if the infant lacks joy and playfulness, or is excessively irritable and constantly crying or fretting, the day care worker may wish to inquire into the mother-infant adjustment. At this age especially, the absence of cooing and babbling may reflect a poor tutorial relationship with the mother as she sets the stage for the development of language.

During the day teachers may wish to spend special time evaluating such children's ability to amuse themselves and to delay gratification. If the observations over a period of several days indicate that this may be an early problem child, teachers may wish to help the mother evaluate the importance of timing and the developing capacity for the infant to wait. Observations in the day care center may reveal a lack of joyful interaction between the mother and the infant (between the ages of six to nine months) and a lack of stranger anxiety in relation to the day care workers. Stranger anxiety reflects the children's developing capacity to differentiate individuals. If lack of stranger anxiety persists, it should be viewed as an indicator of the need for a child development evaluation by a professional either by consultation within the day care center or by referral. Similarly, the child's lack of response to the mother's efforts at soothing, especially if this is associated with a lack of babbling, should alert the day care worker to problems. Day care workers may find the mother unable to accept and to foster the infant's capacity to soothe herself or himself, or to accept the stranger anxiety that is a healthy developmental sign. It may be necessary for the day care worker to explain the needs of children this age. Other causes for concern might be observed miscommunication between mother and child, such as a mother's lack of awareness of the impact of a stranger, or a mother's inability to let the staff care for her child even in the face of necessity.

For children of 9 to 18 months, day care workers should be concerned about the developing capacity for walking. If there are no signs of either early walking or curious exploration, teachers should question the possibility of a maturational lag. Similarly, a tense child in constant motion, or a child who is not babbling and vocalizing, should alert the professional that something may be amiss. In these instances, one may find a mother. If such efforts cannot be used by the mother, then referral to a child development specialist may seem indicated.

Similarly, the mother of a three- to six-month-old infant might be too clinging or, conversely, too casual with the baby. Perhaps one might observe her inappropriate or poorly timed responses to the child as well. Looking at the child, we may find little or no smiling response or extremes of body tone. At this point there should be concern for the mother child dyad. Additionally, if the infant lacks joy and playfulness, or is excessively irritable and constantly crying or fretting, the day care worker may wish to inquire into the mother-infant adjustment. At this age especially, the absence of cooing and babbling may reflect a poor tutorial relationship with the mother as she sets the stage for the development of language.

During the day teachers may wish to spend special time evaluating such children's ability to amuse themselves and to delay gratification. If the observations over a period of several days indicate that this may be an early problem child, teachers may wish to help the mother evaluate the importance of timing and the developing capacity for the infant to wait. Observations in the day care center may reveal a lack of joyful interaction between the mother and the infant (between the ages of six to nine months) and a lack of stranger anxiety in relation to the day care workers. Stranger anxiety reflects the children's developing capacity to differentiate individuals. If lack of stranger anxiety persists, it should be viewed as an indicator of the need for a child development evaluation by a professional either by consultation within the day care center or by referral. Similarly, the child's lack of response to the mother's efforts at soothing, especially if this is associated with a lack of babbling, should alert the day care worker to problems. Day care workers may find the mother unable to accept and to foster the infant's capacity to soothe herself or himself, or to accept the stranger anxiety that is a healthy developmental sign. It may be necessary for the day care worker to explain the needs of children this age. Other causes for concern might be observed miscommunication between mother and child, such as a mother's lack of awareness of the impact of a stranger, or a mother's inability to let the staff care for her child even in the face of necessity.

For children of 9 to 18 months, day care workers should be concerned about the developing capacity for walking. If there are no signs of either early walking or curious exploration, teachers should question the possibility of a maturational lag. Similarly, a tense child in constant motion, or a child who is not babbling and vocalizing, should alert the professional that something may be amiss. In these instances, one may find a mother who is unable to accommodate to the child's exploratory behavior or to the temporary regressions that are appropriate for these ages. Particularly during these ages, the professional should feel free to support the mother's continuing availability, and vacations or other absences should be questioned in terms of their impact on the growing, separating, and individuating child.

Although many day care settings pay particular attention to the younger infant, it is important to view early infant development in a spectrum that includes the period between 18 and 36 months. The impulse ridden child, the child with general inhibition, and the child unable to respond by babbling to verbal communication may be a child crucially in need of a developmental evaluation. Also, at this age the inability to recover from injections and other physical manipulations may reflect a weak personality structure, especially when the mother seems either tuned out or overwhelmingly frustrated by the blossoming toddler. One may, during these months, also see the signs of maternal infantalization through overindulgence with a bottle or undue concern about eating. When the child is at this age especially, the mother should be encouraged to remain flexible in the face of the changing needs of the child and should be encouraged not to use timetables such as this very one! The child from 24 to 36 months may display classical symptoms of problems necessitating referral. The toddler who shows excessive difficulty in separating from the mother, the one who is showing little or no language development, should all be considered for referral.

Opportunities for the caregiver

The assessment chart can serve only as a shorthand reminder of the process of development. We have long since learned to evaluate a child's development only in terms of her or his unique developmental line. Sometimes, however, we assume that children will grow out of it instead of recognizing developmental lags and clarifying the reasons for them. In addition, some concepts presented are based on White middle-class ideas of normality so we cannot be certain that they apply to all mothers and children. It would be hoped that a calendar of evaluation might be set up for each of the children in the child care center, so that each child can be viewed against her or his own developmental line and life experience using the background of the chart as a signpost. If an individual calendar for evaluation is set up for each child, one may observe the signposts of dysfunctioning for a few children among the many being cared for in the center. Once a clarification of special need is made, one can vary the setting or make suggestions to the parent. The staff of a day care center is in a unique position to recognize those parent-infant relationships that can be nurtured with supportive intervention. It is hoped that the developmental chart will act as a stimulant to this process.

References

Spitz, R.A. *The First Year of Life*. New York: International Universities Press, 1965.
Thomas, A.; Chess, S.; and Birch, H. "The Origin of Personality." *Scientific American* 223 (1970): 102-109.

Craig T. Ramey

4

Consequences of infant day care

The proper care for infants and other young children is of great controversy in this country. The last major attempt by the United States Congress to provide comprehensive services to young children and their families brought this controversy clearly into focus. Former President Nixon cited two main reasons for his veto of the Mondale-Brademas Child Development Act. First, he argued that the bill was too expensive. Second, he noted that he was against the bill because it contained provisions for expanded availability of group day care for young children, particularly infants. This increased availability was believed by the Nixon administration to be detrimental to the child's growth and development and a threat to the stability of the nuclear family. That no similar comprehensive plan for the systematic care of preschool children has been successfully implemented since Nixon's veto in 1971 indicates that the subject is still a controversial one and that the necessary votes for passage are not at hand.

Much of the controversy concerning group day care results, I think, from overly simplistic ideas about how day care for infants and toddlers might affect children's development and their relations with family members. Parents are frequently encouraged to phrase the question in the form of whether to place the child in some form of group day care *or* to rear that child at home. Essentially the same question is debated in many guises by pediatricians, psychologists, educators, social workers, and other professionals concerned with the development of young children. Two points about this question distress me.

First, the question ignores the fact that more families are choosing to use some form of day care. Thus, families need information and advice on what to look for in obtaining high quality day care. Debating whether or not it should exist is becoming an increasingly irrelevant activity. It is a little like debating whether our society supports motherhood. No matter what stance is taken, the phenomenon will continue to occur.

Second, the *either/or* form of the question, that is, either day care *or* home rearing is an overly simplistic conception of the issue and is not very constructive. A better way to frame the problem is how to provide effective forms of child care that have demonstrable benefits and minimal disadvantages to the child and the family. It is my hope that when the social history of child care is written, the present controversy over home rearing versus the use of systematic day care will take its place beside the many other pseudo issues in childrearing that dominated much of our thinking during the early part of the twentieth century. However, if the day care versus home rearing issue is to join such issues as breast- versus bottle-feeding and genetic versus environmental influences as pseudo issues, then educators and scientists need to educate the public and governmental officials to ask more appropriate questions. Further, the public needs to be better educated in the use of scientific and educational information so that more rational choices based on publicly available evidence can be made. It is all too frequent that current competition for public and governmental support for or against day care takes the form of assertion and counter-assertion with appeals to unsupported "natural laws," a frequently romanticized past that is inaccurately portrayed (see Howard 1980), and overly simplistic conceptions of services.

The following summary of what we have learned from our research at the Frank Porter Graham Child Development Center on infant and toddler day care during the past ten years should be helpful in stimulating thinking about the provision of care for young children within group settings. Before introducing and summarizing the data, I want to describe the day care program and its operation. The program is primarily for families with low incomes. Therefore, to the extent that low-income and high-income families differ, the consequences of providing day care *may* also differ. This statement does not mean that the results *will* differ, just that they *might* differ, and so we should be cautious about overgeneralizing from the sample of families.

A particularly important feature of the program is that we have formed an experimental and a control group by randomly assigning families to a day care condition at the birth of the child. Families who were not randomly chosen for day care constitute the control group. This particularly powerful design feature allows us to make statistical comparisons between the experimental and control groups and to attribute differences between them to the factor that we manipulated—namely the process of attending a day care center. To date over 120 children have been assigned to either the control group or the experimental group. Experimental children begin to attend the day care center when they are between 6 and 12 weeks of age. No attempt is made to alter the caregiving arrangements for children in the control group. In order to control some of the variables that may confound the experimental test of day care, however, we have provided a number of services for both experimental and control group families. First, because infants and toddlers attending day care receive excellent nutrition, we have supplied iron-fortified Similac to control families during the first 15 months of the child's life. Second, we either provide pediatric care for families or help them obtain care through local clinics. Third, all participants are given family support social services on a request basis. In combination with random assignment to groups, these attempts to equalize potentially confounding conditions are designed to ensure that the primary difference between the two groups is the systematic infant curriculum and preschool program delivered through day care.

Day care environment

Physical setting

Children attend the nursery and toddler programs in a large building that also houses a public school kindergarten and first grade classroom and the administrative and research staff of a large child development center. Infants are cared for in a nursery on a different floor from the toddlers until they reach about 13 to 15 months of age. The nursery, which usually enrolls 10 to 14 infants, contains two sleeping rooms with seven cribs each, two play and curriculum rooms, a hall area onto which the four rooms open, and a kitchen and teacher work area adjoining the hall. Sleeping rooms are separate from rooms in which other activities are conducted to ensure that the infants' sleep is not interrupted.

Once infants can walk well and are judged to be socially ready by their teachers, they are transferred to the toddler program. This floor houses three groups of children ranging in age from about 14 to 40 months of age. A partially enclosed area approximately 10 × 10 meters for each group is created by means of low, movable bookcases or other furniture, though children can usually see or hear children in the other groups. In addition to these work areas, the floor has a teacher work area, a lunch area, and an area used for gross motor exercise, as well as bathrooms, storage rooms, and a teacher meeting area. This floor also has a number of doors that open onto an outside play area surrounded by a cement wall.

In the summer or fall of the year before entry into the public schools, at which time children are approximately four years old, they are transferred to a different floor of the building. Here the classroom is organized much like kindergarten classrooms in the public schools. Eight to ten children are supervised by a lead teacher and an aide. Curriculum activities focus on reading and math skills, and children work in activity centers often without direct supervision.

Equipment and toys

The nursery contains the typical accoutrements associated with infants below one year. These include high chairs, cribs, large playpens, climbers, swings, walkers, and a variety of toys and books.

The areas for toddlers and preschoolers contain more complex toys and equipment including a large jungle gym in the gross motor area, an art area with assorted art materials, a science area with aquariums and other animal housing, play areas for dress up, a book corner, and an area containing manipulative materials such as stringing beads, puzzles, and toys for sorting and stacking. The outside area features large sandboxes, swings, balls, tricycles, jungle gyms, and other large structures for climbing.

Teaching staff

A teacher-infant ratio of 1:3 is maintained in the nursery; a ratio of approximately 1:4 is maintained in the toddler and preschool program. The nursery is organized to promote contacts between all teachers and all infants, with the single planned exception that a teacher is designated as responsible for each infant's educational curriculum every two weeks.

In the toddler and preschool programs, each class of eight children has two teachers. Lead teachers have training in early childhood education and previous experience as a preschool or elementary school teacher. The second teacher in each group is a teacher's aide often working to obtain the Child Development Associate credential.

Daily routines

Some children arrive at the center as early as 7:30 a.m.; all are there by 9:15 a.m. Children begin leaving at about 3:30 p.m.; all are gone by 5:15 p.m. The center is open 5 days per week, 50 weeks per year.

Just because desirable consequences can occur for children in group day care does not mean that they will occur. We, as educators, must be vigilant in our attempts to ensure high quality care.

The typical nursery day is more or less determined by individual infants. Infants sleep when they are tired, eat about every three or four hours, engage in organized curriculum activities once or twice each day for about 15 minutes, and play and move about for the remainder of the day. Infants are also regularly taken for walks or rides in carriages.

Upon moving to the toddler floor, a more structured schedule is gradually set for the children. Though the exact schedule varies according to season, age of children, and day of week, the following sequence of events is typical. Children play together in large groups of 10 to 20 from the time they arrive until 8:30 a.m. They then are divided into their regular groups of 8 children each. After a snack, they begin curriculum activities. As children get older, these activities last up to an hour in large or small groups and focus on academic skills.

By about 11:15 or 11:30 a.m., children go outside or to the gross motor area for 30 to 45 minutes of free play. At this time, they are exposed to as many as 25 children ranging in age from 14 to 40 months. After free play, children eat lunch, clean up, and take a 2-hour nap. After their nap, they again have educational activities and free play until it is time to go home.

Curriculum development

The nature of the experimental treatment is partially described by approximately 300 curriculum activities that have been developed for this program for children from birth to 36 months (Sparling 1974; Sparling and Lewis 1978). The framework for generating materials and activities in the curriculum is based on four sources: (a) Piagetian developmental theory; (b) previously established developmental facts and milestones, such as those observed by Gesell (1946); (c) parents' statements about what they hope their child will be capable of doing at a given age; and (d) abilities, such as task orientation, that facilitate a child's learning of subsequent material.

Based on these sources, items are developed to include a statement of the behavioral objective, type of materials needed, behavior of the teacher, and expected outcome behavior of the child. Particular items are then assigned to an infant with one teacher assuming responsibility for their implementation. Next, teachers evaluate the adequacy of the item (clarity of goal, ease of administration, child attentiveness). On the basis of this evaluation, items are modified or eliminated. About one-third of the items are also evaluated by outside observers who watch teachers use the item on a number of occasions.

As items are developed and tested, they become part of a pool of items and are used systematically by teachers in their curriculum activities with infants and toddlers.

Curriculum activities

In the nursery, toddler, and preschool programs, the teaching staffs meet biweekly to discuss the progress of each child. During these discussions, three to five curriculum items from the pool are selected for the next two-week period, and a specific teacher is assigned to conduct these activities with each child. In addition, a checklist of developmental milestones is updated as necessary during this meeting. The checklist, of course, serves as a continuous check on each child's progress. Individual activities are then performed with children once or twice each day for 15 minutes as described previously.

In addition to the specific items from the formal curriculum, many routine activities of the day care program should be considered as educational experiences. Indeed, teacher training emphasizes the curriculum aspect of routine activities and stresses the use of spontaneous activities as educational opportunities—counting places and napkins while setting the table, repeating the names of shapes and colors while playing with objects, and, of course, language stimulation through questioning and discussion of play activities.

With the foregoing description of the Carolina Abecedarian Project as background, I would now like to briefly summarize available information concerning the status of four major issues in infant and toddler care.

Health care

The first issue is whether the health of infants and toddlers is impaired by group contact at such an early age.

The Frank Porter Graham Center maintains an extensive health services and health research component as part of the day care program. Based on extensive, everyday examinations and comparisons with home reared children, "we feel that our experience suggests that in a well run daycare center with adequate space, staff, sanitation, and medical care, it is possible to care for infants and young children in group daycare without adverse health effects. It does not mean that it is safe to mix young children together in unsanitary, crowded conditions. It does not justify or condone the operation of inadequate daycare facilities" (Collier and Ramey 1976).

Intellectual development

Table 4.1 presents the results of the preschool day care program on intellectual development as measured by scores on the Bayley Mental Development Index and the Stanford-Binet Intelligence Scale. Statistically significant differences were found at every point after the 12-month test (Ramey and Campbell 1981); at 48 months the mean IQ for day care attending children was 96 and for their controls it was 84. Further, there is a significant decline in IQ for control children implying that the day care experience was instrumental in maintaining normal intellectual progress for these low-income children.

In order to examine the specific processes that might be affected by educational day care, the McCarthy Scales of Children's Abilities (1972) are periodically administered. The data in table 4.2 demonstrates superior performance by the day care children at 42 months of age on four of five subscales of the McCarthy Scales. Day care children scored significantly higher than their controls on the verbal, perceptual-performance, quantitative, and memory scales. They did not, however, score significantly higher on the motor scale. These results suggest that

Table 4.1.

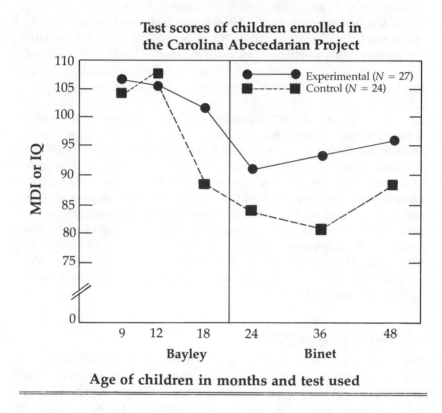

Test scores of children enrolled in
the Carolina Abecedarian Project

Age of children in months and test used

the effects of systematic and educational day care were quite pervasive,
and that day care influenced the development of a broad variety of
cognitive abilities.

Mother's attitudes toward childrearing

One possible consequence of a family placing an infant in group day
care is that the primary caregiver may or may not have certain caregiving
experiences, and that those experiences may result in a different and
perhaps detrimental set of attitudes toward childrearing. To examine
that possibility we measured the mothers' attitudes toward childrearing

Table 4.2.

Means and standard deviations for children's scores at 42 months on the McCarthy Scales of Children's Abilities ($N = 50$)

Subscale	Group			
	Experimental $N = 26$		Control $N = 24$	
	M	*SD*	*M*	*SD*
Verbal (V)	50.07	6.96	46.00	7.60
Perceptual-Performance (P)	46.26	7.49	41.92	8.72
Quantitative (Q)	51.74	7.31	43.83	9.54
Memory	51.74	5.07	48.58	6.94
Motor	50.00	6.96	47.33	7.24
General Cognitive (V+P+Q)	99.18	11.47	89.92	12.96

using Emmerich's (1969) version of Schaefer and Bell's (1958) Parental Attitude Research Instrument. This attitudinal assessment instrument uses a self-report format and yields scores concerning the following attitudes: fostering dependency, seclusiveness of the mother, supression of aggression, excluding outside influences, suppression of sexuality, marital conflict, rejection of homemaking role, irritability, encouraging verbalization, equalitarianism, and comradeship and sharing.

Responses of mothers were analyzed when the children were 6 and 18 months of age. A comparison of mothers whose children were in day care with those of the control group revealed that there were no significant differences in maternal attitudes at either measurement occasion. There were changes between 6 and 18 months in that at 18 months mothers reported themselves as being less concerned with fostering dependency, suppressing sexuality, and being *more* concerned with encouraging verbalization and equalitarianism as well as being more irritable. However, these changes tended to be true of all mothers and did not differentiate the day care group from the non-day-care group. Thus, day care does not seem to have affected these maternal attitudes during the period of infancy.

Attachment between infant and mother

Ramey, Farran, and Campbell (1979) and Farran and Ramey (1977) have reported a set of experiments that are the most direct tests in the scientific literature of whether children in day care have attachment relations with their mothers similar to ones exhibited by children who did not begin day care during infancy. Ramey, Farran, and Campbell (1979) reported data to show that day care attending infants and their mothers and non-day-care attending infants and their mothers interacted very similarly in both a laboratory situation and in their own homes when the children were both 6 and 20 months of age. Further, the changes in behavior between 6 and 20 months were the same for both groups. Thus, no evidence could be found that day care has had any major effect on the mother-child relationship in either a positive or a negative fashion during the period of infancy as assessed by observations of their behavior.

In the Farran and Ramey (1977) experiment the question was simply whether day care children between 9 and 31 months would show evidence of attachment to their mothers in an unfamiliar situation and whether that attachment was as strong or stronger than that shown toward the child's teacher. All current major theories of attachment are in agreement that attachment is indicated by children seeking, at least initially, to be near their mother in an unfamiliar situation, by behaving differently toward the mother than other persons when both are present, and by seeking the mother's help to solve problems when they cannot be solved alone. Using these criteria, children were observed in a novel situation that contained their mother, their teacher, and a stranger. The evidence was overwhelming on each of the three criteria that the children were attached to their mothers. Further, this attachment was stable as early as nine months of age and persisted throughout the first two-and-one-half-years of life. Thus, those data clearly indicated that day care children were attached to their mothers and that the child's teacher had not supplanted the mother's role.

Summary and conclusion

Thus, in summary, it appears from the data that children from low-income families can be cared for in group care during the day beginning in early infancy without adversely affecting their health, their mothers' attitudes toward them, or their attachment to their mothers. Further, it also appears that high quality day care provides substantial intellectual benefits that are detectable as early as the second year of life. These are important consequences of a growing system of care that remains controversial and much embattled. However, a word of caution is in order. Just because these desirable consequences *can* occur for children in group day care does not mean that they *will* occur. We, as educators, must be vigilant in our attempts to ensure high quality care. The main task is to specify the ingredients that, when properly blended, will yield the quality of care for children and their families of which this country can be proud.

References

Collier, A.M., and Ramey, C.T. "The Health of Infants in Daycare." *Voice for Children* 9 (1976): 7-22.

Emmerich, W. "The Parental Role: A Functional Cognitive Approach." *Monographs of the Society for Research in Child Development* 34, no. 8 (1969).

Farran, D.C., and Ramey, C.T. "Infant Day Care and Attachment Behaviors Toward Mothers and Teachers." *Child Development* 48, no. 3 (September 1977): 1112-1116.

Gesell, A.L. "The Ontogenesis of Infant Behavior." In *Manual of Child Psychology,* ed. L. Carmichael. New York: Wiley, 1946.

Howard, A.E. *The American Family: Myth and Reality.* Washington, D.C.: National Association for the Education for Young Children, 1980.

McCarthy, D. *McCarthy Scales of Children's Abilities.* New York: Psychological Corporation, 1972.

Ramey, C.T., and Campbell, F.A. "Educational Intervention for Children at Risk for Mild Retardation: A Longitudinal Analysis." In *Frontiers of Knowledge in Mental Retardation,* ed. P. Mittler. Baltimore: University Park Press, 1981.

Ramey, C.T.; Farran, D.C.; and Campbell, F.A. "Predicting IQ from Mother-Infant Interactions." *Child Development* 50, no. 3 (September 1979): 804-814.

Schaefer, E.S., and Bell, R.Q. "Development of a Parent Attitude Research Instrument." *Child Development* 29 (1958): 339-361.

Sparling, J. "Synthesizing Educational Objectives for Infant Curricula." Paper presented at the annual meeting of the American Educational Research Association, Chicago, 1974.

Sparling, J., and Lewis, I. *Infant Learningames: Resources for a Parent/Child Partnership.* Chapel Hill, N.C.: Frank Porter Graham Child Development Center, 1978.

Magda Gerber

5

What is appropriate curriculum for infants and toddlers?

A growing number of infant programs are being established in the United States. Some are designed to provide alternative care environments to the home, while others, referred to as early intervention programs, are geared to stimulate and educate handicapped or other at-risk infants.

An increased number of professional and commercial publications have popularized new research and findings which emphasize that infants are capable of a wider range of activities and learning than was previously believed (see Stone, Smith, and Murphy 1973).

These studies convince many that if infants can learn, we must teach them. Thus many projects emphasize cognitive development and are often specific-achievement oriented. Their curricula are based on levels of performance as defined by various infant studies and tests (Bayley 1969; Gesell 1940; Piaget 1963), and their goals are to enhance achievement. Specific methods are also designed to teach, drill, and facilitate the development of certain milestone acquisitions. Generally the program staff have preconceived ideas as to when, how, why, and for how long infants should be stimulated. Many times the program adheres to the principle of the more the better. In addition, there are home teaching programs intended to educate families to stimulate their infants (Gordon 1970; Painter 1971).

While all infants benefit from early sensory stimulation, it is a must for handicapped infants to prevent or ameliorate future learning difficulties. It is generally believed that if left alone infants would not master tasks parents and/or professionals consider necessary.

Many books, packaged programs, and infant curricula are available

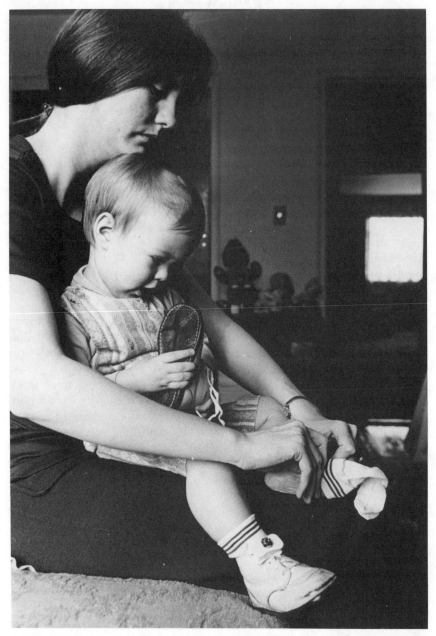

Appropriate curriculum for infants should not be special teaching plans added to daily activities, but rather it should be built into the infant's every experience.

and used as prescriptions in infant programs. These often serve as guidelines or crutches to caregivers who may be inadequately prepared to meet the needs of infants or special children. The caregiver follows instructions to try to elicit a desired response to a prescribed stimulus in the areas of gross motor, fine motor, social-emotional, and language developments. New skills are introduced to the infants—skills one step ahead of their development, skills they themselves cannot master yet. The adult's attention is focused on teaching rather than observing children's reactions to their environment and caregivers.

I am proposing a different view of how infants learn and of how we can facilitate their learning. In the past ten years I have been a consultant to infant programs, initiated and directed model infant programs, and organized Resources for Infant Educarers (RIE), a nonprofit membership organization concerned with improving the care and education of infants. Based on my experiences and my work as a child therapist, I have developed a humanistic-therapeutic approach to working with young children—an approach that has been implemented in comprehensive teaching, training, and demonstration programs. As preventive mental health programs, they are designed to actually demonstrate our theories of caring for normal as well as high-risk infants. The overall therapeutic goal is twofold: (1) to help parents develop, from the very beginning, sound patterns of living with their babies and (2) to train infant caregivers, professionals who provide group care for infants in centers or family homes (Gerber 1971, 1979).

The Pilot Infant Program in North Hollywood and the Demonstration Infant Program in Palo Alto, California vary considerably from the types of programs described earlier. Our approach has been developed in more than a quarter century of research and clinical work with infants who were reared at the National Methodological Institute of Residential Nurseries in Budapest, Hungary, popularly called Loczy. Loczy, founded in 1946 by Emmi Pikler, M.D., is a residence for normal infants from birth to three years of age, with a capacity to serve 70 infants. Four basic principles from the philosophy of Loczy are:

1. All infants derive security from a *predictable environment* and the opportunity to *anticipate* and *make choices*. This is absolutely essential for infants living in an institution.

2. Infants need an *intimate, stable relationship* with one constant person (a mother figure). This relationship can best be developed during *individualized caregiving activities*.

3. *Respect* is shown by treating infants as active participants rather than as passive recipients in all interactions.

4. Infants *do not need direct teaching or help* to achieve natural stages of gross motor and sensorimotor development (Pikler 1971).

The approach to infants at Loczy is predicated on achieving a balance between adult stimulation and independent exploration by infants. Infants are stimulated by their caregivers during all activities including feeding, bathing, and dressing. These are unhurried pleasurable times for both adults and infants. Because these are necessary daily routines of infant care, stimulation is constant and consistent. In contrast, the staff of Loczy does not interfere or promote gross motor and fine motor development but rather relies on maturation and development at the infant's own pace (David and Appel 1973).

In the two California programs, the emphasis is similarly on *observation, anticipation,* and *selective intervention*. Parents and caregivers observe their children to learn about individual characteristics of the child and to realize what can reasonably be expected of the baby at any developmental level. This in turn helps mothers or other caregivers to synchronize their behavior with the child's needs, tempo, and style. Anticipating each other's reactions fosters mutual understanding, acceptance, and basic trust for both adult and child; thus anticipation becomes the forerunner of communication. Selective intervention means knowing when *not* to intervene, and this is more difficult than intervening indiscriminately.

We have identified six conditions under which healthy, normal infants can develop to their full potential.

1. A mother figure must be available to respond to physical and emotional needs.

2. The mother correctly perceives and accepts the child.

3. The baby's inner rhythm (sleep, hunger, etc.) is synchronized with the family's daily routine. Family members mutually plan the day's activities for as little conflict as possible between the infant's and family's needs.

4. Ample space is available to facilitate locomotion.

5. Objects are provided to facilitate manipulation.

6. Other children within the same age range are present to observe and imitate, and with whom to interact and socialize (optional).

Our goals are influenced by the concept of a fully functional human being as one who has many of the following characteristics: realistic trust in self and the environment; perception of one's inner needs and an ability to communicate them; the ability to make choices, including knowing and accepting the consequences of those choices; flexibility and the capacity to learn from past experiences; the ability to deal actively with the present and plan for the future; free access to one's creative talents and resources; and a goal-oriented approach and enjoyment from the process of problem solving, whether physical, emotional, or cognitive. We critically examine all our childrearing practices in order to determine which facilitate and/or hinder the emergence of the following desired characteristics in infancy.

Trust develops when the primary caregivers allow children to anticipate what is going to happen to them. Adults must convey their trust in infants and view children as initiators as well as recipients of activities.

Infants are absorbed by their *inner feelings* of satisfaction or dissatisfaction, and they try to communicate these needs. If caregivers do not sensitively observe infants, they may not respond to the children's communications but rather to their own interpretations of the infants' needs. For example, a mother who is cold may cover a crying infant without trying to find out whether the baby is warm or cold.

Making appropriate choices in life is a learning process lasting from birth to death. Few people realize at what an early age infants are able to make proper choices if given the opportunity. Adults must differentiate between situations according to whether the infant has a real choice or not. If there is a real choice (e.g., "Do you want to be picked up now?"), and the child responds negatively or with disinterest, the baby would be left alone. If the child has no choice, the caregiver does not ask but states the intended action (e.g., "I am going to pick you up now. It is time to go."). The child is then picked up.

Flexibility of the body and mind develops throughout repeated exploratory exercises of infants in free play. Infants who are restricted by mechanical devices such as infant seats, bouncers, walkers, and swings, or are encouraged to assume positions that they are not yet ready for, are not moving freely. Propping up infants into a sitting position before they can sit up alone will neither accelerate motor development nor help the child to become flexible or autonomous.

While some research (Ainsworth 1967; Geber 1958) both in the United States and in Africa indicates that children may sometimes walk earlier if they are given practice in walking, there is no evidence that children who walk a few weeks earlier than they might otherwise have done gain any benefit.

The greater importance of the *quality* of motor and sensorimotor activities has been realized by many professionals in the field of remedial education (Barsch 1967; Radler and Kephart 1960). Yet children's motor abilities have often been judged according to their crude level of achievement in sitting, standing, and walking.

We do not attempt to speed up these landmarks for several reasons:
(1) "Training in any particular activity before the neural mechanisms have reached a certain state of readiness is futile" (McGraw 1963, p. 130). So why the effort?
(2) If we compare the amount of time human beings spend moving horizontally on the floor to the time they spend sitting, standing, and walking, the time we can gain in achieving these upright postures is insignificant. So why the rush?
(3) We witness many older children with motor, learning, and behavior problems who, under the name of therapies, have to go through hours and hours of exercises to learn postures and movements which infants perform spontaneously. Why not let infants exercise at the proper time?
(4) Forcing children into a posture or motor skill for which they are not quite ready can even harm them; they might learn distorted positions when their back or leg muscles are not strong enough to support them. So why take the risk?

Observing the great variety of movements and exploration that infants can perform on any level of neuro-physiological development makes one wonder why we attempt to reduce this rich repertoire into the more stereotyped movements which will occur once they are walking. We believe it is not the movement itself but what the children learn when they move about themselves and about their bodies in relation to the space around them, which is important.

We observed how our infants develop in relation to their surroundings. We saw them adjust their posture when trying to get on, in, or under objects; these movements were purposeful; they wanted to reach objects put on high shelves or to climb into a feeding chair, etc. We observed them use their motor abilities (whether dragging, creeping, crawling) to discover space around them and eventually develop a cognitive inner map of the different areas of the center. Simultaneously, their skill at pushing and pulling doors and gates enabled them to move from one place to another or to communicate a desire to do so.

We also observed a lag between the cognitive and motor abilities of some of our infants; for example, Chris, quite capable of crawling from area to area, was frustrated when the bars of the fence separated him from an object that he wanted; at this point he did not have the concept of going around a barrier to get an object which he could see in front of him. We later witnessed his "aha" experience when he first discovered that he could go around; with a delighted face, he repeated the movement again and again.

Pikler (1971) has critically described commonly used interventions such as helping, teaching, exercising, which supposedly are needed to promote the progression of gross motor skills. "When the mother considers it timely (according to schedules) she introduces a new posture to the child" (Pikler, p. 55). Obviously infants feel uncomfortable, are unbalanced, unfree, and fully dependent on the adult to rescue them from their predicament. Next infants may be "exercised by an adult or with the aid of an apparatus such as a special chair, swing, baby-walker, etc., to attain the ability of remaining in the new posture or to move according to the new way" (Pikler, p. 55). Eventually children become less rigid and awkward in the positions in which they are placed.

> . . .*after* the child has learned to be prone, he learns to turn prone and back again. After having learned to sit, he learns to sit up and get down; after having learned to stand, he learns to stand up and get down; and after having learned to take some steps independently, he learns to stand up without support and to start and stop walking and to get down. Only after he has learned these, is the child able to use the advanced motor skills in everyday life on his own initiative. Only after this third period does he really become independent in the more advanced postures and motions. (Pikler 1971, pp. 55-56)

Pikler then describes how the children at Loczy attained all stages of motor development "without any direct interference by adult or aid of supporting equipment" (Pikler, p. 56).

If children can develop all required motor skills with, as well as without, adult help (about 2,000 infants have been raised at Loczy) what are the benefits in *not* helping them? From my personal observations of infants in both situations described I have found that infants moving on their own are constantly busy moving, exploring, choosing objects, and overcoming obstacles with caution; have longer attention spans; are peaceful; and enjoy their autonomy.

During the sensorimotor stage, explorations are optimal learning experiences and should be one of the two most important parts of the curriculum. Independent, self-absorbed infants who need much less adult intervention make the other important part, a special individualized interaction, possible. The caregiver in charge of a group of peacefully exploring infants can devote undivided attention to the one infant she or he is caring for. In this way infants' basic need for a warm, attentive, special human relation and their need for autonomy are met. Adults have more time to just observe, which will make interventions more appropriate and the caregiver's knowledge of the children more accurate. Both infants and adults feel more relaxed and fulfilled. A relationship of mutual trust develops. This trusting and respectful approach becomes a pattern of interaction and goes far beyond its effect on gross motor development.

Infants do naturally have *access to their own resources* unless we superimpose tasks that are beyond their capabilities. It is truly fascinating to observe infants *solving their own problems* with concentration, endurance, and good frustration tolerance. This happens if adults are available rather than intrusive, and if they learn to wait and see whether children can work it out alone before offering help. Freely exploring children select their own problems and are internally motivated to solve them in their own way, continuously learning without experiencing failure. Though some individual modifications are necessary when working with high-risk children, providing learning experiences without failure is even more important for them than it is for the average child.

While emphasizing the infant's need for *autonomy*, one must keep in mind the utmost importance of the relationship that infants develop with their primary caregiver. An intimate trusting relationship is the prerequisite for children's healthy separation and individuation. Only after they get "refueled" during the unhurried times spent with their caregiver will they be willing to let go of the caregiver and explore the environment.

In this chapter I have discussed infants' needs and adults' goals for them and suggested how to synchronize them. If our goal is an authentic individual, then we should let each child be an authentic infant. Meeting the needs of infants is not an easy task for the family, and it is even more difficult in infant centers. Even good families find that infants are time- and energy-consuming and frequently their needs conflict with those of the parents'. Constancy—so important to the infant—is threatened by disruption of the family and/or the parents' need or desire to work. Nevertheless, in their own families infants usually experience care and closeness from the same primary caregivers. Even in the best of institutions, however, infants are exposed to all kinds of inconsistencies, to many different caregivers and caring styles, and subject to constant change.

Appropriate curriculum for infants should not be special teaching plans added to daily activities, but rather it should be built into the infant's every experience. The types of programs offered as well as curricula should evolve as a joint effort between caregivers and infants.

The caregiver provides space, objects, and loving care; the infant explores the space, manipulates the objects, develops trust and self-confidence. The guidelines for any and all intervention must be based on observation, empathy, sensitivity, and respect for the infant.

References

Ainsworth, M.D. *Infancy in Uganda: Infant Care and the Growth of Love.* Baltimore: John Hopkins University Press, 1967.

Barsch, R.H. "The Infant Curriculum: A Concept for Tomorrow." *Exceptional Infant* 1 (1967): 543-568.

Bayley, N. *The Manual for the Bayley Scales of Infant Development.* New York: Psychological Corporation, 1969.

David, M., and Appel, G. *Loczy ou Le Maternage Insolite.* "Loczy An Unusual Way of Caring." Trans. M. Gerber. Editions du Scarabee. Paris: Centres d'entrainment aux methods d'education active, 1973.

Geber, M. "The Psycho-Motor Development of African Children in Their First Year and the Influence of Maternal Behavior." *Journal of Social Psychology* 45 (1958): 185-195.

Gerber, M. "Infants' Expression—The Art of Becoming." In *Conscious and Unconscious Expressive Art, Psychiatry and Art, Vol. 3,* ed. I. Jakab. Basel: Karger, 1971.

Gerber, M., ed. *Resources for Infant Educarers.* Los Angeles: Resources for Infant Educarers, 1979.

Gesell, A. *Gesell Developmental Schedules.* New York: Psychological Corporation, 1940.

Gordon, I.J. *Baby Learning Through Baby Play: A Parents' Guide for the First Two Years.* New York: Saint Martin's Press, 1970.

McGraw, M.D. *The Neuro-Muscular Maturation of the Human Infant.* New York: Hafner, 1963.

Painter, G. *Teach Your Baby.* New York: Simon and Schuster, 1971.

Piaget, J. *The Origins of Intelligence in Children.* New York: Norton, 1963.

Pikler, E. "Learning of Motor Skills on the Basis of Self-Induced Movements." In *Exceptional Infant, Studies in Abnormalities, Vol. 2,* ed. J. Hellmuth. New York: Brunner/Mazel, 1971.

Radler, D.H., and Kephart, N.C. *Success Through Play.* New York: Harper & Row, 1960.

Stone, L.; Smith, H; and Murphy, L.B., eds. *The Competent Infant.* New York: Basic Books, 1973.

Romayne Sternad

6

A program for infants with developmental delays

Programs that serve developmentally delayed children from birth to three years and their parents need to be based on broad professional knowledge about infants, about handicapping conditions, and about parenting. Standards for such programs have been articulated both nationally and locally by such groups as the United Cerebral Palsy Association National Collaborative Infant Project (Connor, Williamson, and Siepp 1975) and the Task Force on Funding and Quality Standards for Infant Development Programs (Brandt et al. 1977). The thrust of a delayed development program is total family support: amelioration of handicapping conditions in the infant, education in parenting, and preventive mental health for the family.

An effective program for developmentally delayed infants and families adheres to the following principles.

1. *Parents have the most important and pervasive influence on their infant's development.* Although the infant and parent may have become estranged from each other due to the baby's early medical problems and consequent separation, a close reciprocal relationship can be rebuilt and nurtured (Klaus and Kennell 1976). Caring professionals can build on the positive in the infant-parent relationship, supporting the bonding process rather than supplanting it. The importance of the parent's role in the infant's developing motivation to learn should not be underestimated. Because parents know their baby's personality, they understand the meaning of her or his responses. They are a rich source of information to the helping professional who often seeks the parents' view. Parents need to be involved in every step of the program—interacting with the infant in play and daily care, planning objectives, and helping to evaluate the infant's progress (Levitt and Cohen 1976).

2. *Parents do not automatically know how to help their infants develop and learn.* Parenting does not come naturally even to parents of infants without problems (Gerber 1974), although most parents are eager to learn parenting skills. Parents can learn observation techniques and selective intervention strategies to use in daily care that will facilitate the infant's more normal development (Shearer and Shearer 1972; Quick, Little, and Campbell 1973). As the parents become more attuned to the infant's abilities and needs, they are more actively involved in their baby's daily growth, becoming the chief motivators for the infant. The program's benefit to the infant is long-lasting when the parent is committed to help the infant develop.

3. *Early intervention is essential for infants with developmental problems* (Brandt et al. 1977; Connor, Williamson, and Siepp 1978; Richardson et al. 1975; Schafer and Moersch 1977; Shearer and Shearer 1972). Infant programs seek referrals as early as problems are identified, often before there is a firm diagnosis. Early intervention can modify existing handicapping conditions while preventing secondary disabilities both in the infant's and the family's functioning. Attention to the parents' concerns helps to dispel anxiety about the unknown. By participating in an infant program, parents find in other parents an important resource for practical and emotional support. If a family is left without professional help during the first year of doubt and worry about their baby's normalcy, parents may isolate themselves in despair or apathy. The support system of an infant program offers realistic help and hope.

4. *A transdisciplinary team approach to the infant and family is essential.* In a transdisciplinary team approach, one primary staff member is the intermediary between the family and a host of professionals and agencies (Connor, Williamson, and Siepp 1978). Too many officials can overwhelm a family. Too much handling of the infant is not healthy. The primary advocate interprets the advice from staff members of various disciplines such as: child development, special education, infant care, physical therapy, speech and language pathology, public health nursing, and social work. The team coordinates other community resources interested in the family and simplifies the contacts, whenever possible.

An effective program

The Infant Program for Developmentally Delayed at Community Association for Retarded, Inc., in Palo Alto, California, has incorporated these four principles since 1972. The Infant Program is an observation

Anyone who works with a delayed infant soon realizes that the child is a person first, a person within a family next, and finally a person with special problems.

and intervention service for infants from birth to three years who show any kind of delay. No diagnosis is required. Referrals come from the medical community, social workers, Regional Centers for Developmental Disabilities, and by word-of-mouth. Four components are offered: an in-center program (maximum group size is six infants), a home program (maximum group size is four infants), regular home visits, and weekly parent group discussion and education sessions. Parents or parent-substitutes participate in two group sessions as teacher aides with the infants and in parent discussion groups. Infants attend in small groups for two or three sessions per week. Over the past five years the program has grown from 14 to 40 families served per year, with an average of 11 to 22 infants being served at any one time. Conditions of the infants included Down's syndrome and other chromosomal abnormalities, cerebral palsy and other central nervous system defects, cortical blindness, hearing impairment, congenital defects, and mild developmental delays. A multidisciplinary staff consisting of a full-time director and teacher; a part-time teacher assistant; program specialists in social work, physical therapy, occupational therapy, and speech and language; and volunteers and student interns, provided an adult to infant ratio of one-to-two, often one-to-one. The Infant Program carried out a dual purpose: strengthening the family and normalizing the development of each infant.

Focusing on the infant

While acknowledging that parent involvement is paramount in the long-range perspective, teachers need to focus on infants in order to help them develop to their fullest potential. Teachers can draw up an appropriate plan of action that both parents and staff can follow—a plan that will assist but not hamper the infant's progress. There are four important steps: knowing how infants learn, studying the individual infant, individualizing the program, and training adults in helpful approaches to infants.

How do infants learn? Infants learn very early from their mother's caregiving, by interacting with mother, and gradually extending this reciprocity to other members of the family and to other adults (Brazelton 1969). Social interaction between baby and caring adult is a prerequisite to learning. The close emotional ties vital to the welfare of both mother and baby are called the mother-infant bond, a mutual admiration pact (Klaus and Kennell 1976). The infant program staff can foster this bonding by helping the mother to be aware of the infant's cues, by sharing their mutual enjoyment, and by building on the positives in the baby's actions and the mother's nurturance. Handicapped infants have the same capacity as "normal" infants to love and be loved, although it is not as obvious. Parents may have to work harder and wait longer for a response. The "feedback loop" of contact and reward may not be as smooth or as predictable as with parent and infant who have an untroubled beginning, yet it can and should be encouraged.

Infants learn by observing and interacting with other infants (Gerber 1974). They watch and imitate each other. They discover and explore each other. They play next to each other as though unaware while still being observant. They struggle over the same toy, give up or defend a possession. They listen to each other and at times reflect another's emotions by crying or showing an empathic expression. They offer toys and take them back. They engage in follow-the-leader. All of these experiences are stored in memory for future reference. In an infant program, infants are sometimes motivated to try a new behavior only after watching another infant model that behavior. For this reason, normally functioning infants, frequently more physically active, are invited to attend the program to act as models for the delayed infants.

Infants learn by exploring the environment. They enjoy variety and challenge in their world within a stable framework. When they feel comfortable and secure in a safe environment, they follow their own interests, proceeding from the known to the untried. An infant, if allowed to, can solve problems, such as how to get one's leg out from the side of a chair or how to pull a pulltoy that has tipped over. Sometimes an infant returns to the infant session after several days and, remembering an earlier problem, tries a new solution. Infants learn from trial-and-error experimentation with objects. As toddlers, they learn through symbolic play, reenacting their interpretation of real life scenes they have witnessed. They learn by generalizing an old solution to new problems. Adults can set the stage for learning by providing intriguing objects and challenging situations that match the infant's level of interest and skills. Adults need to recognize when learning opportunities arise, remaining available to help only when needed.

Studying the individual infant. Every infant is unique. Anyone who works with a delayed infant soon realizes that the child is a person first, a person within a family next, and finally a person with special problems. In order to know infants fully, one must observe them in different settings: at home with parents and siblings, in the infant session with and without parents, during a formal assessment with teacher and parent, when the infants are well and rested, when they are tired, hungry, etc. The study of infants continues over a period of weeks with assistance from parents and staff members. Through this careful ongoing study, an infant's levels of functioning in physical, social, emotional, intellectual, language, self-help, and health development are determined. Conditions are noted under which various responses occur. A profile emerges of the infant's strengths and weaknesses, personality, style, tempo, and responsiveness (Brazelton 1969). Using this profile, the teacher can plan specific experiences while anticipating that certain behaviors will develop. The picture is constantly changing, however. With maturity and experience, the infant's development may spurt in some areas and plateau in others. Studying the infant is an ongoing process. Formal assessments may be helpful every three to six months, but daily anecdotal records with parent and staff reports are essential to accurate planning for the infant and family.

Individualizing the program. From the systematic study of the infant, the teacher draws up an Individual Program Plan (IPP), a set of behavioral objectives in each developmental area for use as a guide in daily care of the infant. The IPP may also delineate problem areas and intervention strategies. Together parents and teacher review this plan and revise it as necessary. After about three months, the IPP is evaluated in terms of the infant's progress and delays. A formal one-hour infant assessment is made with the parents present during the initial study and at the three-month and six-month evaluation. A comprehensive tool designed for handicapped infants is used, such as the Early Intervention Developmental Profile (Schafer and Moersch 1977) or the Developmental Progression Chart (Richardson et al. 1975). Observations are pooled from staff and parents, and the cycle of study and planning begins anew.

Daily activities in the program are thought out with the needs of each infant in mind. It is important to keep the group size of infants and the numbers of adults small to avoid confusion and noise. In an infant session with six infants, three mothers, three staff and volunteers, one-to-one attention can be given as needed. However, the infant does not need continual interaction with an adult. An atmosphere is created which makes clear that the infant room is the "infants' world." Infants need time and space to become comfortable in familiar surroundings, to explore and rediscover their environment, and to notice each other. A therapeutic environment does not require constant handling of the infant, but it does require selective intervention. A familiar and trusted adult who knows an infant's abilities and needs can offer precise help at the right moment, enough to facilitate the baby's next step while encouraging independence. Continuity of staff and volunteers is important. Visitors are restricted to observing the session through a window because when infants have to adjust to strangers, they become cautious and inhibited.

The focus of the infant session, then, is on the needs of each infant. This requires certain adaptations and restrictions on adult behavior.

Training adults. The attitudes and actions of adults influence the infant's learning. The following suggestions to adults who work with delayed or normal infants will help to ensure a meaningful experience for the infant. Demonstrations and weekly discussion sessions are held to convey these approaches to parents and teachers.

1. In getting acquainted with infants, let them approach you. Be available and interested while waiting for infants to signal that they want

to get to know you. Infants need time to adjust to a new person or a new place.

2. Sit in the background and observe at times. Infants need space and a safe area to explore. Active movement by infants occurs in open spaces with inviting toys which are placed slightly out of reach. Infants learn most as active participants; they learn least when being acted upon (Gerber 1979).

3. Intervene only when necessary, i.e., when the infant is in danger or distress, when it is time for feeding or diapering. Offer aid or comfort but do not impose it. Move very slowly around and with infants. Allow them time to accommodate to change.

Explain what is about to happen. If an infant needs to be picked up, approach the child from the front and explain first what you are going to do. Offer your hands. This enables the thinking process of anticipation to develop. Keep routines (and sequences within routines) predictable. Infants can anticipate a familiar routine when they know what to expect.

4. Talk to infants simply and clearly. Interpret for the baby what she or he is doing and what is happening. Infants begin to make sense of their world when events are consistently explained. The adult provides a language model for the infant. By limiting adult-to-adult conversation around infants, adults can simplify the auditory environment so that language is easier to learn. Infants must abstract meaning out of the language that they hear (Gonzalez-Mena and Eyer 1980; Chomsky 1968). Language and learning are fostered as the responsive adult establishes a meaningful dialogue with the infant based on everyday experiences (Forrest 1980).

5. Let infants work out their own solutions to problems (within safe boundaries). Infants learn through trial and error. Solving a problem, no matter how small, builds competence. Be aware of problem-solving situations the infant may become interested in so that you do not interrupt investigation. Adjust your own actions to allow for growing independence.

Adults set the stage for learning. By their actions, adults can enhance or inhibit infant growth and development. Although some structure and adult-directed activities are necessary in the infant program, a balance can be achieved between structure and flexibility, between adult direction and infants' free choice. In an "infants' world" atmosphere, delayed infants show greater initiative and more curiosity and interest in each other and their surroundings than they do in a more controlling, adult-centered atmosphere.

An effective program for developmentally delayed infants maintains a separate focus on the infant while serving the family, with the goal that each infant may develop to her or his maximum potential.

References

Brandt, J.; Mayo, P.; Morales, S.; Powell, S.; Lowry, M.; Ubbenga, J.; and Lim, N. "Task Force on Funding and Quality Standards for Infant Development Programs: A Report." Unpublished report to the Governor of California, San Francisco, 1977.

Brazelton, T.B. *Infants and Mothers: Differences in Development.* New York: Delta Publishing, 1969.

Chomsky, N. *Language and the Mind.* New York: Harcourt Brace Jovanovich, 1968.

Connor, F.P.; Williamson, G.G.; and Siepp, J. *A Program Guide for Infants and Toddlers with Neuromotor and Other Developmental Disabilities.* New York: Teachers College Press (in cooperation with UCP Association), 1978.

Forrest, T., M.D. "Language Development—New Directions—Pikler Rediscovered." *Educaring Newsletter, Resources for Infant Educarers* 1, no. 3 (Summer 1980).

Gerber, M. "Notes and Quotes on Madge Gerber," ed. C. Wilson. *After Birth* 2, nos. 10-14 (1974). Los Angeles, Calif., 1974.

Gerber, M. "Respecting Infants: The Loczy Model of Infant Care." In *Supporting the Growth of Infants, Toddlers, and Parents,* ed. E. Jones. Pasadena, Calif.: Pacific Oaks College, 1979.

Gonzalez-Mena, J., and Eyer, D. W. *Infancy and Caregiving.* Palo Alto, Calif.: Mayfield, 1980.

Klaus, M.H., and Kennell, J. H. *Maternal-Infant Bonding.* St. Louis: Mosby, 1976.

Levitt, E., and Cohen, S. "Educating Parents of Children with Special Needs—Approaches and Issues." *Young Children* 31, no. 4 (May 1976): 263-272.

Quick, A.D.; Little, T.L.; and Campbell, A.A. "Early Childhood Education for Exceptional Foster Children and Training of Foster Parents." *Exceptional Children* 40, no. 3 (November 1973): 206-208.

Richardson, R.; Ogle, R.; Tudor, M.; Fey, K.; McGagin, C.; and Chang, V. "San Juan Handicapped Infant Project Handbook." Carmichael, Calif.: San Juan Unified School District, 1975.

Schafer, D.S., and Moersch, M.S., eds. *Developmental Programming for Infants and Young Children* (3 volumes). Ann Arbor, Mich.: University of Michigan Press, 1977.

Shearer, M.S., and Shearer, D.E. "The Portage Project: A Model for Early Childhood Education." *Exceptional Children* 39, no. 3 (November 1972): 210-223.

Rose Bromwich
Dorli Burge
Wallie Kass

Ellen Khokha
Eleanor Baxter
Suzanne Fust

7

A Parent Behavior Progression

The powerful influence of parents' attitudes and behaviors on the development of their infants is now widely acknowledged and has been underscored by recent research on parent-infant interaction (see Chapters 2 and 10). When mutually pleasurable interactions between parent and infant begin early, a spiral is set off that leads to satisfaction in parenting and at the same time to optimal development of the infant. The Parent Behavior Progression (PBP) is founded on the principle that when parents achieve mutually satisfying interaction with their infants and acquire sensitivity and responsiveness to their infants' needs in different areas of development, they create an environment in which infants are able to develop to their fullest potential.

In the past, infant specialists were satisfied to assess only the infant's development and behavior for the purpose of setting short-term goals and planning interventions directly with infants. Today these specialists are aware that parenting behaviors must also be considered if optimal development of children is the aim. If parenting behaviors have a major influence on infant development, then the achievement of those parent behaviors which foster that development should be goals of parent-infant education and intervention.

Reproduced with minor changes from "The Parent Behavior Progression Manual" (Rose Bromwich, Ellen Khokha, Dorli Burge, Eleanor Baxter, Wallie Kass, and Suzanne Fust 1978).

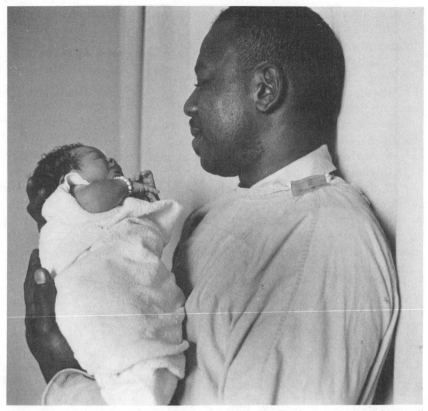

*When mutually pleasurable interactions between parent and infant begin early, a spiral is set off
that leads to satisfaction in parenting and at the same time to optimal development of the infant.*

The aim of the PBP is to sensitize infant development specialists to the
feelings, attitudes, and behaviors of parents and thus enable them to
work more effectively with these parents toward experiencing greater
enjoyment, satisfaction, and competence in their parenting role. It
serves as a tool that leads staff to: (1) support positive behaviors already
in the parent's repertoire, and (2) help the parent acquire new behavior
patterns that enhance infant-parent interactions and the infant's development. The Parent Behavior Progression* has been empirically derived from five years of home intervention experience by the educational

_____

*Parts of the manual and forms 1 and 2 can be found in *Working with Parents and Infants*
 (Bromwich 1981).

staff of the University of California, Los Angeles Infant Studies Project. For details on administration and scoring, contact the authors.

Framework

The progression from level to level of the PBP suggests the behavioral sequence that many parents follow as they grow with their infants. It consists of six levels, each of which is defined and then elaborated on in the form of descriptive statements of parenting behaviors. The first three levels of the progression, although containing cognitive components, have been identified as the affective base. The first three levels demonstrate that parents are actively providing growth-promoting experiences for their infant. The parents' enjoyment and knowledge of their child— their sensitivity to their child's needs and cues resulting in mutually satisfying interactions—constitute the foundation for the more complex parenting behaviors of the second three levels. In levels I, II, and III, the affective base (Bromwich 1976), the growing pleasure of the parents in the child leads to interest in reading and responding to cues, which, in turn, leads to mutuality or reciprocity of interaction. The parents are then able to provide their infant with an environment, play materials, and language and social experiences that foster the child's development (level IV). The parent's behaviors become more complex as they cue in to the subtleties of their infant's needs. They continue to progress in parental competence as they learn and profit from their own experience and/or from intervention (level V). Finally parents independently generate a wide variety of activities for their infant, anticipate her or his more complex needs in the next stage of development, and are able to view the baby's needs in relation to their own needs and those of the rest of the family (level VI).

This sequence or progression of levels should not however be thought of as a rigid structure to follow in setting goals for intervention. It does not imply that behaviors at level I are acquired before behaviors at subsequent levels. In fact, behaviors at level I are often the natural consequence of behaviors at levels II and IV. For example, when dealing with a mother who, for any number of reasons, does not experience any enjoyment of her infant (level I), it is often much easier to begin intervention efforts by involving her in some activity with her infant (level IV). When she sees the positive effect she is having on the infant, she feels more adequate in the mothering role. A more positive feeling toward one's self as parent if often an important first step toward a parent's enjoyment of, and sensitive responsiveness to, her or his infant.

The Parent Behavior Progression

The behaviors listed here apply to parents of infants from birth to 9 months.* They also describe the desirable behaviors to be expected of parents with older handicapped and developmentally delayed infants who are functioning below the 9-month level. An additional form (not included here) for parents of infants between 9 and 36 months of age is structured in basically the same manner as the birth to 9 months form. Parent behaviors can be either observed or reported. Feminine and masculine pronoun references on this form are used only for editorial simplicity and in no way reflect stereotyped concepts of parents or children.

Level I

The parent enjoys her infant

Enjoyment by the parent does not need to be reciprocated by the infant at this level. The parent can get pleasure from her baby on her terms, without regard to what the baby is experiencing, even if this enjoyment is limited to brief periods of the day or only to certain types of interactions. This is in contrast to level III, where the enjoyment has to be reciprocated by the baby (mutuality).

Parent Behaviors

A. Pleasure in watching infant

1. Parent shows or reports pleasure in watching the infant at least some of the time.

    example: "Sometimes I like to sneak in and watch her lying in her crib."

2. Parent shows or reports pleasure in infant's physical appearance.

    example: "It tickles me that he looks so much like his grandfather."

3. Parent shows pride in the infant by ascribing to him qualities that the parent values.

    example: "She's a tough little girl. I think she's going to be somebody in this world."

---

*Form 1 of the Parent Behavior Progression has also been reproduced in the Appendix in *Working with Parents and Infants* (Bromwich 1981).

4. Parent spontaneously talks about the things the infant does that please her.

   example: "She looks up when I come in the room. I think she knows me!"

The following three behaviors would not be expected to appear until the baby begins to smile or show pleasure in some manner.

5. Parent shows or reports pleasure in watching the infant respond pleasurably to other adults or children.

   example: "He gets so excited when his daddy comes home."

6. Parent shows or reports pleasure in watching the infant play.

   example: "I notice that she can really kick her mobile to get it to move now. That's really exciting."

7. Parent shows or reports pleasure in infant's *enjoyment of his own activities*.

   example: "I love when he gets all excited and happy in his bathtub!"

B. Pleasure in proximity—including physical contact

8. Parent gives evidence of enjoying the presence of her infant—having the infant near her.

   example: Mother says she puts the infant in his seat on the counter while she does the dishes because she likes to have him with her.

9. Parent reports that she looks forward to doing something with her infant (not necessarily alone with infant—others may be present also).

   example: "I really enjoy taking him to my Mom's where everybody fusses over him."

10. Parent gives evidence that she enjoys physical contact with infant (without necessarily playing with him).

    example: Father spontaneously picks up his baby, hugs her and holds her on his lap for a few minutes.

11. Parent gives evidence that she enjoys some aspects of the physical care of the infant.

    example: "It's fun bathing him even though he is so floppy and I have to hold his head up."

C. Pleasure in interaction

12. Parent seeks eye contact with her infant much of the time when she is attending to him.

    example: While changing infant's diapers, mother looks into his face as she softly talks to him.

13. Parent gives evidence that she enjoys engaging in some type of play or playful interaction with her infant, even if only on her terms—physically, vocally, or with toys.

example: After her infant wakes up, mother plays peek-a-boo with her through the bars of the crib before picking her up.

Level II

The parent is a sensitive observer of her infant, reads his behavioral cues accurately, and is responsive to them

Level II consists of two elements—(1) the parent's reading of the infant's cues and (2) the parent's responses to those cues. It is possible for the parent to be aware of the meaning of some of the infant's behavior or to read his cues without being responsive to them. This is, of course, insufficient for a desirable interaction between parent and infant. The ability to observe *and* read behavioral cues accurately is basic to the development of sensitive responsiveness.

Parent Behaviors

A. Reading biological cues

1. Parent is able to read the infant's signals of distress (crying, whimpering, fussing).

    example: "That's his 'Hurry up, I'm starving' cry."

2. Parent gives evidence of knowing the infant's biological rhythms with respect to sleeping, eating, elimination.

    example: "I can't plan her feeding schedule too tightly because she doesn't always get hungry at the same time every day."

3. Parent recognizes signs indicating whether the infant is safe and comfortable (satiated but not too full, physically secure, comfortably warm).

    example: Father reports his baby seems happier when he holds him snugly.

B. Reading infant's social-affective and temperamental cues

4. Parent reports on the infant's responses to herself and to others.

    example: "She always seems to quiet down when someone talks to her."

5. Parent makes reference to infant's temperamental and behav-

ioral characteristics, i.e., attentiveness, activity level, intensity, reaction to change, etc.

example: "She really stares at that new mobile we put up over her crib." (attentiveness)

example: "When she laughs, I can hear it in the next room!" (intensity)

example: "Every time I give her a new food, she spits it out." (reaction to change)

example: "Unlike his sister who is always in motion, he enjoys sitting in one spot exploring a toy." (activity level)

C. Reading infant's response to environmental stimulation

6. Parent reports details of the infant's response to his physical environment.

   example: "The baby likes going for a ride—she stops crying the minute the car starts moving."

7. Parent talks about the amount of stimulation the infant can handle and profit from.

   example: "My first baby just loved when his father used to 'rough-house' with him, but this one doesn't like it at all—she starts crying."

D. Responding to infant's needs and cues

8. Parent adapts caregiving practices in response to infant's cues related to his biological needs.

   example: "He seems quite happy playing past his usual lunchtime—so I've been feeding him a little later."

9. Parent is responsive to infant's changes in state or mood. (Exception: When an infant has unusual difficulty in inhibiting crying, the parent would not be expected to show the same sensitivity to his crying behavior.)

   example: When the baby begins to fuss, the mother goes to her, changes her position, and talks to her soothingly.

10. Parent adapts the amount and intensity of stimulation to what the infant can handle and profit from.

    example: When the baby gets restless in the same room as siblings watching a loud TV program, mother puts baby in a quieter part of the house and calms him.

11. Parent takes into account infant's level of development and behavior in providing for his safety.

    example: Parent removes fork from baby's reach and substitutes a short wooden spoon.

Level III

The parent engages in a quality and quantity of interaction with her infant that is mutually satisfying and that provides opportunity for the development of attachment

At level III the parent is aware of, values, and gets enjoyment from the *infant's pleasure* in their interaction with each other. Mutuality of enjoyment and a transactional quality is evident in their relationship. At this level the parent also understands the developmental value of a considerable amount of parent-child interaction during the periods of the child's greatest alertness, or, with the increase of mutual enjoyment, she simply spends more time with the child when both can enjoy it most.

Parent Behaviors

A. Parent or stable caregiver time with infant

1. Parent provides situation with some stability of caregiving where the same adult(s) cares for the infant during his wakeful periods of the day.
2. Parent plans her day or the infant's day so that she can spend time with him giving some attention to him during his waking hours (not necessarily in interaction or alone with him).

    example: "I try to do some of my housework while the baby is asleep so that I can spend more time with her while she's awake."

B. Mutuality of enjoyment in interaction

Behaviors listed here are not usually expected to appear until the infant is approximately four months developmentally. By that time most infants will have behaviors such as smiling, cooing, and babbling to show pleasure.

3. Parent and infant enjoy spending time in each other's company (not necessarily engaged in an activity with each other).

    example: "I really get a feeling that she enjoys watching me, and I enjoy having her in the same room with me."

4. Parent and infant interact pleasurably during some caretaking routine.

    example: "When I diaper her she stares at me with those big eyes and I make little sounds. Pretty soon she starts smiling and that really makes my day!"

5. Some noncaretaking interactions between parent and infant give pleasure to both.

   example: "I love to kiss his tummy and I know he loves it too because he laughs out loud."

6. Some *pleasurable interactions* are intiated by parent, some by infant.

7. Sequences or chains of pleasurable interactions between parent and infant suggest mutuality in the relationship.

   example: Baby coos, mother nuzzles baby, baby coos back, etc.

Level IV

Parent demonstrates an awareness of materials, activities, and experiences suitable for her infant's current stage of development

Behaviors at this level deal concretely with what the parent actually provides for or does with the infant in the areas of play, language, and social interaction. The parent not only knows what toys are most appropriate to the infant's skill level but also *how to use these materials* in interaction with him. She identifies and plans experiences for the child that are developmentally appropriate, motivating to him, and therefore satisfying.

Parent Behaviors

A. Providing and structuring environment for satisfying experiences

1. Parent provides environment in which infant can engage safely in motor activity at his skill level.

   example: Mother lets her infant climb up and down the doorstep while she watches him.

2. Parent positions infant to allow wide range of vision and movement (young or handicapped infant).

   example: Parent puts wide-awake young infant, who cannot lift his head, on his back so that he can follow visually and move his limbs.

3. Parent provides for some variety in the infant's physical and social environment.

   example: Parent puts infant outdoors where he can watch his father do the gardening.

One should not overgeneralize about cultural mores in relation to individual families. The importance of sensitivity to individual styles and patterns of interactions within a particular family cannot be overestimated.

4. Parent provides the kind of space for the infant that he needs for his level of play.

   example: "I put an old bedspread on the floor in the corner, and she loves playing there with her things."

5. Parent provides materials (not necessarily toys) at infant's skill level for adaptive play.

   example: Mother gives eight-month-old baby cereal and finger foods he can practice picking up.

6. Parent allows infant to mouth, touch, or play with a variety of things he discovers around him.

   example: Mother allows baby to crumple pages in an old magazine that he finds on a low shelf.

7. Parent gives infant access to sufficient play materials to lead to profitable play and removes materials not of interest to him.

   example: Mother of six-month-old hangs a plastic mirror on side of playpen and removes some of the stuffed animals.

B. Interacting with infant to enhance his play

 8. Parent is aware of infant's tempo in play and paces appropriately.

   example: Mother allows infant time to play with object in which he shows interest before giving him another one.

 9. Parent facilitates the infant's play with objects.

   example: When baby drops rattle, mother puts it within reach.

C. Providing for language experience

 10. Parent responds to infant's sounds.

   example: Mother imitates baby's sounds.

 11. Parent talks, sings, or hums to infant even if he does not give a vocal response.

   example: Parent of deaf child makes certain to have face-to-face contact while talking and singing to him.

D. Encouraging social-emotional growth

 12. Parent deals with infant in an affirmative manner the majority of the time.

 13. Parent accepts attachment and separation behaviors and responds to them appropriately. (Not applicable to parent of infant before approximately seven months of age.)

   example: Mother explains that her baby seems to warm up faster to a visitor when she can sit on mother's lap for a while.

Levels V and VI consist of more complex behaviors across all areas of parenting. Many parents who have normal and easy-to-care for infants will develop these behaviors, based on their parenting experience. Other parents will need outside help for a variety of reasons, be it problems of the parent herself, social and environmental circumstances, a difficult and unresponsive baby, or any combination of these.

Level V

The parent initiates new play activities and experiences based on principles that she has internalized from her own experience, or on the same principles as activities suggested to or modeled for her

The parent generalizes from an explanation, suggestion, or observed activity by developing other activities related to the same developmental goal. She reaches this level when she sees that a particular activity is enjoyed by her infant and understands how it contributes to his developmental progress. The parent may or may not be sufficiently aware of the underlying principles to articulate them at this level, but she is able to apply them.

Parent Behaviors

A. Providing more effectively for cognitive (play), language, and social learning

1. Parent provides infant with a variety of developmentally appropriate materials for different sense modalities and which encourage different schemas (e.g., holding, shaking, exploring visually, banging).

   example: Mother makes texture ball out of different fabrics for baby to feel.

2. Parent enhances the quality of play and the infant's satisfaction from it by introducing alternative ways of using materials.

   example: Parent of infant who only mouths objects puts her hand around his and helps him shake his rattle.

3. Parent finds ways of increasing the infant's interest level by the way she organizes play materials or situations.

   example: For baby that seems distracted by lots of stimulation, mother removes other toys before presenting new ones.

4. Parent modifies her style of verbal communication with infant as she observes his differential responses.

   example: Mother shifts her baby's position so that he can see her face when she notices this increases his interest in her language.

5. Parent begins to differentiate between those infant behaviors that she should try to modify and those she should adapt to as she looks for a comfortable modus vivendi for herself with the baby. She experiments with ways of making some of the infant's behavior more tolerable for her without restricting him unnecessarily.

   example: Infant begins dropping his food on the floor. Mother cannot change his behavior so she spreads newspaper under and around his chair when he eats.

Level VI

The parent independently generates a wide range of developmentally appropriate activities and experiences, interesting to the infant, in

familiar and in new situations and at new levels of the infant's development

Level VI is characterized by behaviors that tend to establish the basis for continued desirable parenting. Here the parent is able to perceive the infant functioning within the framework of the family and is able to generate a variety of experiences to meet the physical, intellectual, emotional, and social needs of the growing infant. The parent is aware of what to expect next in the infant's development and plans to try to meet his increasingly complex needs. Also, built into this level is the ability of the parent to be aware of and respond to her own personal needs as well as those of other members of the family.

Parent Behaviors

A. Anticipating next steps in development

    1. Parent keeps pace with her infant's changing skills and interests and plans activities that will continue to challenge him.

       example: Mother observes infant's attention to the consequence of his banging an object and gets him a cause-effect toy.

    2. Parent anticipates infant's changing responses to people and places and plans ahead to try to meet his emerging needs. (Not applicable to parent of infant before six months developmental age.)

       example: "It is getting harder for him to sleep just anywhere, so I will take along his blanket and other familiar things when we go places."

B. Considering the infant in context of family

    3. Parent recognizes infant's interest in watching family social interactions and finds ways to include him more in family activities; she encourages other family members to do the same.

       example: Mother allows four-year-old sibling to help feed the baby even though it takes a little longer.

    4. Parent tries to respond in a balanced manner to the infant's needs as well as her own and those of the rest of the family.

       example: Mother contacts nearby community college to find someone capable of taking care of her young infant so she can get some time for herself and with her husband on a regular basis.

    5. Parent exercises her own judgment before following suggestions of other "experts" (pediatricians, relatives, peer group, books for parents, etc.).

example: "My mother-in-law cannot understand why I let him make such a mess but I enjoy watching him try to feed himself."

Using the PBP

The PBP should be used by educational or clinical staff experienced in working with infants and their families in an ongoing program, and *not* by independent evaluators from outside the program. In order to utilize this instrument in an appropriate manner, the information needed has to come from observations and conversations in the context of an ongoing relationship between parent and staff. The statements describing behaviors in the PBP should not be used as a basis for questions in a formal interview or parent conference.

The staff has to determine for each individual family which behaviors can and should be realistically aimed for in intervention. It was necessary that behaviors in the PBP describe only desirable attitudes, feelings, and actions so that these behaviors could serve as possible goals of intervention. Some may interpret this as a limitation, especially if they feel that they also must note parenting behaviors judged to be detrimental to the infant and the parent-infant relationship. We suggest that such behaviors be recorded separately; the PBP is not constructed to identify undesirable parenting practices. On the other hand, the absence of the majority of behaviors, especially between levels I and IV (which represent the more basic caregiving practices), would indicate a pattern of parenting that needs intervention. In our experience it has sometimes been more effective to add positive behaviors to the parent's repertoire than to try to eliminate undesirable ones. When the parents become aware of alternatives to their customary way of interacting with their infant that are more satisfying to all, these alternatives frequently become incorporated gradually into their pattern of parenting. Subsequently the negative behaviors tend to drop out on their own.

We do not mean to imply that the parent's ability to express negative feelings about the infant, and sometimes even to the infant, is not an important part of a healthy relationship between the parent and child. Healthy parent-infant interaction involves the parent *reading* the infant's cues as well as the parent *giving* cues clear enough for the infant to read. A parent who is unable to express some anger verbally and facially when feeling it gives mixed messages to the infant that confuse her or him and interfere with emotional development. Many parents (especially those with difficult or deviant babies) may need help to be able to express to other adults some of their disappointments and frustrations with their infants.

We are quite aware that the PBP behaviors do not necessarily reflect the mores and childrearing practices of a number of cultures or subcultures with whom this instrument might be used. The staff should become familiar with the cultural influences on the childrearing patterns of the parents in their programs. This knowledge would give the staff some basis for making judgments about which PBP behaviors could be expected in a particular family or should be realistically viewed as intervention goals. However, one should not overgeneralize about cultural mores in relation to individual families. The importance of sensitivity to individual styles and patterns of interactions within a particular family cannot be overestimated when working with families.

It should also be clearly understood that no parent is expected to show all the behaviors at the six levels of the PBP or at any one level, no matter how competent he or she might be. It should be taken into account that some parents are, for example, much more communicative about their interactions with their infants than others.

Also parents differ in style. For example, two mothers might exhibit different combinations of PBP behaviors and still be considered equally competent.

A natural effect of infant intervention is the parents' increased attention to the infant. In some cases this may have the effect of decreasing their attention to other family members. Therefore we believe that it is the responsibility of an intervention staff to try to support the parents in maintaining a balance in their response to the needs of all the family members. Moreover, it is at least as important for the staff to encourage the parents to consider and attend to their own personal needs.

Many parents of handicapped or deviant infants tend to be under tremendous emotional stress, especially within several months after they become fully aware of their children's problems. Infant specialists working with these parents should guard against being intrusive, emotionally or physically, in their eagerness to help. It is often unrealistic to expect many behaviors at the first three levels of the PBP, especially during periods of intense stress. It is usually more productive to focus on behaviors at level IV that deal more specifically with things that the parent can *do* with and for the infant. Here it is especially helpful to find out what type of contact the parent enjoys most (or minds least) with her infant. The staff might do well to help the parent expand her effectiveness and sense of adequacy in these areas rather than move into areas where the parent may feel uncomfortable. Intervention that allows the parent to set her own direction and pace in her interactions with her handicapped infant is most likely to lead ultimately to mutually satisfying transactions between parent and child.

At the risk of being redundant, we want to emphasize again that the best justification for using the PBP is to sensitize intervention staff to the feelings, attitudes, and behaviors of parents, to become aware of the parents' strengths, and to work toward helping them achieve greater enjoyment, satisfaction, and competence in their role. In other words, this instrument should *not* be used to judge or classify parents as "supermothers" or "zookeepers." We are confident that those who will be using the Parent Behavior Progression are as concerned as we are regarding its appropriate use with parents.

References

Bromwich, R.M. "Focus on Maternal Behavior in Infant Intervention." *American Journal of Orthopsychiatry* 46 (1976): 439-446.

Bromwich, R. *Working with Parents and Infants: An Interactional Approach.* Baltimore: University Park Press, 1981.

Bromwich, R.; Khokha, E.; Burge, D.; Baxter, E.; Kass, W.; and Fust, S. "The Parent Behavior Progression Manual." (unpublished), 1978.

Judith S. Musick
Roseanne Clark
Bertram Cohler

8

The Mothers' Project: a program for mentally ill mothers of young children

Mental illness among mothers of infants and toddlers presents a challenge for the field of child development. Unlike mental illness among people in other social roles, mental illness among mothers of young children has serious consequences not only for the mother's own life but also for the development of her children. Because most mothers provide virtually all of their infant's care, a mother's psychopathology may be communicated to her child, leading to impairment in such areas as the capacity to appraise and act in accord with reality and the capacity to develop close relationships with others. Such impairment in the child's cognitive and social-emotional development may combine with increased genetic risk to predispose the child of a mentally ill mother to far greater vulnerability to subsequent mental illness than exists among children of well mothers in the community.

Even for the ordinary devoted mother, in American society the task of caring for an infant while at the same time fulfilling obligations to husband, friends, neighbors, and her own parental family is replete with stress and potential conflict. The composite picture that emerges particularly clearly from the studies of Cohler (1974a, 1974b) and Cohler et al. (1970, 1974a, 1974b, 1975a, 1975b) of women who become psychiatrically ill during the first years after childbirth is of women who from their own childhoods have been unable to achieve closeness with others. Largely unable to trust others or to achieve reciprocal and interdependent relationships, these women are unable to assume the multiple differentiated roles expected of an adult in contemporary society. Because of very primitive emotional needs, they are unable to achieve mutuality with their husbands and are unable to obtain satisfaction from the roles of wife, homemaker, and mother.

For the woman with longstanding conflict regarding nurturant care, the responsibility of caring for an infant evokes feelings of intense resentment and conflict. Other women, able to accept the infant as an organism in need of supplies, are able to care for their infant but are unable to respond to the young child's demand for a social relationship. As a group, mentally ill women strongly believe that infants are not capable of differentiated social relationships. Rather, the child is viewed as a part of the mother herself, making individuation of a child from mother a particularly difficult task among mentally ill women. Consistent with this inability to differentiate one's own needs from those of the child, mentally ill mothers deny, to a significantly greater extent than well mothers, any concern regarding child care. Their greater inability to tolerate ambivalent feelings regarding the maternal role increases their sense both of rage and of vulnerability and helplessness which they express regarding the care of infants and small children.

The most effective intervention program for mentally ill mothers would be one in which support would be provided in helping them deal with conflicted and ambivalent feelings regarding child care, while at the same time providing support and assistance as they learn the skills involved in caring for children. In addition, because her own needs and those of the child are so closely intertwined, the mother should be encouraged to develop a sense of separateness, including a separate life for herself, in addition to the time spent in her role as mother. Finally, psychotherapeutic intervention, accompanied by more directed efforts in the development of mothering skills and increased capacity to respond to the child as an interdependent person, should be accompanied by couple and family therapy involving husband and, if necessary, other members of both her own and her husband's extended families. In sum, traditional psychiatric treatment following hospitalization should be supplemented by rehabilitation directed at the mother's roles as mother, wife, and homemaker, encouraging development of a wide sphere of competence together with greater and more varied sources of life satisfaction, including some independent activity outside the home such as work. For the sake of both mother and child, it is especially important to provide direct assistance to the mother in her relationship with her child.

It is best to begin these intervention efforts as early as possible after the birth of the child since these children are at high risk of the subsequent development of social-emotional and intellectual (attention, language, concept formation, abstract thinking abilities) impairment (Anthony 1974a, 1974b, 1974c, 1978; Garmezy 1974; Rolf and Hasazi 1977).

As a result then of what we know about the development of these vulnerable children, and the role of the mother-child relationship in affecting both the child's development and the mother's own conception of herself as a woman and mother, it is difficult to conceive of an effective program of intervention that would not be aimed at three targets: (1) the mother's own psychiatric rehabilitation; (2) a special therapeutic nursery program for the child; and (3) evaluation and clinical efforts with the mother-child *relationship* itself. The Thresholds Mothers' Project is such a program. In this chapter we will describe the clinical program for and research findings on the interactional patterns of these mothers and their young children.

The clinical program

The Mothers' Project is a National Institute of Mental Health funded clinical research and intervention program for psychotic (schizophrenic, schizo-affective, manic-depressive, and psychotic depressed) women and their children under five years of age. Mothers and children attend an intensive clinical intervention program on a daily basis for a period of 12 to 15 months. This program includes group and individual therapy sessions, a didactic child development course, and social and vocational programs for the mother, as well as a therapeutic nursery for her child. The program was structured both to provide therapeutic intervention for these high-risk families and to afford the clinical and developmental research teams the opportunity to conduct ongoing assessments of the mother, the child, and the mother-child relationship. This group will be compared to a comparison group receiving treatment in the home as well as with a third group of women, who have never experienced a psychiatric illness, and their young children. The well mothers, recruited from the community, are matched with the experimental groups on six variables: age and sex of youngest child, mother's age, marital status, race, and SES (mother's education and father's occupation).

The Mothers' Project is a part of Thresholds, a psychiatric rehabilitation agency housed in an old mansion on Chicago's north side. While it is an integral part of the agency, it offers additional services designed specifically for the needs of mothers and children that are not part of the program for Thresholds' other nonmother patients. The rehabilitation program at Thresholds described by Dincin and Cohler (1975) is the foundation upon which the Mothers' Project rests. Mothers participate in most aspects of the Thresholds program, which is characterized by an emphasis on behavior, a utilization of the experiential approach, and the prevention of rehospitalization. The work readiness program, and the many facets of the social rehabilitation program, such as problem-solving groups; evening, weekend, and summer programs; therapeutic family camping; skill rehearsal; and social placement, form a core of activities around which a large portion of the mother's time is spent. In addition, a number of mothers have taken advantage of the academic program at Thresholds to improve their basic skills and complete their high school education.

In addition to the social and vocational rehabilitation program of the agency, very intensive and specialized clinical intervention program components have been designed to provide for the unique needs of this population. The staff of the Mothers' Project includes Thresholds' case workers and vocational rehabilitation counselors, psychiatrists, and a psychiatric nurse. In addition, a specialized team of clinical and research personnel including clinical and developmental psychologists, a psychiatric social worker, a teacher/therapist, an assistant teacher, a driver/videotape consultant, a pediatric nurse practitioner consultant, a student teacher, graduate student research and testing assistants, and several volunteers make up this large and diverse staff.

The specialized program is twofold, encompassing interventions that are therapeutic and those that are educational. This multiproblem group of women requires much in the way of empathic and nurturant experience in order to be able to take advantage of the educational and skill building aspects of the program. This is necessary before a mother is able to relate to her child in the more positive and growth-fostering ways about which she is learning through her participation in the project.

Soon after a mother and child enter the program they are given an intensive battery of personality and intellectual assessments. The information derived from these assessments is used along with expressed maternal perceptions of current problems, nursery observations, family history, mother's current level of functioning in the social and vocational program, and videotapes of mother-child interaction to develop a treatment plan for the mother, the child, and both of them together. (Details about the assessment process are available upon request from the authors.)

The mother

Mothers' Group. This therapy and peer support group meets one-and-one-half hours per week with the psychiatric social worker and the clinical research psychologist. The group is diverse in terms of psychological functioning, symptomatology, level of cognitive functioning, age, social class, racial and ethnic group, and marital status. In spite of this heterogeneity, the group provides a forum for discussing common life stresses, problems of readjusting to the roles of wife and mother, medication compliance, and core issues such as the relationship to one's own mother and fears of the effect of the illness upon the children.

Child Development Course. As the program was developing, we became aware of the mothers' general lack of basic child care knowledge. The need for another group with a more structured and didactic approach became apparent. The Child Development Course meets weekly and is supervised by the project director and the nursery teacher/therapist. The format and topics covered are varied.

Guest speakers have included a pediatric nurse practitioner (one class per month) who covered nutrition, childhood illness, and how to avoid accidents; a Family Service Bureau social worker (one class every two months) who covered topics such as stresses on the working mother, childhood sexuality, and finding and using community resources for you and your child; a parental stress volunteer who dealt with issues of child abuse and neglect; and the parents as resources volunteer (one class every three or four months) who made hand puppets and other toys from common materials.

Special sessions are also held on child development expectations. Films or filmstrips are shown at one session per month. Field trips have been made to a toy lending library, an Educational Resource Center, preschools and day care centers, and public libraries.

Other programs. In addition to the Mothers' Group and the Child Development Course, there are Friday Mothers' Field Trips (one Friday per month) to such places as the Flower Show at the Conservatory, the Evanston Children's Clothing Association Annual Clothing Sales, museums, and art galleries. Mothers also enjoy going out to tea with staff on Friday afternoons at one of the neighborhood restaurants. The mothers are seen individually and in marital and family counseling if needed.

The milieu approach of the agency, in conjunction with the clinical staff of the project, provides an atmosphere that is ever ready to cope with the multiple crises in the lives of these women and children. All staff members, including the driver (who at times has had to dress and feed children and coax a mother out of bed), serve a therapeutic function.

The child

The therapeutic nursery. The nursery of the Mothers' Project is designed to provide an educational and therapeutic environment for the young children of mentally ill mothers. The nursery serves as both a remedial and preventive program for ten children who are at high risk for developing emotional and intellectual problems. In addition, each mother spends one-and-one-half hours per week in the nursery working with her child.

Staffed by a head teacher/therapist and an assistant teacher, and aided by volunteers and student teachers, the nursery is in session five mornings a week from 9 to 11:30 a.m., and three afternoons a week from 1 to 4 p.m.

For the children, the nursery is designed to provide a safe, consistent environment that offers educational stimulation and emotional support. The children vary in age from birth to five years and come from a broad range of socioeconomic groups and ethnic backgrounds. The children also differ in the kind of family networks and parenting experiences they have had. What is common to all these children is that each is the child of a mother with some form of mental illness that inevitably has affected her abilities to be an adequate parent for her young and vulnerable child.

Certain areas of development are of special concern for those who work with the children of mentally ill mothers. *Language* is usually delayed and may be used inappropriately for communication. *Attentional skills* are marked by lack of ability to focus and sustain attention to relevant stimuli in the environment, both animate and inanimate. *Attachment* and *separation* issues are poorly negotiated, since there is usually a striking lack of healthy mutual bonding between mother and child. There is instead either a sense of great distance and mutual mistrust or a symbiotic fusion between mother and child when boundaries are blurred and the child does not act as, or perceive herself or himself to be, an autonomous, separate individual. These are the primary issues we consider in programming for the nursery. However, the program is adapted to meet the needs of individual children. For a three-year-old child who

As the mothers come to feel better about themselves, as they learn to trust the staff and each other and to take in the caring environment, they become better able to relate to their children as separate and valued individuals.

is attached symbiotically to his mother, skills in mastery and independence are especially important in promoting more adequate individuation. For a two-year-old who communicates by hitting, grabbing, or grunting incoherently, language skills are essential for developing better peer relationships and less frustrating relationships with adults.

For a tuned out, poorly relating, environmentally delayed seven-month-old, we work intensively on helping to establish bonds of love and mutuality with mother and with one special member of the nursery staff. We simultaneously work on providing the child with experiences of sensitive responsive interaction as the adults in the nursery introduce the baby to the stimulating world of objects, events, and people.

The nursery curriculum is varied and based upon a philosophy of individualized planning for each child that encompasses reality testing, responsiveness, and the development of a trusting relationship within a safe, structured, and predictable environment. This environment serves, we believe, as the basis from which more adaptive learning and coping skills can be developed by these children. Indeed, the nursery is such a powerful therapeutic tool that we must often reassess the children's development after only one month of attendance, because they change so drastically during that time. For example, one toddler was assessed at entrance and found to be borderline retarded with precursors of autistic behavior. Several weeks later we realized she needed a reevaluation and found that her score on the Bayley examination increased strikingly. In another case, the two-and-one-half-year-old child of one of our most seriously disturbed mothers entered the nursery as primitive as a feral child: licking mirrors, grunting, eating with his fists, and unable to be still long enough to attend to any task, object, or person. Within several weeks the nursery and clinical staff became aware that a competent, extremely winning, and clever child was emerging. Within the nursery's safe, structured environment, a child's potential strengths are allowed to develop. Although all of the children are to some degree delayed and/or deviant in certain areas of development, we do have strong evidence that they are functioning at a much higher level than when they entered the program and are making significant gains in learning and adaptive skills.

The foundation upon which all nursery planning rests is the all-staff weekly committee meeting. To this meeting the nursery staff bring their own clinical observations, progress notes, and description of the child's (and mother's) behavior in the nursery. They also bring a completed nursery assessment form on one child. This form has been developed and refined to give an accurate picture of a child's strength and weaknesses. These forms are filled out on each child four times per year and are used for research as well as nursery planning purposes. The information from the nursery assessment form is used in conjunction with that derived from the development and personality assessments completed at entrance to the program. This information is also used as an early screeing mechanism helping in the diagnosis and treatment of problems existing for the child that may lead to abuse (hyperactivity, nonresponsiveness, etc.) or severe learning disorders (motor, speech, language, and intellectual dysfunctions).

The mother/child dyad

Mothers in the nursery. A special time is set aside each week for the mother to visit with her child in the nursery and to be observed interacting with her child by project staff. Special assistance is provided for the mother in helping her to learn how to determine and meet her child's needs and to realize a more mutual relationship. As a result of observing the nursery teachers and psychologists with the children, the mothers are exposed to the spirit of the tolerant approach to child care and to specific ideas for the handling of their children. The nursery provides a partial separation of mother and child. Mothers may also work with children other than their own in the nursery. For example, one mother had been hospitalized and therefore separated from her toddler a number of times since the child's birth. This mother was basically a stranger to her child who had been raised by multiple surrogates during the first 18 months of her life. She was unable for many months to interact with her own child for more than a very brief period, literally fleeing from her at any opportunity. In this case, the mother's initial sessions in the nursery were spent helping one or two older children to whom she could relate more easily, because they were less dependent. Gradually, we began to acquaint her with her own child, pointing out her child's developing competences and taking every opportunity to let her see how her child was becoming more attached to her. We model a tolerant, observant, and enthusiastic approach to being with children, and as time passed, this mother-child pair came to know and love one another. The first time her daughter cried as her mother left the nursery was a moving experience for mother and staff alike, signaling her growing attachment to her mother.

A mother's time in the nursery is tailored to her capacity to relate to her child as well as her personal skills and abilities. For example, one mother plays the guitar and sings beautifully. She is often asked to assist with music. We try to find activities that can be mutually enjoyed by mother and child—reading a story together, having a pillow fight, tickling, putting together a puzzle, puppets, pretend play. We have found that mothers grow in their capacity to understand and care for their children as they experience success in the nursery.

Lunchtime intervention. Mothers and children eat lunch together daily, the mothers having full responsibility for their children during the 11:30 a.m.-1:00 p.m. time period. Lunchtime is supervised by two Mothers' Project staff members. It is their responsibility to monitor the atmosphere and to provide nurturance as well as modeling for mothers interacting with their children in a positive and constructive way.

Mothers go to the nursery to pick up their children at 11:30 a.m. Lunch is served in the agency dining room from 11:30 a.m. to 12:15 p.m. From 12:15 until 1:00 p.m. mothers and children either go to the park across the street or, in inclement weather, they use the nursery and other rooms in the agency.

The mothers find this time with their children to be very stressful, as the feeding of infants and eating times for older children are areas of much symptomatic behavior. Struggles for autonomy, testing the mother's ability to set limits and *give* to her child are issues that must be negotiated on a daily basis. Indeed, for the mothers themselves, food, and the issues surrounding eating, appear to be related to their own desperate neediness. We often see a mother shoveling a large amount of food into her own mouth while her child sits next to her quietly hungry. One mother who was experiencing guilt over her separation from her child and what she considered to be her inability to relate to her child would stuff her child's mouth with food, having little or no awareness of his inability to swallow as fast as she was feeding. Almost all of the mothers manifest very inappropriate ideas about what is a suitable amount of food to expect a young child to eat and will fill the plate of a toddler with portions suitable for a very hungry adult. This behavior is seen in middle-income and low-income mothers and is therefore viewed as symptomatic of deeper issues than merely seeing that the child is well fed.

There are occasions when after several observations (and careful consideration of issues involved at our weekly staffmeeting) a decision is made, and plans are developed for staff intervention at lunchtime. An attempt is made to begin where the mother is in her relationship with her child and to recognize and appreciate cultural differences in approaches to child care and discipline. There are two basic rules to which all mothers are asked to comply: (1) no hitting and (2) during the lunch period they are responsible for their children and must stay with them. If they need staff support, it will be provided.

Videotape intervention. The work with the mothers in the nursery and at lunchtime is supplemented by regular videotaping of the mother and child together. These videotapes, made when the mother and child enter the program and at regular three- to four-month intervals thereafter, are used as the subject of discussion with the mother regarding her relationship with her child. The advantage of the videotape over the classroom sessions is that the tape can be stopped so that the mother and her staff worker can talk together about the mother-child interaction and current issues in their relationship to each other. When the mother-child interaction becomes the focus of discussion between a mother and her worker, the mother's feelings about child care and the maternal role acquire a sense of immediacy that is missing in the ordinary contact between a mother and her therapist in the consulting room.

The video consultant (Jill Metcoff, a psychiatric social worker, who has an extensive background in the uses of videotape in mental health settings) and the mother's worker meet to plan the session after the worker and the mother have jointly decided upon an issue or problem on which to work. In addition, when preparing for the video intervention, case material from the weekly staff meeting is used in conjunction with the ideas and observations of the worker and the video consultant.

The goals for the videotape intervention are to sensitize the mother to her child's cues and to help her respond based on her child's needs, not her own; to help her recognize her child as a separate individual; to support her in her role as an adult decision maker who helps structure her child's environment, sets limits, and introduces the world of objects and people to her child; and to increase her opportunities for positive interaction with her child.

The video intervention is a situation that fosters and focuses on interaction within an environment that is consistent, safe, protective, and individualized for each mother. Mothers can have experiences of mastery within this situational and time-limited exercise in which they work on important developmental tasks such as separation/individuation; specific parental behavior such as limit setting; and general competencies such as learning to observe and communicate better. During this time, no matter what the task, a warm affective exchange is encouraged between mother and child. The outcome is extremely rich, both for the staff and for the mothers and children.

The Mothers' Project staff use the material from the video intervention in conjunction with other observational material and, with the research videotapes (three- to five-minute segments of feeding and structured and unstructured play), plan the future direction and focus of the therapy. The mother and child have shared an enjoyable experience and have a sense of mastering a task or learning something new together. Finally, the mothers are helped to reflect on their role and their feelings about it.

About a week after the video session, the mother is asked to choose her favorite segment from the taping and share it with all the other mothers at the follow-up group session. The mother explains to the group why she likes the particular segment. This generally initiates a group interchange of ideas and feelings about mothering. The video consultant acts as a group facilitator but encourages the mother to be the leader. These sessions have been found to be very special occasions for all concerned, especially the mother who is the star of the day.

Research findings

The results to be presented have been drawn from behavioral analyses of two, five-minute videotaped sequences of feeding and unstructured play of each mother-child pair. Videotaping of mother-child interaction is done at: (1) the pretest (within two weeks of entrance into the program), (2) the post-test (when the child is discharged from the program), and (3) the follow-up (approximately one year after post-test data). The rating scale, coding system, and data analysis have been drawn from pretest tapings, before intervention.

These videotapes are coded and scored by trained independent raters on the rating scale we have developed for analyzing mother-child interaction (Musick et al. 1979). This rating scale is based, in part, upon the work of Clarke-Stewart (1973) as well as upon our extensive research and clinical observations of the interactional patterns and behavioral characteristics of mentally ill and well mothers and their young children. We have developed a scale that encompasses a number of categories of behavior not previously included in scales of this kind. We view these categories as critically important in understanding what goes wrong in the mother-child interactions between mentally ill mothers and their children (table 8.1). We will continue to revise and refine this instrument in order to be able to better rate maternal and child behavior.

Our findings are based on a preliminary analysis of the interactional patterns of 36 mother-child pairs: 18 mentally ill and 18 matched well mothers and their children. Most children were from one to three years of age, but some data from four-year-olds have also been included.

Significance or trends were found in 12 categories—6 in feeding and 6 in structured play categories. Within the feeding categories it was found that mentally ill mothers were less involved with their children during feeding than were well mothers. They were also less able to read their child's cues and to respond empathically to their children. Mentally ill mothers did less structuring of the environment and taking the role of an adult caregiver during feeding. They initiated social interaction fewer times and were less consistent during feeding than were well mothers. There was also a significant difference between the two groups on the variable of reciprocity during feeding, with mentally ill mothers and their children displaying fewer bouts of interaction, less dialogue, and less contingent responsivity and engagement on the part of both mother and child.

Within the unstructured play categories, mentally ill mothers structured the environment less, had less contact with their children, spoke or vocalized to their children less, and were less consistent than were well mothers. The children of mentally ill mothers displayed more negative emotion and less communicative competence than did the children of well mothers.

Although no significant differences were found on the variable of expressed positive emotion during feeding, 50 percent of the mentally ill mothers expressed *no* positive emotion while this was true of only 16.7 percent of the well mothers. Also, 22.3 percent of the mentally ill mothers displayed inappropriate behavior during unstructured play, whereas none of the well mothers did. These and other similar findings point to the need for a more complete analysis of the data.

The differences found between groups of mentally ill and well mothers and their children were not consistent across situations. It seems apparent that feeding and unstructured play tap very different issues and capabilities in these mothers. Feeding, or eating with one's young child, a situation usually characterized by a sharing, giving, social interaction, is difficult for these women who have been given so little themselves, whereas the unstructured play situation requires that a mother feel comfortable in her role as an adult caregiver. She must be able to step in and assist her child at times and step back and allow the child to explore and create at other times. The mentally ill mothers were found to either under- or overstructure this free play situation.

Preliminary findings based on both the clinical and research programs

Table 8.1.*
Variables for rating disturbed mother-child interaction

Variables	Type of interaction
Mother	Tone of voice
	Amount of expressed positive emotion (touch, smile, affection, hug, expressed enthusiasm)
	Amount of expressed negative emotion (apathy, scowl, anger)
	Mother's involvement with child (connectedness)
	Mother's expressed attitude toward child
	Mother reads child's cues and responds empathically (appropriate, sensitive)
	Contingent responsivity (includes frequency and latency of responses as appropriate for situation and based on child's behavior)
	Appropriateness of mother's behavior (reality oriented vs. disturbed; evidence of distorted or disordered thinking, confused thinking, affect inappropriate to situation)
	Encouragement, praise of child, mirroring (imitation)
	Affection
	Structures environment/takes role of adult caregiver
	Amount of contact with child (touch, hold, gaze)
	Amount of verbalization
	Consistency of maternal behavior over five-minute segment
	Social initiative (number of times mother initiates social interaction)

indicate that it is not that the mentally ill mothers lack mothering skills or knowledge, but rather that the underlying affective relationship is characterized by a striking lack of connectedness. As we approach the conclusion of our program we have come to feel that information on parenting and assistance in parenting skills will be less meaningful than the mother's ability to become genuinely engaged with her child. Initially the mothers are either detached from their child—unempathic, unresponsive to the child's needs, and unable to respond contingently or appropriately—or they are fused with the child and unable to acknowledge or empathize with their child's needs as separate from their own. One mother was still breast-feeding her four-year-old child and ornamenting him with religious medals to ward off demons and devils. She could not respond to any advice about how this might either infantalize or make a laughingstock of her child, or how it might not be

Variables	Type of interaction
Child	Amount of expressed positive emotion (touch, smile, enthusiasm, affection-giving, sharing, pride in accomplishments
	Amount of expressed negative emotion (crying, whining, throwing, obstinancy, hitting, scowling)
	Child's activity level
	Readability
	Communicative competence (use of gesture or language to make wants known)
	Attentional abilities (situation-relevant)
	Responsivity of child to mother
	Compliance/noncompliance
Mother-Child	Joint attention/activity
	Affective quality of interaction
	Reciprocity (dialogue, bouts in interaction) characterized by contingent responsivity and engagement on the part of both mother and child

*A manual for using this scale is available upon request from Musick and Clark.

good for him because his needs were not viewed as separate from hers. Another mother fed her infant at arm's length while she averted her gaze because, as she later told us in Mothers' Group, "I'm afraid I might give him my sickness." This child represented the "bad" parts of herself and she frequently attributed malevolent motivations to him. When he stuck out his lower lip at two months of age she said, "He's really out to get me."

Mentally ill mothers are unable to nurture their children—to be playful, joyful, or engaged with them—because they themselves are so desperately needy and without internal structure or resources.

Interacting with the mother's inability to care for her child in an affectively warm and sensitive way, there may be certain temperamental and/or behavioral characteristics of the child that make her or him somewhat hyperkinetic or hypokinetic. The children are often somber or unrelating and have difficulty in communicating their needs. They may be hard to understand when they try to speak and may give very unclear messages by gesture or words. They may also be somewhat unpredictable as well as unreadable and unable to effectively use adults as resources. Finally, the children generally display attentional disorders on a number of levels; in developmental testing, in the nursery, and across a variety of situations. Although the children show marked improvement after only a few weeks in the nursery, these temperamental and behavioral characteristics by no means disappear overnight. They are, no doubt, the behavioral consequences of possible genetic and biological vulnerabilities interacting with the environmental stresses of living within a multiproblem family, with a distant or bizarrely behaving mother from whom one has been separated on a number of occasions.

In addition to teaching and modeling effective parenting, we have shifted our emphasis and are now directing our primary intervention efforts toward fostering the mother-child bond. We help a mother become attached to the child she may not know well because of frequent separations. Perhaps she went into the hospital when her child was 15 months old and was not able to stay out for any length of time until he was almost 2. The child she must begin parenting again is almost a stranger to her, with different skills, interests, likes, and dislikes.

We work on learning how to observe and read cues sensitively and appropriately. We point out to a mother her child's developing competencies and growing attachment to her. At the same time we are working with the child in the nursery and with the mother-child interaction, we are focusing on nurturing the mother and helping her to value and find worth in herself so that she can more effectively have her own needs met. As the mothers come to feel better about themselves, as they learn to trust the staff and each other and to take in the caring environment, they become better able to relate to their children as separate and valued individuals.

References

Anthony, E.J. "From Birth to Breakdown: A Prospective Study of Vulnerability." In *The Child in His Family: Vulnerable Children,* Vol. 4, ed. E.J. Anthony, C. Koupernik, C. Chiland, and A. Freud. New York: Wiley, 1978.

Anthony, E.J. "Introduction: The Syndrome of the Psychologically Vulnerable Child." In *The Child in His Family: Children at Psychiatric Risk,* ed. E.J. Anthony and C. Koupernik. New York: Wiley, 1974a.

Anthony, E.J. "A Risk Vulnerability Intervention Model for Children of Psychotic

Parents." In *The Child in His Family: Children at Psychiatric Risk,* ed. E.J. Anthony and C. Koupernik. New York: Wiley, 1974b.

Anthony, E.J. "The Syndrome of the Psychologically Vulnerable Child." In *The Child in His Family: Children at Psychiatric Risk,* ed. E.J. Anthony and C. Koupernik. New York: Wiley, 1974c.

Clarke-Stewart, K.A. "Interactions Between Mothers and Their Young Children: Characteristics and Consequences." *Monographs of the Society for Research in Child Development* 38, no. 153 (1973).

Cohler, B. "Character, Mental Illness, and Mothering." In *Mentally Ill Mothers and Their Children,* ed. H. Grunebaum, J. Weiss, B. Cohler, C. Hartman, and D. Gallant. Chicago: University of Chicago Press, 1974a.

Cohler, B. "The Maternal Attitude Scale." In *Tests and Measurements in Child Development,* ed. O. Johnson and J. Bommarito. Rev. ed. San Francisco: Jossey-Bass, 1974b.

Cohler, B.; Grunebaum, H.; Weiss, J.; and Abernathy, V. "Social Relations, Stress, and Psychiatric Hospitalization among Mothers of Young Children." *Social Psychiatry* 9 (1974a): 7-12.

Cohler, B.; Grunebaum, H.; Weiss, J.; Gallant, D.; and Hartman, C. "Child-Care Attitudes and Psychopathology among Formerly Hospitalized and Non-Hospitalized Mothers." Unpublished manuscript, The University of Chicago, 1974b.

Cohler, B.; Grunebaum, H.; Weiss, J.; Hartman, C.; and Gallant, D. "Life-Stress and Psychopathology among Mothers of Young Children." *American Journal of Orthopsychiatry* 45 (1975a): 58-73.

Cohler, B.; Robbins, D.; Hartman, C.; Shader, R.; Grunebaum, H.; Weiss, J.; and Gallant, D. "Social Adjustment and Psychopathology among Formerly Hospitalized and Nonhospitalized Mothers. I: The Development of the Social Role Adjustment Instrument." *The Journal of Psychiatric Research* 12 (1975b): 1-18.

Cohler, B.; Weiss, J.; and Grunebaum, H. "Child-Care Attitudes and Emotional Disturbances among Mothers of Young Children." *Genetic Psychology Monographs* 82 (1970): 3-47.

Dincin, J., and Cohler, B. "Rehabilitation of Mentally Ill Mothers." Research Grant Proposal PHS-2590-1, 1975.

Garmezy, N. "The Study of Competence in Children at Risk for Severe Psychopathology." In *The Child in His Family: Children at Psychiatric Risk,* ed. E.J. Anthony and C. Koupernik. New York: Wiley, 1974.

Musick, J.; Clark, R.; Cohler, B.; and Dincin, J. "Interactional Patterns of Schizophrenic, Depressed, and Well Mothers and Their Young Children." Paper presented at the annual conference of the American Psychological Association, New York, September 1979.

Rolf, J., and Hasazi, J. "Identification of Preschool Children at Risk and Some Guidelines for Primary Intervention." In *Primary Prevention of Psychopathology Vol. I: The Issues,* ed. G. Albee and J. Joffe. Hanover, N.H.: University Press of New England, 1977.

Portions of this chapter appear in Musick, J.; Stott, F.; Cohler, B.; and Dincin, J. "Posthospital Treatment for Psychotic Mothers and Their Young Children." In *Family Therapy and Major Psychopathology,* ed. M. Lansky. New York: Grune & Stratton, 1981.

Laura L. Dittmann

9

Where have all the mothers gone, and what difference does it make?

Where have all the mothers gone? Out. Out to work. More than half of those with school-age children, about 40 percent with children under 6, and one-third with infants under 3 are employed, and the numbers continue to rise. Two-thirds of these are working full time. For a number of years, the greatest increases have taken place with mothers who have the youngest children. And who is left at home? Nobody. The other adults, including the father, have been disappearing, too. Today more than one child in every six under 18 years of age is living in a single parent family, with the one parent holding down a job.

What difference does it make? Considering how widespread this trend has been, one would expect to find a good deal of information on the effects, but astonishingly little is known about the long-range impact of alternative child care arrangements upon the child, the parents, and the society in which we live. A headline in the *American Psychological Association Monitor* proclaimed "Day-care is given a clean bill of health," yet the authors of a review in *Child Development* (Belsky and Steinberg 1978) caution, "To even say that the jury is still out on day-care would be . . . both premature and naively optimistic. The fact of the matter is, . . . the majority of evidence has yet to be presented, much less subpoenaed" (p. 946).

This chapter will focus therefore on what is widely accepted as fact about the needs of children, review research on the effects of alternative care, and finally, offer some recommendations for change.

What are your own convictions about Mother's Place? Personally, I must admit to a nagging ambivalence on this topic. Enlightened readers would doubtless be outraged at the suggestion that women have a place assigned by biology, a cage that snaps shut at the birth of the first child and which does not open until seven or ten years later when the youngest child goes off to school permitting her to reenter the Big World Out There. Yet, as a group, you are also cognizant of the special need of the young child for *individualized nurturant* care and aware of the magnitude of these two adjectives when translated into day-by-day activities!

Government agencies and lawmakers are similarly conflicted. They disapprove of working women and piously talk about the strength of the family when voting against legislation that would make subsidized day care available to all families, regardless of income level. Providing adequate day care, they fear, would lure women out of the home. At the same time, they forget that 80 percent of the households enrolled in the Aid to Families of Dependent Children program are headed by women whom they encourage, subtly threaten, and set up dollar incentives for, to get out and work. Under this plan, costs in the long run are actually increased because the children of this mother who goes out to work also need day care that is subsidized by the taxpayer.

One way legislators avoid controversy about whether women should be working or not, or whether to make it possible for them to leave their children in decent surroundings, is to hide day care support in legislation on other matters. In 1971, the House of Representatives tacked funding for the employment of welfare recipients in child care centers onto the Burial Benefits Bill for Military Personnel. Furthermore, they did not provide for training these welfare mothers in the job of caring for children, which gives evidence of the low regard they have for this job. Such legislation and ancient convictions about a woman's place conflict with today's economic and societal realities.

The needs of children

Research is being done in both England and the United States that vividly demonstrates how competent babies are from birth to enter into social interaction with others and to respond to and shape the world around them. This research includes the importance of the father as a person in his own right as well as a support to the mother. Thus, we are actually discussing the *role* of mothering, not the sex or even the blood tie to the child. Fathers, baby sitters, mothers, child care workers—they are all the same to the baby. Fraiberg has paraphrased a description of the role we are discussing:

> WANTED: Mature woman. Child care.
> Children two and five. Employed
> mother. Light housekeeping. Live
> in. Must love children. More for
> home than wages. Call after 5:00 p.m.
>   Kenney 220-7482

Alas, for the Kenneys as they wait for the phone to ring. This devoted nanny will not be found. I believe she was last employed by David and Agnes Copperfield, London, circa 1850, having been the childhood nurse of Mr. Copperfield since the untimely death of his father. For a modest wage this cheerful, red-cheeked woman performed all household duties, consoled and advised the widow, and mothered the orphaned child. This goodly woman literally burst with maternity. Her hearty embraces, recalled by Copperfield the younger, caused the buttons of her bodice to fly off in all directions. (1977, p. 78)

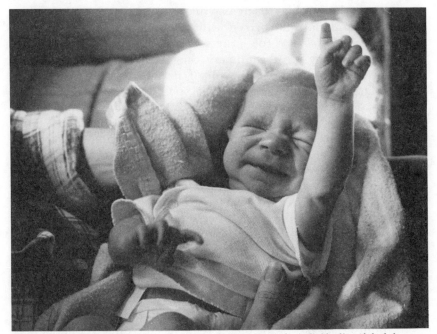

Every baby needs continuity of care from a person sensitive to the individuality of the baby.

Elsewhere, this role has been defined (Bronfenbrenner 1976) as an "enduring, irrational involvement of one or more adults in care and joint activity with the child." In other words, somebody has to be crazy about the child and be willing to stick around.

Of course a father would do nicely for this job. In fact, more fathers are taking on the mothering role. For purposes of neuterizing the concept, we can call it *primary caregiver*. In one University of Maryland class on infant development, there were three men, two of whom were primary caregivers for their babies. With these graduate students, a reversal in breadwinner/caregiver roles had occurred. Mother had gone out to work; Daddy attended classes and took care of the baby. In addition, there was one woman in the class who had assumed the outside-of-the-home job, while her husband had become the baby-tender. With the presence of these role switchers, all of us in the class became sensitized to the literature that talked about fathering and mothering in the old stereotyped clichés. We corrected our statements about the behaviors of the parents in the light of primary versus secondary caregiving roles. We accepted the interesting finding (Field 1978) that the stylistic manner mothers use in conversing with their babies—a higher tone of voice, drawing out the syllables, using playful sing-song words and repetitive clusters of sounds interspersed with clicking, humming, cooing—*motherese* or *baby talk*—is role-, not sex-related. Fathers do exactly the same thing if they are the primary caregivers. The role triggers an elaborate effort to obtain the attention of the baby, to rouse the infant by means of tones and alteration of normal speech patterns that communicate most effectively with the baby. The baby's response reinforces this kind of behavior. Clearly, it is the awareness on the part of the father that makes these tricks work and his eagerness to communicate with the child for whom he is responsible that calls forth this behavior, usually thought of as maternal.

But the tendency to equate the female with the primary caregiving role is hard to give up. When the final papers for this class were handed in, one of the fathers and the one mother wrote about sex behaviors just as they have always been portrayed in the literature.

When roles are reversed, relationships between the parents are likewise affected. Traditionally, the father has come home from work wondering what the mother has been doing all day. Why didn't you get the ironing done? Why is the house a mess? The breadwinner mother in my class confessed that she has exactly these feelings when she comes home from a hard day at the office. What has the caregiver father been doing all day? Why didn't he get to the store? Caregiver father replies,

"Well, the baby didn't wake up from her nap until late, and by then it was time to start dinner. So we have to go to the store tonight." Tension, stress. Not sex- but *role*-linked.

Every baby should have a primary caregiver, wherever she or he is being cared for. There is a growing consensus that every baby needs continuity of care from a person sensitive to the individuality of the baby. Even the experts, Margaret Mead for example, who have taken the position that much of the literature on mother-infant separation is spurious seem to prescribe a substitute who sounds very much indeed like the old-fashioned mother.

Mead (1976) comments, "The campaign on the evils of mother-child separation is just another attempt by man to shackle women to the home" (p. 160). Yet in another context she pleads for help at home, stating that the nuclear family is now being asked to do what an entire clan used to accomplish. Mead did not have a clan, but she did hire an English nanny, who had been governess to the Governor-General of Canada and had married a butler who had disappeared after a stormy marriage and left her with a daughter to support. This nurse brought her daughter along, by this time an adolescent, so there was the nucleus of an extended family, at least. And in the summers, they moved in with the Larry Franks and their five children plus a new baby. Mead (1975) comments, "In the summer months I had an opportunity to realize what it had been like to bring up a child in a household in which there were many willing hands ready to hold the baby and someone to do the endless chores and to sleep with the baby at night, so that the mother's contacts with her child were both intense and relaxed" (p. 293).

In writing about the working mother, Michael Rutter (1976) cites another British investigator, T. W. Moore: "There is no evidence that children suffer from having several mother figures so long as stable relationships and good care are provided by each" (p. 160). Rutter adds that this applies equally to mothers who are not working, to which I agree wholeheartedly.

The Clarkes (1976), in their book *Early Experience: Myth and Evidence*, summarize: "No mother of a very young child should feel bound to remain at home (provided satisfactory alternative caretaking arrangements can be made); equally, no mother should feel that her responsibilities diminish after her child becomes older" (p. 272).

Finally, Fowler (Fowler and Khan 1976, p. 5) says, "The core of the problem, i.e., whether or not a child can thrive in day-care, is the finite availability of adult energy and adult attention." This sounds suspiciously like saying that it depends upon whether or not a mother-type person, a primary caregiver, is available.

If even the critics of the idea agree on the importance of a good mother substitute or primary caregiver with reasonable stability in the relationship, we should take a few moments to examine what it is this person does for, or with, the child. Apparently, there are two levels to keep in mind. One has to do with the role of the attentive caregiver in making the world become a predictable, but interesting, place to be; creating a responsive environment in which expectable events take place, reactive to the input of the baby; and later on, to provide challenge and responsibility appropriate to the child's enlarging capacity and understanding. The second is in terms of modulating and modifying the events and stimuli to fit the needs of that particular child. Babies differ in a host of dimensions: activity type, amplitude of the child's motions, availability of energies, degree of alertness and wakefulness, distinctness of state, zest and energy reserves under stress, what quiets the baby (sucking, rocking, rhythmical sounds), the soothability of the child, and the capacity for self-soothing. These qualities persist over time, expressed in differing behaviors, of course, as the child grows older, but remain of comparable underlying quality. Primary caregivers vary too—in their ability to understand the baby's cues, in their investment in trying to do so, and in their availability and emotional involvement. If there is a reasonably good fit or match, the baby and caregiver begin to attain synchrony very early in the life of the baby—a kind of regulatory stability. You may be familiar with the exquisite observations of Brazelton, Tronich, and others (1974) as they describe the "ballet" or cycling in which mothers and their babies engage.

In the first year of life, these delightful communications take place in the context of routine care as well as in playful moments. Gradually, the baby takes in gestalt complexes of pleasure-pain stimuli on a contingency basis; these are vaguely remembered, and with this, anticipation begins. For instance, in the second month babies will suck when put into the feeding position (and it should be approximately the same position from one feeding to the next via the same caregiver); in the third month, infants usually are able to wait when they hear the refrigerator door or the running water that warms the bottle. The sequence is: (1) conditioned reflex; (2) primitive memory and with it anticipation; this is associated with the capacity to delay—the first steps toward acceptance of reality. When the infant is able to wait for and confidently expect satisfaction, it is possible to speak of the beginning of an ego.

Early capacity for attention and concentration takes place, and the number of cues that are fitted into coherent pictures is widened when individualized and consistent caregiving takes place. Of course, some mothers chronically misinterpret the baby's signals. Some mothers will respond indiscriminately to all cues with a bottle, bringing a pacifier, or jangling a toy, or some other automatic, if inappropriate, response. Continuity and consistency is not automatically good or synchronized with the desires or needs of the child. However, I suggest that even misguided responsiveness and predictability are assets to the baby. At least the infant can count on something.

And when, for example, this something is a response to the child's cries, the baby becomes less tearful. Rather than becoming spoiled, by the end of the first year of life those infants who have been responded to promptly when they cried become resourceful in getting attention in other ways, and respond to a variety of behaviors from their mothers such as vocalization, a glance, or a smile, rather than expecting to be picked up most of the time (Bell and Ainsworth 1972).

Once babies begin to walk they enter into an exhilarated conquest of the world. Toddlers are practically oblivious to falls or frustrations such as having a toy snatched by another child. They are even ready to accept substitute caregivers more comfortably than before. Then it suddenly dawns on this exuberant child that "the world is not her oyster," that she must cope with it more or less on her own as a relatively helpless, small, and separate individual, and she once again becomes very dependent on this mother person, or primary caregiver, in a new way that carries awareness of one's own vulnerability (Mahler 1976). She begins to woo the mother or primary caregiver but presents a contradictory picture that is difficult for the adult to handle. While toddlers are not so dependent and helpless as before and fight to become even less so, they even more insistently demand that the mother be readily available to share every aspect of their life. She falls and hurts herself—and howls when she becomes aware that the mother is not by her side. He wilts and becomes fatigued but perks up immediately when he contacts the mother, enabled to move quickly on with his explorations and absorbed in his own affairs. Mother and baby seldom achieve the "ballet of infancy"; there is more friction and basic conflict. The mother welcomes the growing independence of the child yet resists letting go; the baby needs and refuses nurturance. Verbal communication becomes more and more necessary for them to function together, as gestures and preverbal mutual glances no longer suffice.

If the mother is not threatened by the rejection of the child and continues to be quietly available, the child is apt to be able to handle ambivalences comfortably and can afford to be more imitative, to test reality, and to develop a personal coping style. The less emotionally available the mother becomes during this so-called hatching process, the more insistently and desperately the child attempts to recapture her, and the less energy is available to her for evolution of the many important cognitive tasks ahead. There are clear implications for day care in this finding. If mothers interpret the child's periodic shouts for independence as evidence that their child does not need them anymore, there can be a pervasive dampening effect on the child who has reached too far and been left hanging out there on a limb.

As time goes by, the pattern of interaction should become progressively more complex. The environment should be filled with space and objects to explore, relationships to establish, beginning experiences with causality, a chance to learn about the properties of the physical world, and increasing challenge in the use of language and mental operations. The child can accept separation from the primary caregiver for progressively longer periods of time, even welcome it—but the whole long, long day is another matter. I noted with wry amusement the title of a workshop session for day care workers: "Noon to Six—The Years Between," testimony to the fatigue that settles down on child and caregiver alike. The caregiver half of the pair must be considered as well. Experiences with the baby mold and shape the caregiver's attitudes and behaviors.

Klaus and Kennell (1976), with follow-up work by Hanes and others in Sweden and Guatemala, have exciting accounts of the importance of the first hours after birth as a critical time for awakening nurturant, individuated responses from the mother. Extended time with the baby—free from the pressure of being observed or of getting somewhere or the superimposition of a schedule such as the hospital regime—is important for the caregiver. In this situation, the caregiver becomes bonded, attached, hooked to the baby. Brazelton et al. (1974) have called this need to our attention, stating that mothers should plan to be with the baby for at least three or four months until the baby's physiological rhythms have stabilized and the mother can begin to feel competent as a nurturing person. As the baby becomes more readable and predictable, the mother can respond more accurately; then the baby is satisfied and responds to the mother, reinforcing her and setting the stage for the rhythmic exchange between the two to bring growing assurance and confidence to both. There can be spontaneity, delight, joy.

When this exquisite communication becomes established, the primary caregiver, the mother, can truly empathize and feel for the baby and her or his needs. She can select a more appropriate substitute caregiver. She can better prescribe for the baby in the hands of a substitute. She can modulate change and make decisions about her own comings and goings that may not be so heavily distorted with guilt.

For the mother's sake, then, there should be time for the baby. Quality and unfettered time. We have lately been cheering ourselves by the assurance that quality in caregiving exchanges means more than quantity. But it seems somewhat overoptimistic to me that one could expect to compress all of the quality time available into 10 or 20 minutes at the end of the day. In more normal relationship patterns, there are a few seconds or minutes here and there—a pause to play, an encounter in the course of routine care—liberally sprinkled over the day, a dipping in and out of contact, around real-life needs and demands. Both infant and caregiver need to have unscheduled time together, both routine and playful, both stressful and casual.

Effects of alternative care

Babies need someone around who knows them well, can match their readiness to next steps, can read the child, anticipate trouble, modulate the demands. But *what happens to the child in day care?* Research should supply ready answers, but instead there is a good deal of information about atypical care, including short-range and perhaps not too significant outcomes. First of all, most of the research is conducted in university-based, adequately funded day care centers. Yet most children do not attend these model centers. One-fourth of them are cared for by a baby sitter in the child's own home—by a baby sitter being paid $1 an hour! One-sixth are cared for in someone else's home, in what is called family day care. About 8 percent of the children are in nursery school or preschool. Only 3 percent are in center-based programs, of which high interest, adequately funded research programs are an infinitesimal proportion. Yet our information is in the reverse order. We know the most about this latter group (Belsky and Steinberg 1978, p. 930). And policy is being shaped on the basis of model, not more typical, programs.

Furthermore, the work concentrates on immediate outcomes, outcomes of a narrow range. As Bronfenbrenner (1977) points out, much child development research is "the science of strange behavior of children in strange situations with strange adults for the briefest period of time" (p. 513).

These studies, flawed as they are, in general do not find measurable intellectual differences of lasting quality between day care and home-

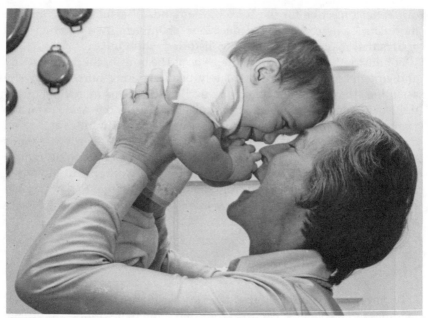

Caregivers would find their roles much more satisfying if they were able to perceive babies in all of their splendid competencies, and would receive more pleasure as they become able to elicit even more interesting responses from the child.

reared children unless the child comes from genuinely depriving circumstances (see Chapter 4). Even then, a disturbing finding emerges (Fowler and Khan 1976): The effects of a program designed to improve the child's cognitive development may peak after a year or more. An increase in IQ from 107 to 114, in the months from 11 to 37 months of age, began to taper off, leveling at 100 by the time the children were 5. The researchers suggest that there was a reduction in the interest of the parents in the child's education, as they let the experts take over, and pointed out also that there was an unusually high turnover rate in the center staff.

Tyler and Dittmann (1980) studied differences in the behavior of 18-month-old children in two kinds of settings—homes, including family day care, and group or center care. We found the child in a group more apt to resort to self-comforting behavior such as thumb sucking and hair twirling. There was less speech between caregiver and child in the group. There was greater range of emotional expression in the homes, both joy and delight as well as anger and irritability. Physical affection was low in both settings; less than 3 percent of the time was spent in affectionate playfulness. Toilet training? No indeed. The caregiver tended to flop the child down on the floor wherever he was, change the diaper, right the child who did not clamber up alone, and the whole event—wordless and swift—was over in 30 seconds. Grim efficiency was the word of the day.

Many of the family day care mothers preferred to keep the children on a bottle rather than encouraging them to develop more mature eating patterns, since a bottle does not spill, and the child could wander around with a built-in comforter at hand. The conclusion of White (1975) that not one in ten of our children is being challenged to capacity rings true.

Other research points to some behaviors for the child in group care with worrisome, long-range implications. Reports note decreased cooperation and more verbal and physical aggression toward peers and adults (Schwartz, Krolick, and Strickland 1973). The children seek proximity to peers and resist adult authority. The day care child spends more time in the large muscle activity area of the center and less in the expressive and cognitive areas (Lay and Meyer 1973). Day care children are characterized as more self-assertive, less conforming, less impressed by punishment, less averse to dirt, and more prone to toilet lapses (Moore 1964). Negative interactions with teachers increased with the amount of exposure to group experience in nursery and kindergarten (Raph et al. 1964).

To sum up, children in day care programs are placed in an environment that lacks the variety and meaning of the typical home. There tends to be a restriction in emotionality—a kind of bland neutrality. The objects played with are made for children and often confined to plastic materials. The children themselves often reflect the characteristically stressed American values of aggressiveness, impulsivity, and egocentrism. This begins to sound like the child the public school teachers are complaining about. However, these characteristics were not observed in home-reared children to the same extent.

Burnout and exhaustion are common complaints among day care teachers. Family caregivers are isolated from contacts with other adults and usually paid lowest of all caregivers.

The steps to be taken

So, what is to be done about this? Obviously we cannot go back to the old days, whether good or bad for child or mother. Telling mothers to stay home is no solution. An increasing number are principal or sole wage earners. Mothers have to work to supplement fathers' incomes just to make ends meet. Mothers have to work for reasons other than financial: they feel obligated to share their expertise; to make use of their education; to stay in a favorable position on a career track; or to enjoy the payoff of a job in prestige, status, and social relationships.

In seeking a solution, we can turn to an ecological frame of reference such as that conceptualized by Brim (1975) and Bronfenbrenner (1977), using a systems approach, a matter of layers or levels impinging on one another, none free from the impact of change or events taking place in adjacent layers.

We have been talking from the standpoint of the basic layer, the microsystem, the family, relationships among individuals, the time people are able to spend with each other, what they must do to live. In the microsystem, our economic structure dictates that people have to earn a living. In addition, the impact of the women's movement is felt. In 1978 in Washington, D.C., there were more abortions than live births; there were more out-of-wedlock births than births to married couples. These events in the microsystem are the result of forces embedded in the matrix surrounding individuals and families today.

On the next level, there is the culture of the neighborhood, TV and radio, stores, schools—these make up a middle layer, or mesosystem. In this middle layer also are the agencies, work places, professionals, and mass media that affect and are affected by the neighborhood or town. And finally, there is a macrosystem, the outer ring consisting of the structures of our society: the social, political, legal, economic, educational, and communication systems. If we think in terms of these levels, each working on the other to determine events and beliefs, we no longer need to say that it is just too bad that mothers do not stay home anymore—tough as it is, there is nothing we can do about it. We *could* decide that infants and children must have an enduring relationship with a primary caregiver who has time to be a human being and who feels sufficiently psychologically affluent so that there is a surplus of energy and love to give away. We could begin to find elements in each level of the interconnecting systems that could help to make this come about. Let me mention briefly four things we could be doing.

1. We should continue to study infants and children. It is hard to explain today why until the last decade or so most astute scientific workers bought the idea of infancy as a time of blooming, buzzing confusion. The more one learns about the responsiveness and capabilities of newborns—their ability to discriminate between people, to match faces and voices, to regulate sucking to focus on an interesting picture, to select among stimuli on the basis of familiarity or

complexity—the more opportunities for meaningful interaction with a baby occur. The study of how one infant differs from another becomes equally absorbing. Caregivers would find their roles much more satisfying if they were able to perceive babies in all of their splendid competencies and would receive more pleasure if they became able to elicit even more interesting responses from the child.

These new findings from the study of children should be widely distributed, not just to serious students of child development, but through newspapers, magazines, TV, films, etc., to legislators, caregivers, parents, high school students, and others. This strategy could change the behavior of individuals in the microsystem.

2. Appreciation of how quickly any change in both caregiver and in baby takes place (Klaus and Kennell 1976; Bell and Ainsworth 1972) would make these earliest months become important in their own right. We no longer need to wait to see the outcome of good care until school age or later, blurred over by the intervening experiences and years. Awareness of the rapidity with which change in caregiving practices creates change in the baby will enable us to regard early childhood as a more precious time. Far beyond survival, regulation of physiological rhythms, feeding, and routine care, infancy would be regarded as basic to future cognitive and social development. The preschool years would be recognized as a time of astonishing growth in problem solving, development of mental strategies, language proliferation, aesthetic appreciation, and increasing discrimination.

The low status of those who give care to children might be one of the elements to be changed in this mesolayer. The federal government, in the *Dictionary of Occupational Titles* published by the Department of Labor, clearly expresses its imperfect understanding of the complexity of the task. Child care, in general, is rated lower than parking lot attendant and restroom cleaner. In terms of the market place, those who care for the youngest children are given the least status. Infant caregivers work, on the average, an hour longer each day, are paid $1 less per hour, and have the lowest qualifications of all child care workers.

3. As the span of life increases and technological changes require career shifts and retraining for new careers, the period of productivity outside the home, or in the home, could be broken up into smaller packages, into shorter time units. Already the fact that an applicant for doctoral studies has spent some years out of school is considered a positive qualification by some academic departments. If the pressure to move in steady increments from one stage of productivity to another could be lessened, young parents could grasp the early years of creating

a family as important in themselves instead of attempting to launch simultaneously the family and career, each of which are almost full-time commitments. Part-time jobs, role shifts, movement in and out of the work force could result in the mesosystem.

4. If this point of view became widely accepted, it would be necessary to acknowledge the costliness of raising a child. Family income maintenance would be a matter of course. Acknowledgment that babies cost money, time, and effort would ricochet throughout the system. On a personal level, we might be able to acknowledge the demands that having a baby entails. This is not always the case, now. Recently a student happily confided to me that she was pregnant. "But my baby sitter won't like it," she continued. "My first child is only 18 months old, so that will mean she will have two babies under the age of 2 to look after." To me, this happy mother-to-be is abdicating, or denying, what producing a baby means.

On a mesolevel, the services of many people will be seen as necessary to raise a child. Junior and senior high school students, foster or genuine grandparents, volunteers from many sources will become involved. Increasingly, today, I hear my friends announce with respect to their own daughter's pregnancy, "Well, she can't count on me for baby-sitting. I've done my share of that, and I don't want to be thought of as Grandma. I look over my shoulder for my own mother when I hear the word Grandma." Even grandparents are asking to be excused from the commitment and time it takes to raise the next generation.

Parenting is not regarded as productive work. In general, work in the home is given no monetary value. Work that does not carry monetary reward goes unrewarded and unsung. We are the only industrialized nation in the world that does not acknowledge the cost of being a parent in payment of a family allowance. If we accepted the validity of work in child care, then work hours in the factory, office, or shop would be adjusted to accommodate this valuable service. The mass media might no longer regard babies and children as a consumer group to be exploited but a national investment required to raise a healthy citizen. Even more unbelievable, we might reject the idea that individuals should be permitted to make a profit on the business of taking care of children.

For almost five years (1974-1979), the Department of Health, Education and Welfare studied the question of whether or not standards for child care outside of the home should be established, and, if so, of what these regulations should consist. Cautiously, they decided that it was proper to propose some regulations. Before the regulations could be implemented, however, the Reagan administration moved to reduce or eliminate regulatory functions of the federal government, referring such matters back to the states or to the businesses involved.

The position is taken by the Reagan administration that families should be able to select freely the conditions under which their children are spending many of their waking hours. But is it freedom to choose when most of the day care available is barely acceptable? Rarely indeed is there a first-class choice that a parent can afford! Often, parents are unaware of conditions that do exist. One caregiver, for example, took half of the children in attendance at her center on a long bus ride when the local inspector announced a visit in order to bring the ratio of children to adults to a more acceptable level.

The idea of providing subsidy for day care, particularly for those not in poverty, has consistently raised alarm in this and preceding administrations. The cost of the Mondale-Brademas Child Development Act was expected to reach 2 billion dollars in 1971. President Nixon vetoed this bill as wildly excessive, as well as threatening to family life. When reintroduced the following session of congress, the provisions were scaled down to reduce the expected cost to around 1 billion dollars. This measure was defeated in the House of Representatives.

In 1980, Senator Alan Cranston introduced a bill to address the needs of children in day care, aimed primarily to assist families whose incomes fell in the 8,000 to 15,000 dollar range. He used the existence of 2 million children under age 13 who were looking after themselves as their parents worked, of whom 20,000 were children under 6 years of age, as his rationale. Cranston thought in terms of 1 to 2 billion dollars, which caused the Carter administration to complain about excessive costliness. This bill was withdrawn as Cranston became convinced that he could not muster sufficient support either from the day care constituency or from the general public. Once again, the effort to assist families either through regulation of quality of day care or through subsidy of costs has been rejected. As a country, we seem unable to make it possible for mothers to be at home to care for their children, or to assist them in paying for and finding adequate conditions for the children when mothers leave home to earn a living.

In conclusion, I plead that we should state our conviction that babies need a primary caregiver and then set to work at the various societal levels to make this attainable. We have been busy counting how many mothers are at work, at home, or otherwise occupied; we have been looking at what happens to babies after a year or so in one kind of care or another, but we have yet to implement a study to tie the microlevel, mesolevel, and macrolevel together in asking:

How can we ensure that every baby will have a loving and nurturant primary caregiver? Someone who will be there, committed to an irrational involvement with that child?

How can we use every minute of the child's first years in the most satisfying way for both caregiver and child?

References

Bell, S. M., and Ainsworth, M. D. E. "Infant Crying and Maternal Responsiveness." *Child Development* 43 (1972): 1171-1190.

Belsky, J., and Steinberg, L. D. "The Effects of Day Care: A Critical Review." *Child Development* 49 (1978): 929-949.

Brazelton, T. B.; Tronich, E.; Adamson, L.; Als, H.; and Wise, E. "The Origins of Reciprocity: The Early Mother-Infant Interaction." In *The Effect of the Infant on the Caregiver,* ed. M. Lewis and L. A. Rosenblum. New York: Wiley, 1974.

Brim, O. G. "Macrostructural Influences on Child Development and the Need for Childhood Social Indicators." *American Journal of Orthopsychiatry* 45 (1975): 516-524.

Bronfenbrenner, U. "Who Cares for America's Children?" In *The Family, Can It Be Saved?*, ed. V. C. Vaughan and T. B. Brazelton. Chicago: Yearbook Medical Publishers, 1976.

Bronfenbrenner, U. "Toward an Experimental Ecology of Human Development." *American Psychologist* 32 (1977): 513-531.

Clarke, A. M., and Clarke, A. D. B. *Early Experience: Myth and Evidence.* New York: Free Press, 1976.

Field, T. "Interaction Behaviors of Primary Versus Secondary Caretaker Fathers." *Developmental Psychology* 14 (1978): 183-184.

Fowler, W., and Kahn, N. *A Follow Up Investigation of the Later Development of Infants in Enriched Group Care.* Urbana, Ill.: Educational Resources Information Center, 1976. (ERIC Document Reproduction Service No. ED 093 506)

Fraiberg, S. *Every Child's Birthright: In Defense of Mothering.* New York: Basic Books, 1977.

Klaus, M., and Kennell, J. *Maternal-Infant Bonding.* St. Louis: Mosby, 1976.

Lay, M., and Meyer, W. "Teacher/Child Behaviors in an Open Environment Day Care Program." Mimeographed. Syracuse University Children's Center, 1973.

Mahler, M. S. "Rapprochement Subphase of the Separation-Individuation Process." In *The Process of Child Development,* ed. P. Neubauer. New York: Jason Aronson, 1976.

Mead, M. *Blackberry Winter: My Earlier Years.* New York: Pocket Books, 1975.

Mead, M. Quoted in Clarke, A. M., and Clarke, A. D. B., *Early Experience: Myth and Evidence,* p. 160. New York: Free Press, 1976.

Moore, T. "Children of Full-Time and Part-Time Mothers." *International Journal of Social Psychiatry.* Special Congress Issue 2 (1964): 1-10.

Raph, J. B.; Thomas, A.; Chess, S.; and Korn, S. J. "The Influence of Nursery School on Social Interactions." *American Journal of Orthopsychiatry* 38 (1964): 144-152.

Rutter, M. "Parent-Child Separation: Psychological Effects on Children." In *Early Experience: Myth and Evidence*, ed. A. M. Clarke and A. D. B. Clarke. New York: Free Press, 1976.

Sander, L. W.; Strechler, G.; Julia, H.; and Burns, P. "Primary Prevention and Some Aspects of Temporal Organization in Early Infant-Caretaker Interaction." In *The Process of Child Development*, ed. P. Neubauer. New York: Jason Aronson, 1976.

Schwartz, J. C.; Krolick, G.; and Strickland, R. G. "Effects of Early Day Care Experience on Adjustment to a New Environment." *American Journal of Orthopsychiatry* 43 (1973): 340-346.

Tyler, B., and Dittmann, L. "Meeting the Toddler More than Halfway: The Behavior of Toddlers and Their Caregivers." *Young Children* 35, no. 2 (January 1980): 39-46.

White, B. *The First Three Years of Life*. Englewood Cliffs, N.J.: Prentice-Hall, 1975.

Douglas B. Sawin

10

Fathers' interactions with infants

Over the past several years we have seen a dramatic increase in interest in the father's role in the family during early infancy and in his involvement in caregiving and affectionate behavior with young infants (Lamb 1976; Walters 1976). Concomitantly, we are seeing a breakdown of traditional stereotypes that have depicted the father as a kind of vestigial appendage of the mother-infant dyad (Nash 1976). The father is becoming recognized as a significant and integral component of the family unit during infancy and, in that capacity, is seen as having an important influence on the relationship between the mother and infant and on the child's development.

In light of the extensive attention to the father in current research on the family in infancy, we must critically examine our approaches to conceptualizing and studying the father during this early period of infant life. The purpose of this chapter is to do so from three perspectives: (1) a current trait theory of masculinity and femininity (Spence and Helmreich 1978); (2) differentiated levels of inquiry into fatherhood; and (3) the social ecology of the infant (Bronfenbrenner 1975, 1977).

Several considerations argue for this kind of critical reexamination. The first of these is the finding from observational studies of parent-infant interaction in the early months of life that fathers are very active partners in these interactions and very few stable, behavioral differences are evident between mothers and fathers (Parke and O'Leary 1976; Parke and Sawin 1976, 1977). Further, the few significant differences between mothers and fathers have not been large. Perhaps even more important, analyses of the contingency of the parents' responses to behavioral cues from the infant (i.e., parental sensitivity and responsiveness) indicate that fathers are as responsive to most of their infants' behaviors as are mothers (Parke and Sawin 1975, 1977). These findings are quite discrepant from traditional views of fathers' behavior with infants (Parke and Sawin 1976) and thus support a reconsideration of the father in his child's infancy.

In addition, these findings suggest that there may be more variation in parenting behavior among parents (i.e., individual differences regardless of gender) than there is between groups of fathers and groups of mothers (i.e., groups of parents classified by gender). This is particularly true for such behavioral variables as holding patterns; tactual, auditory, and visual stimulation; and affectionate behaviors such as smiling, patting, and stroking. The implication of these findings is that a better understanding of the determinants of patterns of parent-infant interaction is not best served by classifications of parents defined or conceptualized on the basis of the parents' biological sex alone.

Parenting from the perspective of masculinity and femininity

Why are there so few differences between mothers' and fathers' characteristic styles of interacting with their infants? Cross-cultural and historical evidence, paternal behavior in subhuman primates and other animals, and biological considerations (physical, hormonal, and other genetic differences between males and females) would lead us to expect that parent gender would be associated with highly differentiated behavior by human mothers and fathers in parent-infant interactions (see Parke and Sawin 1976 for a brief review of these issues, and Lynn 1974; Nash 1976; Redican 1976; and West and Konner 1976 for more extensive reviews).

An answer to this question may be found in a recent trait theory of masculinity and femininity developed by Spence and Helmreich (1978). This approach focuses on individuals' conceptions of themselves on clusters of *instrumental* and *expressive* personality characteristics. Since, according to stereotype and to self-report, men are more strongly instrumental than women and women are more expressive than men, these characteristics are identified as masculine and feminine respectively.

These investigators have demonstrated not only that these dimensions are essentially independent within each sex, but also that sex differences are quantitative rather than qualitative. That is, the average man is not nonexpressive but merely somewhat less expressive than the average woman; similarly, the average woman is not noninstrumental but merely somewhat less instrumental than the average man. This dualistic model, which treats these personality characteristics as separate dimensions, acknowledges that an individual may have both masculine *and* feminine traits to varying degrees and that personality measures of gender-related traits must be constructed to permit the assessment and classification of individuals along both masculine *and* feminine dimensions. Using this strategy, Spence, Helmreich, and Stapp (1975) proposed a fourfold classification scheme based on the self-evaluations of personal attributes by respondents. These classifications are *masculine* (high masculine—low feminine), *feminine* (low masculine—high feminine), *androgynous* (high masculine—high feminine), and *undifferentiated* (low masculine—low feminine).

The implications of this approach for understanding the patterns of parenting that mothers and fathers adopt in relation to their infants are evident from a recent study by Bem, Martyna, and Watson (1976). College men and women were classified as masculine, feminine, androgynous, or undifferentiated based on their responses to the Bem Sex Role Inventory and according to the classification scheme proposed by Spence, Helmreich, and Stapp (1975). At a later date, each of the subjects were observed during a ten-minute period in which they were left alone with a human infant on the pretense that the investigators were studying infant responsiveness. A summary measure of behavioral nurturance was derived for each subject based on a time sampling of a variety of affectionate behaviors; smiling at the infant, talking to the infant, kissing and nuzzling, ventral holding, affectionate stimulation (tickling, patting, stretching). No differences were found in the nurturance of men and women in their interactions with the infant. However, a significant main effect was found for the classification of the subjects on the psychological dimensions of masculinity, femininity, androgyny, and undifferentiated. Post hoc tests revealed that (1) feminine men and women were more nurturant than masculine and undifferentiated men and women; (2) androgynous men and women were more nurturant than masculine and undifferentiated men and women; and (3) both androgynous and feminine men and women and masculine and undifferentiated groups were not different in their nurturance of the infant. These data indicate that the adults' personal construct notions about their masculinity and femininity were more strongly related to how nurturantly they behaved with the infant than to their biological sex. Note that these findings indicate that the men and women who scored above the median on the femininity dimension (i.e., the feminine and androgynous subjects) were significantly more nurturant with infants than men and women who scored below the median on femininity (i.e., the masculine and undifferentiated subjects). Also important is the fact that the subjects who scored above the median on the masculine dimension, if they also scored above the median on the feminine dimension (i.e., the androgynous subjects), were no less nurturant than the subjects who scored above the median on the feminine dimension but not the masculine dimension (i.e., the feminine subjects). This finding indicates that self-reported masculine personality characteristics represented by high instrumentality did not preclude or interfere with the expression of the feminine expressive behaviors of those men and women who saw themselves as both instrumental and expressive (i.e., androgynous).

Findings such as these, and the cogent arguments and construct validity of the personal attributions approach in the work of Spence and Helmreich (1978), suggest that the dualistic model of the psychological dimensions regarding masculinity, femininity, and androgyny may be more useful for describing parent characteristics and behavior in relation to infants than the role classification of *father* versus *mother*. Parent personality characteristics defined by this scheme would be expected to account for additional variance in parent behavior with infants (among parents and between groups of parents) beyond the variance accounted for in comparisons between groups defined by sex of parent.

In reference to fathers' relations with their infants and children, the personal attributes that comprise androgyny may reflect a flexibility or adaptability (Spence and Helmreich 1978) that permits the father to behave in ways that have been traditionally thought to be masculine as well as those that are feminine, depending on the situation or the task at hand. That is, androgynous fathers may be just as prepared as masculine men and more prepared than feminine people to adopt instrumental parenting roles in the circumstances where those behaviors are required. Similarly, androgynous men may be just as able as feminine individuals to adopt an expressive role involving sensitivity to others' emotions, responsiveness, affection, and nurturance in contexts where those behaviors are appropriate. I refer particularly, of course, to fathers' behavior toward their infants.

In light of the foregoing discussion and of the failure of observational research to find the kinds of differences between mothers' and fathers' patterns of interaction with infants that would be expected on the basis of historical, cross-cultural, and comparative approaches to parent behavior with infants, the utility of distinguishing several levels of inquiry becomes evident. For purposes of research and discussion of parenting styles with infants, three levels are proposed: (1) parent roles as they are defined by society; (2) parent characteristics defined in terms of individual and personal self-concepts of parenthood; and (3) parenting defined in terms of the actual behavior and activities engaged in by the parents. These levels of inquiry and their relevance for studying fathers will be elaborated upon.

The father: levels of definition and inquiry

Historical, cultural, and sociological approaches

At this level, fatherhood is defined in terms of structurally given demands. This is the classic definition of roles—normative expectations or rules for behavior, duties, and responsibilities including taboos. These role expectations are normative in the sense of shared values and expectations by a majority of individuals in a given culture. They define the role ascribed to fathers in a given culture or society at a given time. This approach generally defines fatherhood in relation to, or in contrast with, motherhood. Defined in this way, parenthood is something outside of the individual—it is a set of pressures and facilitations that channel, guide, impede, and support parents' functioning in the family.

Self-concepts and personal expectations approaches

Here, fatherhood is defined as the individual father's orientation or conception of the kind of parent he is or wants to be in the family system, i.e., his inner definition of his functions in the family and his relationship to the infant and the mother. Defined in this way, fathering or parenting is an aspect of the person—the person's cognitions and feelings about himself and how he wants to be as a father. These self-concepts may or may not correspond to cultural norms or may do so only to varying degrees.

Behavioral approaches

Fathering is defined here on the basis of the action or behavior of the individual father toward other members of the family. Here, as in the preceding definition, fathering is defined in terms of the person; in this case, in terms of behavioral characteristics of the person (i.e., in terms of what he does) rather than in terms of the prevailing norms for fathering (i.e., what he is "supposed" to do) or his self-concept of his fathering activities. This behavior may or may not correspond to cultural norms and/or the father's self-concept.

Much of the research on fathers during the infancy of their offspring has operated with a unitary conception of fathers and fatherhood as though there were an isomorphic relation, or at least a great degree of convergence among these levels of fatherhood. There seems to have been an implicit assumption that the self-concept that fathers held for the kind of parent they are or want to be was an internalization of the cultural prescriptions for fathers and that the ways that fathers behaved with their infants were determined by these internalized norms.

Although it is not unreasonable to expect some convergence between these levels of dealing with fatherhood, to assume a priori that there is a close convergence between them, and that assessment of fatherhood at one of these levels serves as a substitute or accurate predictor of fatherhood at the other levels, is premature and apt to be misleading. Instead, the relation among the three levels of dealing with fatherhood should be maintained as an empirical problem for study and, in the meantime, we should make the distinctions indicated by these definitions in both our theory and research into fatherhood in infancy. We should eliminate the single unitary conception of the father and give independent status to the three different levels of defining fatherhood.

Some evidence in support of distinctions among levels of inquiry into fatherhood

Historical, cultural, and sociological approaches

What is a father? He is a man, he works primarily outside of the home, and he is the material and perhaps the emotional supporter of the mother. He has traditionally been depicted as uninterested and uninvolved in infant care and affection (Parke and Sawin 1976). He does not become an active parent until his infant grows older.

This is a fair characterization of the conventional Western definition of the father during infancy. Further, this description of the father is consistent with the most prevalent social theory of parental roles (Parsons and Bales 1955). In this theory mothers and fathers are distinguished by their functioning in the family. Fathers serve primarily an instrumental function and mothers serve primarily an expressive function. It is further argued that the father is the provider for his wife and children, the disciplinarian, teacher of instrumental activity for his children, and the socializer of the children and adolescents for assuming roles outside the family. He is viewed as the representative within the family of the authority of the larger society outside the family. He is, above all, the man of the house.

Such role descriptions of fathers and mothers are consistent with the assumption that women are more suited to the tasks of parenting during their offsprings' infancy. Correspondingly, Nash (1965) noted that the father has become vestigial during the early periods of the development of his children, and Josselyn (1956) noted it is considered inappropriate in our culture for fathers to be nurturant toward their infants. Many cultures believe that fathers are much less capable of appropriate parenting behavior with infants—they lack know-how and are inadequately sensitive to infants' emotional needs for warmth and nurturance.

Based on social scientists' descriptions of these cultural stereotypes and on sociological theory, the picture that we get of the father is a bit like a quarterback of the football team: (1) he is instrumental—he calls the shots and makes things happen; (2) he is tough and strong—he is thus too rough and clumsy to handle infants; and (3) he is primarily concerned with winning the game for his team (family) and not with the emotional well-being of the members of the team in the process—that is the mother's job. Though this somewhat overstated stereotype of the father has firm precedence historically in Western cultures (see Parke and Sawin 1976 for a review of these issues) as well as in more contemporary sociological theory of parent roles (Parsons and Bales 1955), it was noted earlier in this chapter and discussed at greater length elsewhere (Parke and Sawin 1976) that this is not the picture that emerges from observational studies of patterns of paternal behavior in interaction with young infants.

Self-concepts and personal expectations

How do fathers' conceptions of their relationships with infants and wives fit with the prevailing social-cultural stereotype of fathers? In dissertation research conducted with a subsample of fathers involved in a longitudinal study of father-infant interaction during the first several months of infant life (Parke and Sawin 1977), Cordell (1978) interviewed 25 middle-class, White fathers about their conceptions of fatherhood and their relationships with their infants. The interviews were conducted when the infants were three to four months old. The questions were open-ended and the responses were spontaneous. The observational data from the dyadic interactions of these fathers with their infants were also available.

One of the questions asked of the fathers addressed the issue of the kinds of functions they saw for themselves in relation to their young children. The fathers' two most frequent responses (16 of 25 fathers) were

(a) to recognize and be sensitive to the child's emotional needs and (b) to be a companion to the child by showing an interest in her or his activities, spending time together, and sharing the child's happiness or joy. The next most frequent functions mentioned by these fathers (14 of 25) were to be a provider and to socialize and discipline their young children. In contrast, only 4 of the 25 fathers described their function as teacher and only 1 of the fathers saw his function as the male role model or as he also said, "the male parent."

In response to a question about the fathers' conceptions of their functions specifically with their young infants, all of the fathers mentioned routine infant care as being part of their conception of their fatherhood. Twenty of the 25 fathers mentioned infant stimulation, and 11 of the fathers specifically mentioned affection giving. In contrast, only 4 of the 25 fathers included any reference to teaching basic skills as a part of their conception of their function as a father to their infants.

The fathers were also asked to compare themselves as parents to their wives as parents. The question was designed to assess how many of the fathers viewed themselves as the same as their wives, or at least similar, and how many fathers viewed themselves as basically different from their wives as a parent. Only two fathers felt that they were clearly different from their wives due to basic differences between fathers and mothers in their natures or instincts. Most of the fathers noted both similarities and differences between themselves and their wives as parents of their young infants. Three fathers stated that there were no basic differences between them and their wives in relation to their infants.

Though the sample is small and composed of a somewhat select group of fathers, these self-reports indicate that there may be little correspondence between fathers' conceptions of their fatherhood and the sociocultural stereotype of the father presented earlier. Cordell (1978) notes several significant contrasts. The large proportion (16 of 25) of fathers in this sample who specifically mentioned recognizing their children's emotional needs as an important function of their relationships with their children is considerably higher than would be predicted from the sociocultural theories such as Parsons and Bales (1955) theory of parent roles. This expressive function of parenting is almost exclusively seen as the primary function of motherhood and is not usually considered from these perspectives as a dimension of fatherhood. The low frequency with which the fathers in Cordell's sample mentioned teaching or the fostering of basic skills in their children and infants is also notably discrepant with prevailing theories of the father's role in the family.

Self reports indicate that there may be little correspondence between fathers' conceptions of their fatherhood and the sociocultural stereotype of the father.

Behavioral perspectives on fathering

How do fathers behave with their young infants? In what ways are patterns of paternal activity different from or similar to patterns of maternal activity? As described briefly at the beginning of this chapter, findings from observations of parent-infant interactions during bottle feeding and play sessions involving mother-infant dyads and father-infant dyads have yielded only a few differences between the frequencies and durations of mothers' and fathers' caregiving, affectionate, and stimulating behaviors (Parke and O'Leary 1976; Parke and Sawin 1975, 1977). During the neonatal period, mothers engaged in actual feeding (putting the nipple in infant's mouth or attempting to put it there) for a longer total duration during a ten-minute feeding session than fathers (Parke and O'Leary 1976; Parke and Sawin 1975). Mothers wiped their infant's face or hands more than fathers did during feeding sessions in this early period (Parke and Sawin 1975, 1977), and mothers engaged more frequently in routine caregiving (checks, adjusts, grooms) during play sessions in the hospital than did fathers (Parke and Sawin 1977). On the other hand, fathers looked at their infants for a longer total duration during feeding in this early period and maintained more eye-to-eye contact with their infants than did mothers (Parke and Sawin 1975). Fathers also provided more visual stimulation (showed toy) and auditory stimulation (e.g., rattled toy to make sounds for infant) during play sessions in the neonatal period than mothers (Parke and Sawin 1977).

Thus, during the very earliest period of infancy, there appears to be some differentiation between mothers' and fathers' patterns of parent activity with their infants, but the number of behaviors that differentiate mothers and fathers are few, and the absolute amount of difference in the frequency and durations of these behaviors, though statistically significant, is not large. Mothers appear to engage in more of the activities that we think of as routine caregiving, and fathers appear to be more attentive to their infants and provide them with more visual and auditory stimulation.

The next question addressed in this line of research was whether these early differences between mothers and fathers in their interactions with their infants are stable; that is, would they hold over time (the early months of infancy) and contexts (hospital versus home). In the most recent study of this series (Parke and Sawin 1977), observations of parent-infant interactions similar to those made in the hospital during the neonatal period were also made in the families' homes during the fourth week and fourth month following the infants' births.

The differences between mothers and fathers that remained stable over this period were similar to, but fewer in number, than the differences observed during the neonatal period. Mothers continued to engage in more routine caregiving (checks, adjusts, grooms) than fathers, and more of the mothers kissed their infants during feeding and play than fathers. Fathers, as compared to mothers, engaged more frequently in affectionate visual stimulation of their infants in the form of mimicking or imitating their infants' facial expressions and mouthmovements.

Though there are few differences between mothers' and fathers' patterns of interacting with their newborn infants, and even fewer mother-father differences that are stable over the first four months of the infant's life, there is some indication in these observational behavioral data of characteristic differences between mothers and fathers. Notwithstanding, the overall picture that emerges from these studies of parent-infant interaction in early infancy is that fathers are active participants in the care and affection of their infants during dyadic interactions in both feeding and play.

How does this behavioral picture jibe with predominant sociocultural views of fathers? Not very closely. The only correspondence between these two levels of examining fatherhood is the tendency for mothers to engage in more routine caregiving than fathers and the greater number of mothers who kissed their infants during their interactions with them. But overall, fathers were no less affectionate, sensitive, and responsive to their infants than mothers (Parke and Sawin 1975, 1977) and did not show significant differences in the frequency and duration of most parenting behaviors during interactions with their infants (Parke and O'Leary 1976; Parke and Sawin 1975, 1977). The few indications of differentiation between mothers' and fathers' characteristic patterns of interactions with their infants are certainly not as great as would be expected from the sociocultural stereotypes of mothers and fathers.

The correspondence between the patterns of fathers' behaviors in father-infant interaction and fathers' personal construct notions of fatherhood are not so discrepant. That is, there appears to be a greater relation between these fathers, activities in father-infant interactions, and their self-reports of their functions than with sociocultural stereotypes of fathers.

For example, all of the fathers interviewed by Cordell (1978) mentioned routine infant care as one of their activities. Correspondingly, the observed differences between mothers and fathers in these behaviors during parent-infant dyadic interactions were small and evident during the play session but not during feeding sessions over the first four months of infant life. The second most frequent paternal activity mentioned by the fathers was infant stimulation. This was one of the few behavioral differences between mothers and fathers that was more typical of fathers during the neonatal period and over the four months of infancy. Finally, while only about one-half of the fathers interviewed specifically mentioned affection giving as part of their paternal activities, the observations of the fathers' behavior with their infants indicated that fathers were just as affectionate except for kissing their infants.

There is some correspondence between these fathers' self-concepts of their functions with their infants and the behavioral measures of their activities in father-infant interactions, but the correspondence is not identical. Thus, approaching fatherhood in infancy from the self-concept perspective will not necessarily yield reliable and valid indices for predicting fathers' behaviors, though the relation between these levels of examining fatherhood certainly warrants more consideration and research.

In conjunction with these issues, and in response to the emerging perspective of the "social ecology of development" (Bronfenbrenner 1975, 1977), a third consideration in conceptualizing and defining the father needs to be examined. We should view the father not as an isolated element of the infant's social environment, but as one of several interacting components of the social system that constitutes that environment. Each of these persons, or components, plays a role in relation to both the infant and to one another. This matrix of social relations and its impact on infant development cannot be understood by examining only the relation between a single individual and the infant; rather we must examine the entire social matrix of the family. The whole can only be understood in terms of the relations among the parts.

In adopting such a strategy, we should consider such factors as (1) the number of caregivers; (2) the amount and quality of their involvement with the infant; (3) the reciprocal influences and mutual regulation process operating among the caregivers and the infant; and (4) characteristics and behaviors of the infant that influence the behavior of the caregivers and their relationship with the infant and with one another. The remainder of this chapter will be a more thorough discussion of this issue, with a focus on defining and conceptualizing parenting for purposes of research on the family and on infant development.

Parenting in infancy from a social-ecological perspective

This issue will be explicated with some examples from recent research and some anecdotes from our experiences with parents of young infants.

Context or tasks of parenting

In our most recent study of parent-infant interactions in early infancy (Parke and Sawin 1977), we observed parent and infant behaviors in both a feeding session and a play session. As we had expected, there was more variation in parents' behaviors in the play context than in the feeding context. We obtained a greater number of significant effects due to sex of parent, sex of infant, ordinal position of infant, and time of measurement in the analyses of the behavioral data obtained during the play sessions. In addition, the behaviors of mother-father couples were less similar in the play context. There were fewer significant positive correlations between the behaviors of mother-father pairs in the play context than were obtained between the behaviors of mothers and fathers in the feeding context. These findings are not surprising. In the feeding context, the tasks of parents are far more clearly and narrowly defined than in the play context. The primary task of feeding is to make the infant comfortable and be sure she or he gets enough food. This parenting task involves feeding behaviors with which most parents are familiar or are at least aware of, they are fairly routine, and tend to be stereotyped. Thus, feeding situations seem to place constraints on the variations in parenting behavior that become evident in a play context. This suggests the need to evaluate mothers' and fathers' behaviors with their infants in several of the contexts in which they occur in order to obtain a more salient and comprehensive picture of variations in parents' behaviors and thus a better assessment of the infants' social ecology. Observations of feeding interactions alone are almost certainly insufficient for these purposes.

Infant characteristics

There is currently an emerging recognition of the infants' influences on parent behavior (Lewis and Rosenblum 1974). Several infant characteristics have been shown in our own research to elicit differential behavior by parents in parent-infant interactions (Parke and Sawin 1975, 1977). The infant's gender is one such characteristic. During the newborn period, female infants receive more physical stimulation (parent changes infant's position; parent touches/moves part of infant) than male infants, and female infants are held in the ventral position (belly-to-belly) and are more frequently pulled into a well-supported, snuggly, held close position (Parke and Sawin 1975). In examining these sex-of-infant differences in parents' behaviors over the first four months, we found that during feeding sessions parents looked at female infants more frequently and during play sessions female infants were offered a pacifier more than male infants. Further, parents talked to someone other than the infant more frequently while playing with a female infant than with a male infant, and they held their male infants close and snuggly during play more than their female infants (Parke and Sawin 1978).

More frequent than main effects for infant gender over these early months were interaction effects of this factor with parent gender (Parke and Sawin 1977). These interaction effects indicate that infant gender plays a differential modifying influence on mothers' and fathers' patterns of interacting with their infants: fathers behaved differently with sons than with daughters, while mothers' behavior with daughters and sons appears to be reciprocal to fathers'. For example, during play we found that mothers held their sons close and snuggly more frequently and for longer periods than their daughters. Conversely, fathers tended to hold their daughters close to them more than their sons. In contrast, for visual attending and stimulation behaviors, fathers consistently favored their sons, and mothers more often favored their daughters. However, there was little differentiation in mothers' and fathers' behaviors toward their sons and daughters for routine caregiving behaviors. These findings indicate that mothers' and fathers' affection giving is more focused on their opposite-sexed infant, while their attending and stimulation behaviors are more frequent with their same-sexed infant.

Other infant characteristics appear to be relevant to parents' behavior in interaction with their infants. Infant cuddliness, as measured in the Brazelton Neonatal Assessment Scale (Brazelton 1973), was positively correlated to the amount of time mothers looked at their infants during a feeding session in the neonatal period, the frequency with which they engaged in eye-to-eye contact with their infants, the amount of time they held their infants in the ventral position, and the frequency with which they touched/moved (affectionate tactual/kinesthetic stimulation) and, most interestingly, with the frequency of mothers kissing their infants (Parke and Sawin 1975). Similarly, fathers more frequently engaged in eye-to-eye contact with their cuddly infants, held them in the ventral position more, and were more likely to kiss them (Parke and Sawin 1975).

Similar relations were found between parents' behavior and an informal rating of the infant's cuteness made by the Brazelton Scale administrator in this same study. Infants who were rated higher on the cuteness scale had parents who maintained eye-to-eye contact with them more frequently, were more likely to be kissed by their parents, were held in the ventral position more by their mothers, and received more affectionate tactual/kinesthetic stimulation from their fathers (Parke and Sawin 1975).

These findings of relations between infant characteristics such as sex, cuddliness, and cuteness, and parent behaviors in parent-infant interactions indicate the importance of considering the infant as a significant component of the social matrix that determines the quality of the infant's social ecology. The infant is clearly a contributor to the nature and quality of patterns of parent behavior.

Family composition

The number of people involved in infant care is an additional factor that may be a significant component of the infant's social ecology. Of particular importance here is the availability and nature of an extended family arrangement. Since there are little data bearing on this issue, the significance of this factor will be demonstrated with an anecdotal example.

We recently went into the home of a young couple with a two-month-old infant to videotape mother-infant and father-infant interactons in order to prepare training materials for our observers. At the time we were in this home, the maternal grandmother was living with the family. During our visit, she stayed on the periphery of the action, watching her daughter feeding her infant and observing with some amusement our video equipment and recording activities. This passive observation by the grandmother lasted until it was the father's turn to feed the infant. At the instant that the mother began to hand the infant over to the father, the grandmother moved swiftly forward and intercepted the infant before the father could take hold of his infant. After some explanation by the mother to the grandmother that we were there to observe the infant while being fed by the father, the grandmother reluctantly gave up the infant to the father but hovered over the father during the entire time that he held and fed the infant. At any point when the infant appeared to be getting fussy, the grandmother would begin to reach for the infant. When the father finally handed the infant back to the mother, the grandmother recessed into the background again.

The point to be made from this example is that the behavior of other family members living in the home with the new parents will very likely be a significant determinant of the behavior of the parents with their infant. While the presence of other family members may be supportive and contribute positively to the overall quality of the infant's social ecology, it may also serve to determine the amount and quality of involvement that parents, especially the father, have with their infant.

Influence of parents on each other's behavior

The effects of the behavior of one caregiver toward another and the relationship between the caregivers are often evident in the behavior and relationship of each of the caregivers with the infant. Parents influence the nature of each other's interactions with their infants. For example, Pederson (1975) has reported a significant correlation between the father's positive feelings about his wife as a mother with her skill in caregiving with her infant. While the direction of influence of this relationship is not discernible from these data, such findings argue for including the parents' relationship as a significant component of descriptions of the infant's social ecology and as a factor in studies of parenting behavior.

Further support for this argument comes from data obtained by Parke and O'Leary (1976), who observed mothers' and fathers' interactions with their neonates while each parent was alone with their infant and again when the parents were together with the infant. These investigators found that the mother engaged in more exploration of her infant and smiled more when the father was present than when she was alone with her infant. It thus appears that the father's presence during the mother's interactions with her infant had a positive influence on the mother's interest in the infant and on her own affect while interacting with her infant.

Note, however, that the extent to which the father's involvement in the early family triad has a positive influence on the mother's relation with her infant may depend on the way the mother defines her parenting role. If the mother sees herself as the primary or the exclusive caregiver for her infant, the father's efforts to become actively involved in the care and affection of his infant may not be well received by the mother. On the other hand, if the mother defines her role as that of one of two parents who willingly share the care and affection of the infant, the father's active involvement in these activities will be well received by the mother and may even enhance her relationship with the infant. The father's involvement in sharing some of the responsibilities of infant care may provide the mother with rest and relief and allow her to interact with her infant at those times when she is comfortable and relaxed. In addition, the process of sharing per se may enhance both parents' feelings about their infant.

Such sharing of the tasks of infancy appears to have other influences on the parents' behavior as well. In our observations of mothers' and fathers' interactions with their infants over the first four months of the infants' lives (Parke and Sawin 1977), we noted some interesting shifts over time in the parents' behaviors in interactions with their infants that suggested that parents may simultaneously serve as models for each other's behaviors as well as learning from each other. For example, comparisons of mothers' and fathers' caretaking behaviors (e.g., checks, diapers, grooms) during the play session indicated that mothers engaged in more caretaking in the hospital observation, while fathers engaged in more caretaking at the three-week observation. By the time of the three-month observation, however, fathers and mothers engaged in similar amounts of caretaking during play with their infant.

Parents' auditory stimulation of their infants during the play session was characterized by the same trend evident in several of the stimulation variables. At time one, fathers more frequently than mothers jiggled or rattled the toy for their infant to hear, but by time two at three weeks, mothers were providing this auditory stimulation more often than fathers, and at the three-month visit, the differences between mothers and fathers were very small.

Overall, the parent gender × time of measurement (i.e., parent experience and infant age) interactions revealed trends in shifting patterns of mothers' and fathers' interactions with their infants over the first months of infant life in which the direction of the differences between mothers and fathers at each time point was a function of the type of caregiving activity being examined. These trends indicated a shift from early stereotyped behavior (mothers giving their infants more care and affection and fathers giving more stimulation) to reversed or more homogeneous patterns by four months.

These indications of reversals and convergence in parent behavior suggest that mutual modeling effects are operating in the family system during the early period of infancy. It appears that, as parents experience the caring and stimulation of their infant together, they adopt the behaviors of their mates. Parents seem to learn from each other and, at the same time, provide a model for each other's learning.

Summary and conclusions

The purpose of this chapter has been threefold: (1) to suggest the added utility to our understanding of characteristic styles of parenting of classifying parents on the basis of personal attributions to themselves along the psychologically relevant dimensions of masculinity and femininity in addition to classifying parents on the basis of gender; (2) to argue for more carefully conceived and more highly differentiated conceptualizations and inquiry of fatherhood in early infancy; and (3) to indicate the need to view early parenting and infant development from a broad social perspective, namely, the infant's social ecology—a dynamic

Mothers' and fathers' affection giving is more focused on their opposite-sexed infant while their attending and stimulation behaviors are more frequent with their same-sexed infant.

and changing social system consisting of a matrix of social relationships involving all of the persons in the infant's environment, including the infant.

Such strategies for exploring and understanding fatherhood and the family in early infancy require distinctions among socioculturally given roles, the self-conceptions that parents use for defining their own role in relation to each other and in relation to the infant, and behaviorally based approaches that focus on the actual behaviors that parents engage in with infants and the nature and quality of these patterns of parenting. These sources of data are not isomorphic; and they are not necessarily interchangeable—each is important for understanding the family in early infancy, but the extent to which they are interrelated, and the significance of each of these levels as an influence on the other, must be viewed as an empirical question for further study.

In a similar vein, the extent to which the designations of caregivers such as fathers, mothers, aunts, or grandmothers are useful to our understanding of the infant's social ecology and of patterns of parenting behavior is also an empirical question. Recent research on individuals' self-reports of their masculine and feminine characteristics suggests that caregivers' personal conceptions of themselves and their relationships with infants may provide a better means of understanding their behavior with infants.

Finally, a multivariate and longitudinal strategy for conceptualizing and investigating the determinants of patterns of parenting is necessary for a comprehensive understanding of the family in early infancy. This broadened perspective must include consideration of a large number of factors that comprise the infant's social ecology. These include characteristics of all of the family members (including the infant), the nature of the family arrangement, the relations among the members of the family unit, and the second-order effects of each person on the other persons as they are mediated through a third person. Such a strategy places the study of the father in infancy within the context of the entire social matrix surrounding the infant and will allow a better understanding not only of his relationship with the infant and the significance of that relationship, but also of his relationship with the infant in relation to the other significant persons in the infant's environment who may serve to influence both father and infant.

References

Bem, S.L.; Martyna, W.; and Watson, C. "Sex Typing and Androgyny: Further Explorations of the Expressive Domain." *Journal of Personality and Social Psychology* 34 (1976): 1016-1023.

Brazelton, T.B. *Neonatal Behavioral Assessment Scale*. Philadelphia: Lippincott, 1973.

Bronfenbrenner, U. "The Ecology of Human Development in Retrospect and Prospect." Invited address of the final plenary session of the conference on ecological factors in human development held by the International Society for the Study of Behavioral Development, University of Surrey, Guildford, England, July 1975.

Bronfenbrenner, U. "Toward an Experimental Ecology of Human Development." *American Psychologist* 32 (1977): 513-531.

Cordell, A.S. "The Father-Infant Relationship." Doctoral dissertation, University of Chicago, 1978.

Josselyn, I.M. "Cultural Forces, Motherliness, and Fatherliness." *American Journal of Orthopsychiatry* 26 (1956): 264-271.

Lamb, M.E., ed. *The Role of the Father in Child Development*. New York: Wiley, 1976.

Lewis, M., and Rosenblum, L.A., eds. *The Effect of the Infant on Its Caregiver*. New York: Wiley, 1974.

Lynn, D.B. *The Father: His Role in Child Development*. Monterey, Calif.: Brooks/Cole, 1974.

Nash, J. "The Father in Contemporary Cultural and Current Psychological Literature." *Child Development* 36 (1965): 261-297.

Nash, J. "Historical and Social Changes in the Perception of the Role of the Father." In *The Role of the Father in Child Development*, ed. M.E. Lamb. New York: Wiley, 1976.

Parke, R.D., and O'Leary, S.E. "Family Interaction in the Newborn Period: Some Findings, Some Observations, and Some Unresolved Issues." In *The Developing Individual in a Changing World (Vol. 2): Social and Environmental Issues*, ed. K.F. Riegel and J.A. Meacham. Chicago: Aldine, 1976.

Parke, R.D., and Sawin, D.B. "The Family in Early Infancy: Social Interactional and Attitudinal Analyses." Paper presented at a symposium, "The Family System: Networks of Interactions among Mother, Father, and Infant," at the biennial meetings of the Society for Research in Child Development, New Orleans, March 1977.

Parke, R.D., and Sawin, D.B. "The Father's Role in Infancy: A Re-Evaluation." *The Family Coordinator* 24 (1976): 365-371.

Parke, R.D., and Sawin, D.B. "Infant Characteristics and Behavior As Elicitors of Maternal and Paternal Responsivity in the Newborn Period." Paper presented at a symposium, "Direction of Effects in Studies of Early Parent-Infant Interaction," at the biennial meetings of the Society for Research in Child Development, Denver, April 1975.

Parke, R.D., and Sawin, D.B. Unpublished data, 1978.

Parsons, T., and Bales, R.F. *Family, Socialization and Interaction Process*. New York: Free Press, 1955.

Pederson, F.A. "Mother, Father and Infant As an Interactive System." Paper presented at a symposium, "Fathers and Infants," at the annual convention of the American Psychological Association, Chicago, September 1975.

Redican, W.K. "Adult Male-Infant Interactions in Non-Human Primates." In *The Role of the Father in Child Development*, ed. M. Lamb. New York: Wiley, 1976.

Spence, J.T., and Helmreich, R.L. *Masculinity and Femininity: Their Psychological Dimensions, Correlates, and Antecedents.* Austin, Tex: University of Texas Press, 1978.

Spence, J. T.; Helmreich, R.; and Stapp, J. "Ratings of Self and Peers on Sex-Role Attributes and Their Relation to Self-Esteem and Conceptions of Masculinity and Femininity." *Journal of Personality and Social Psychology* 32 (1975): 29-39.

Walters, J., ed. *The Family Coordinator* (Special issue: Fatherhood) 25 (1976): 335-520.

West, M.M., and Konner, M.J. "The Role of the Father: An Anthropological Perspective." In *The Role of the Father in Child Development*, ed. M.E. Lamb. New York: Wiley, 1976.

Bernice Weissbourd

11

Supporting parents as people

"We have a society that claims love and concern for its young, and yet it leaves parents to raise their children virtually unprepared and alone."

The poignancy of this statement becomes apparent when one realizes its author is not a sociologist but a young parent. The statement speaks for the multitude of young parents today for whom parenthood raises the specter of anxiety, confusion, and excessive burdens.

This chapter glances at the psychological aspects of being a parent, presents a brief picture of the social environment in which parents raise their children, discusses directions indicated by these factors for support to parents, and presents a model for providing such support.

The psychological environment of parenting

Parenting is a stage in adulthood increasingly being examined by psychologists, sociologists, and educators as interest grows in understanding the continuum of development throughout the life cycle. After many years of focusing on the development of the child, and looking at the parent primarily as the vehicle for the child's growth, emphasis has now shifted to examination of the parent as a developing person and of the interactional effect of parent and child relationships.

In Gutmann's transcultural studies (1978), he finds that "parenthood seems to represent the point at which individual satisfaction intersects with species' needs. For most adult human beings, parenthood is still the ultimate source of the sense of meaning" (p. 3). Parenting is viewed as a pivotal stage in the life cycle, as an organizing factor of adulthood, reflecting the events of childhood and shaping the later periods of our lives. Erikson (1979) has suggested that the urge to have children is an

Stages in parenting parallel the stages in the child's growth, as each developmental task of the child challenges the parents' attitudes and ability to respond.

impulse linked to, but distinct from, the sexual drive, and comparable to it in importance.

"The child is father to the man" is a familiar adage now reinforced by knowledge that parental behavior is determined by the environment in which the parent as a child was socialized. Adults repeat their early experiences and parent as they were parented and/or consciously make the effort to establish patterns of parenting different from those in which they grew up. Anthony and Benedek (1968) describe parenthood as reexperiencing the past and as a time of reactivating old conflicts and bringing new hopes.

Parenthood viewed in these terms emphasizes the possibilities for individual growth and development rather than a stage in which individuality is submerged and lessened by the responsibility toward a child. It implies sensitivity to the next generation while at the same time it permits an expansion of one's own competence, emotional attachments, and coping skills. It is in itself a developmental process requiring awareness of one's own needs as they may complement or conflict with one's child's needs.

Stages in parenting parallel the stages in the child's growth, as each developmental task of the child challenges the parents' attitudes and ability to respond. Parents of infants whose own experiences have led to a sense of trust in themselves are able to communicate that feeling and respond to children in ways which establish their development of trust. Parents of toddlers deal with issues of control and autonomy with themselves as well as with their children. The individuality of the child, her or his particular personality and temperament that are reflected in the child's unique way of managing developmental tasks, further influence the adaptation and growth of parents. In each of these stages, parenting requires intuition guided by a careful evaluation of the child's needs, developmental tasks, and goals (Anthony and Benedek 1968). It further requires a parent's good feeling about self, a sense of confidence and self-esteem, a sense of self-worth as a person who is a parent.

Lack of confidence inhibits the parents' ability to react and results in interactions with the child that have negative effects and consequently further undermine the parents. Sometimes, it is the lack of knowledge of the meaning of the child's behavior that causes the misinterpretations and misunderstandings that increase a parent's anxiety and frustration. Confidence is built in parents as they experience the satisfaction of seeing a child grow up well, and it is built as parents experience their own ability to manage their lives.

The social environment of parenting

In viewing families today, the scene appears tumultuous and complex. The word *family* itself has new connotations and different configurations (see Howard 1980). There is a wide spectrum of family units. One may be the traditional structure of the nuclear family, with father supporting the mother and children at home. But this model now represents only 1 out of 17 American families. Another, which is assuming significant proportions as the divorce rate nears 50 percent, is the mother and children model, with the father in occasional contact or out of the picture entirely. Less commonplace, but occurring with increasing frequency as court decisions grant custody to fathers, is the male-headed family with the mother in varied degrees of contact with the children. There is the family of the single mother, the woman who either intentionally or unintentionally conceives a child and chooses to bear and rear the child alone. One in 8 children are in that category. There is the single woman who desires to be a parent and adopts a child. In total, there are 10.9 million children growing up in single parent families. The increase in remarriages results in what is now termed the reconstituted or blended family, children living with their own and a new parent including new siblings. As both of the natural parents remarry, children may be sharing time between two sets of parents and two or more sets of brothers and sisters. Finally, there are children living in varied groups of communal arrangements that constitute their family. A kaleidoscope of this picture was seen on a recent application form that read, "Check one: married, single, widowed, divorced, remarried, separated, living together"!

The data on the impact of various family structures on children is not definitive. In situations of divorce, there are strong indications that the effect on the child varies greatly depending upon the frequency and quality of contact with both parents following the divorce. Some research on single parenting shows that children from one-parent households are more frequently associated with low school achievement and juvenile delinquency while other studies indicate little measurable impact on children's lives (Pearlin 1975).

Though the structure of the family is undergoing massive changes, it seems that the content of family life and the way a family functions are greater determinants of children's health. The primary value given to the family as a source of emotional support and personal gratification continues to exist. After reviewing studies on the American family, Rice (1977) concludes that most parents enjoy their children and desire control over their caregiving arrangements, that trends toward outside care have not lessened the impact of the family, that attitudes toward marriage continue to be connected with permanence, and that the family, including the extended family, continues to be a primary source of socialization.

Coloring the picture of the family is the changed status of motherhood. A tangential effect of the women's movement, the role of being a mother has become of little significance compared to that of the career woman who has successfully entered the professional world. To her go the accolades, for she is another proof that women have the imagination, intellectual ability, and vitality to work and excel in the fields heretofore limited to the male members of the population. The similar qualities of creativity, intelligence, and energy required for good mothering have been devalued and often ignored. A recent survey made by an eastern Ivy League college of its women graduates indicated only the professional career positions held. There was no listing of the women who had chosen to have children and be at home with them in their early years. Obviously such a role is not viewed with pride by society's institutions and consequently seldom by the mother herself.

Many women are juggling careers and motherhood in an almost superhuman attempt to succeed at both. Most young women expect to have children and most also expect to work (Smith 1979). Increasingly, mothers have moved into the labor force, and within only the last two decades the magnitude of the rise of working women has been so great that it is now termed a subtle revolution. In 1978, 50 percent of the married women were working, and by 1990 an additional 56 percent increase is expected in the number of working mothers with young children.

The impact of these changes on the lives of parents and children directly affects our concern with support systems for families. The rapid increase in the number of very young children whose mothers are working requires an examination of the alternative care children are receiving, as well as alternative possibilities for mothers to remain at home in these early years, particularly those mothers who would opt to do so if finances permitted. The recognition that families in varied structures, such as single parents or male-headed families, can perform well in childrearing roles but require additional assistance further underscores the need for family support systems. In this discussion we are concerned with the pressures and demands on both men and women resulting from new roles and the uncertainties and anxieties as patterns of family living change from the experienced and known structure of a generation ago.

A picture of families in our society cannot be drawn without including the issues of poverty and the fact that children born into families in severe financial stress will inevitably suffer basic deprivations. Recent reports show that a quarter of American children are born into families too poor to provide for adequate care (Children's Defense Fund 1979). It requires little stretch of the imagination to recognize that parents experiencing stress must have difficulty maintaining calm control and comforting relationships with their children. In a study by Passman (1979) on parental stress, he concludes, "The child too often is the convenient victim for a parent who punishes the child with increasing severity as stress increases" (p. 12). This research was conducted under conditions of minimal stress, and it is not a great leap from that to realize the impact on children when families are beset with the severe stress associated with problems of food, jobs, and housing.

Mixed messages parents receive

We are aware that mixed messages cause difficulties for children (Smith and Davis 1976), but little has been said about their effects on adults. There are many mixed messages entering adult consciousness in our society; the following mentions but a few.

Particular emphasis has recently been given to the significance of the first three years of life and especially to the importance of the mother-child interaction in developing bonds. The implications of positive experiences and good attachments in the very early years to cognitive and emotional development are subjects of intensive research today. The results indicate the importance of significant persons in the child's life who know her or his particular signs of distress, joy, need for affection and play. Yet the all-too-common attitude toward the woman who stays at home with her children is that she is only a mother. The correlation between her status and the significance of the job she does at home is negative.

Parents are constantly being told that their child should feel secure, have a good sense of self, and be able to cope. Parents learn that it is their responsibility to communicate confidence to their children. Yet parents are living in environments that are often difficult and isolating, contributing to making them feel insecure, anxious, and frustrated. Parents not feeling good about themselves have that sense compounded by the knowledge that they must assure their children's positive self-images.

If you must work, parents are cautioned, be sure your children have good quality care, because if they do not, they can be psychologically damaged. The horror stories of poor child care are too familiar to merit repeating. Yet the society does not offer or support good child care. Today 6 million preschool children have working mothers, but there are only 900,000 licensed day care slots. This means that over 5 million children are in care that we know nothing about. Even assuming that some of these children are in good private arrangements or in good extended family situations, the vast majority are probably receiving less than optimal care. The conscientious mother who must work is all too frequently caught in a painful bind.

Policies and institutions functioning in our society sap the strength of the family. Welfare laws, high unemployment rates, unequal paychecks for men and women, and working hours that do not fit school hours often have the effect of making it more difficult, and sometimes impossible, to fulfill one's desire to be a good parent. Yet while policies are made that weaken the family, we say loudly, "The family is our most important institution and should be strong."

The complexities of the society demand interrelatedness and interdependence. The availability of day care, of health care, the proximity of the parents' working place, and the mode of transportation affect the life of the child. *Yet* the credo of the society is to be self-reliant, independent, self-sufficient: Never mind what the society does to you, just believe in the myth that one should not need people or supports. The fact is that true independence and being able to effectively use support systems are not opposites. In actuality, the emphasis on individualism is too often a direct path to isolation.

Finally, the family is constantly reminded that it is the single most fundamental influence on the child's development. It acts as a system for socializing the child and communicating cultural values, and for promoting emotional growth and development of cognitive skills. *Yet* in terms of practical support, our society barely acknowledges the existence of the family role. Only a limited number of communities provide for services of any kind, and generally these are available only to those families having special needs.

Assumptions about parenting

We can assume that people who are parents want to be good parents. If they are not good parents, it is seldom from lack of desire to be good parents but more likely from lack of gratification in their lives and the result of hardships in their own childhoods. Parenting requires emotional maturity and stability in order to give and be responsive to children. Parents need support to develop competence, and to be nurturers — some, most of the time, and all, some of the time.

There is ample evidence to assume that the mental health of children is closely related to that of the parents and, specifically, that the parents' sense of confidence, competence, and self-worth has a direct impact on the nature of the parent-child interaction and therefore on the child's self-image. Particularly in the first three years of life a prime requisite for optimum growth is a mutually satisfying relationship between child and parent.

If we are concerned with children's welfare, we must look at the parents' state of being; the parent, or parent substitute, being the most significant bond a child has. Since parents construe their children's relations to society in ways that are fundamentally the same as their own relation to society, parents experiencing defeat and feeling hopeless project that attitude into their children's lives. It should be considered quite remarkable that sometimes the most destitute parents persist in having dreams of success for their children. Clearly, if communications with the children are to be effectively changed, there must be change in the parents' own *experience* with the world.

Emphasizing the word *experience* is to differentiate it from the words most commonly used in relation to parenting—education, teaching, training. An approach to parents that is based on the conclusion that lack of knowledge is the sole source of difficulties, that information on child development will provide the cure for problems in the parent-child relationship, is functional only when parents are feeling relatively confident in themselves and secure in their life patterns.

For others, particularly in programs directed to low-income families, these words often imply that they lack the skills, the know-how, the intelligence to do an adequate job of childrearing. For the middle-income but insecure parent the training courses often add to the anxieties and uncertainties of which they are already victims. Moreover, for all parents the focus on educating tends to communicate that skills and knowledge of cognitive development can be equated with good parenting.

"The problem is not that she doesn't know what to do, but that she feels as if she can't do it. The advice she gets [from professionals] increases her feelings of failure and guilt" (Heffner 1978, p. 27). The strengths that exist, and are often found amidst great adversity, are the core upon which good parenting can be based, and they need to be underscored not undermined.

Support for parents

Typically a community has health resources, social service agencies, welfare agencies, and recreation programs, but nothing to support the basic function of parenting. Furthermore, the majority of social services, except those for the handicapped and for special problems, come in contact with the family when the child is three years or older. There simply are no places to go for parents to better understand their own feelings and their role with their children in the early years, just those years when the interaction is of crucial importance.

The supportive relationships with other people are frequently missing. The extended family is seldom present. Whatever its problems were, and there were many, it nonetheless was a haven for venting feelings, a system of ties and relationships that created a sense of belonging. One may often have wished to be unencumbered by its invasions and demands, but it remained a base and a place to come home to. Pediatricians tend to complain about anxious mothers' phone

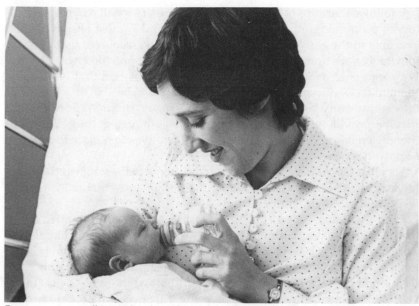

Programs are most effective when focused not solely on teaching skills to parents for teaching their infants, but on creating an environment in which experiences enhance parents' self-esteem and confidence, and therefore affect their behavior toward their children.

calls, and though the newly developing category of pediatric nurses may alleviate some of the problems, it cannot replace the emotional ties of the extended family. And with few exceptions, the neighbor as support is virtually nonexistent. Our social orientation of individualism leads to the practice of each alone caring for and protecting one's own. The effects of this are shown in research indicating that a substantial proportion (36 percent) of variance in rates of child abuse and maltreatment is due to the degree to which mothers are subjected to social-emotional stress without adequate support systems (Garbarino 1976).

Concomitant with the lack of people to support the young parent, there is a plethora of information. Hundreds of books on childrearing, magazine articles, TV parenting shows, parent education classes are available and ready to tell the parent what to do, how to raise a smart child, how to nurse, how to toilet train, how to discipline, and how to be an effective parent (the ultimate challenge). Valuable as this knowledge may be for young parents who doubt themselves and stand on a shaky value base, the often conflicting messages of this vast load of information tend to exacerbate anxieties, and the "musts" on how to be a good parent frequently feed guilt.

It follows that support from society is necessary for all parents, regardless of economic status and ethnic origins, and is most effective when available in the early years. The character of the resources required will inevitably vary from group to group depending upon the levels of need. For some parents it may be the reduction of isolation that will enable them to feel sufficiently gratified in themselves to be able to act on what they know constitutes a good environment for children. For others it may be providing assistance to acquire jobs, housing, and education, thereby enabling success in coping with their lives to replace their sense of powerlessness.

For all, it means offering services that enhance self-esteem and competence, recognizing that lack of confidence inhibits parents' ability to react responsibly to their children.

Family resource centers to support parents can well be justified based on the results of Bronfenbrenner's (1974) comprehensive examination of early intervention programs in which he concludes that "the family is the most effective and economical system for fostering and sustaining the development of the child" (p. 55). He further asserts an ecological intervention "to provide those conditions which are necessary for life and for the family to function as a child-rearing system. These include adequate health care, housing, employment, and opportunity and status for parenthood" (p. 55). Finally, he describes a sequential strategy of intervention including preparation for parenthood before the birth of the child and intervention programs with the prime objective of establishing an optimal reciprocal relationship between infants and parents.

Implementing principles of this kind into programs can perhaps best be translated into a community commitment to construing parent education as supporting parents as people and supporting parents as parents. Key elements of such a program would be that it:

— is available to all citizens regardless of economic status and ethnic origins,
— offers services that enhance self-esteem and confidence,
— is sensitive to cultural diversity and variety in childrearing patterns,
— builds on the strengths of families in order to enhance family functioning,
— reduces parents' isolation,
— assists parents toward coping and managing their environment,
— stimulates parents to develop their own self-help resources,
— is a source for increased understanding of child development and of the significance of the parent/child interaction,

— seeks to promote health,
— serves as an advocate to influence societal forces that affect the lives
of parents and children.

Family Focus: a community-based model

Family Focus is one model program based on these assumptions and designed to serve the family as a whole. Family oriented activities are scheduled in the evenings or on weekends to accommodate working parents, and special efforts are made to provide for the needs of older siblings. Family Focus provides a meeting place, a neighborhood center for multiple age groups and multiple family styles.

With its stress on family advocacy, community interagency linkage, and direct provision of help in behalf of securing necessary support services (health, education, housing, employment), Family Focus fits within the classification of an ecological intervention model. It is flexibly geared to the activities of the community within which it is established, and the extent of its involvement on an ecological intervention level is determined by the needs of the community and the center users.

As a service to families in the earliest years of childrearing, with special emphasis on the parent and establishing positive interactions between parent and child, Family Focus is a primary prevention model. Building on the strengths of parents in these crucial years can facilitate their capacities to provide an environment most favorable to the mental/ emotional and social growth of their child. Support systems ameliorating stress at this time set a groundwork for a good start for both parents and child.

Supporting parents as people

Family Focus is a drop-in center, available to parents at any time during scheduled hours that may be from 30 to 40 hours per week. This is distinguished from a place to go for classes or organized activities, for while it will inevitably encompass both, its quality of open-ended accessibility has unique value to parents. The presence of a place to be with others or to be alone while someone else takes care of your child can be just the relief necessary. The possibility of going where there is a warm welcoming atmosphere created by people who care, where there are no requirements for entry, no forms to fill out declaring your income, state of health, or problems, is both inviting and supportive. The center becomes a place where a parent feels valued as a person whose own needs for fulfillment are recognized and accepted.

The implicit message of a drop-in center, that all parents deserve support, erases special feelings of inadequacy. At the same time, such an environment permits families who might be reluctant to declare themselves at traditional social service agencies to lean on its nonthreatening character and gradually become available for more intensive help.

The peer relationships established frequently lead to the formation of mutual aid networks in which families organize to support each other in ways that lessen the strain of daily living, such as baby-sitting, car pooling, and co-op shopping. The evidence documented in research on depression in women (Pearlin 1975) argues that the incidence of depression decreases with the presence of a strong social network. The center provides a base from which such self-help support groups naturally form.

To adequately address the needs of parents, the center is founded on a firm base of professional expertise and skills. When staff is available to give information as it is sought, assistance when needed, and to serve as a link to other resources in the community, families are strengthened in their ability to cope. Developing trust in staff assures parents that help will be on hand, whether it is for the normal situation of handling the tantrums of a two-and-a-half-year-old or for a crisis situation that has rocked the family. Often for very young parents, staff can assist in planning for such goals as completing school, preparing for and finding jobs, and securing child care. The skills of staff serve to foster the competence of parents toward being masters of their environment.

Parents' sense of self is enhanced by involving parents in every process of the program. When programs are parent-initiated, a respect for parents' point of view is communicated, and increased self-respect emerges for the parent. Parents teach classes in areas of their skills, or discussion groups can have parents as co-leaders with professionals, with each learning from the other. The center is the parents' center, and parents function in planning its growth, making changes, and establishing future directions. Such involvement demonstrates the belief in building on strengths and promotes parents' confidence and competence. Responding to self-determined need reinforces the ability to be self-determining. Therefore, the program grows and develops as parents express their needs and as staff interprets and anticipates what parents seek in order to feel more competent as people. The ability to be responsive, as well as to lead, permits a program to enhance existing strengths.

Each center is linked to community services through an advisory council that represents community agencies working with families, community leaders, and parents. Through these contacts with the community, parents are able to readily get assistance when needed and are, in addition, able to assert themselves in relation to the institutions with which they are involved. It encourages parents to increase their effectiveness in dealing with the people with whom they share the work of childrearing (the teachers, social workers, pediatricians) to make themselves heard, and to move toward competently controlling their own futures. As one parent put it after being urged to talk to the school principal about a situation in which he felt his child had been unfairly treated, "I didn't think I could do it. I made her listen to me and it worked." Whether it is contacting the school administrator or the state senator, advocacy involves a determination to actively take charge of one's life.

Supporting parents as parents

It is generally agreed that effective learning is tied to the relevance of the subject matter to the learner and that learning occurs when the learner is active in the process. When parents' interest and concern determine the timing of classes, group discussions, and activities, the learning is both active and relevant and therefore is more likely to be a source for modifying behavior. On the other hand, as mentioned before, superimposed parent education classes replete with the do's and don't's of childrearing often increase anxiety by raising the spectrum of the possible "awful" things a parent has already done or by setting standards a parent is emotionally unprepared to meet.

Through informal contacts parents often acquire the information they are most ready to learn. Casual social interaction between parents, between parents and staff, and observation of successful encounters other adults have with children can sharply affect parents' behaviors. Group discussions in which parents speak freely of their feelings about being parents and about their childrearing patterns have been most requested in all the communities and most effective. Observable changes occur as parents become responsive to and trusting of the learning environment.

It is obvious that a community center for parents must provide child care of high quality in the kind of environment needed for positive growth and development. Very young children are given the opportunity to expand their spheres into new surroundings, socialize, participate in appropriate activities, and interact with and receive support from other adults. In some instances, children may receive from others the nurturance necessary when parents are temporarily incapable of coping due to crises or problems they are experiencing.

A child care program has significance also for the sake of the parent. Through being able to observe staff interaction with children, it provides a model for parent interaction. Child care becomes a medium for providing parents with information on the basic developmental stages of children, as well as the needs of their individual child.

Groups planned for parents and children together encourage positive interaction by providing situations of mutual enjoyment. Starting from infancy, parents join with their children in age-appropriate activities through which they learn about their children's abilities, how to respond in stimulating ways, and how to understand their children's cues. Good experiences together in the center set the stage for similar ones at home.

The prevention aspect of this child care program is exceptional. It may relieve the parent from the responsibility of child care at a time when tension and frustration make that relief most necessary to prevent the child from being the victim. Child care also serves as an early detection system. Through it parents can be alerted to problems and referred to appropriate resources at the time when a child is very young and able to benefit most from such assistance (see Chapter 3).

Summary

In our highly mobile society, structures of support for the family are declining, with the resultant isolation and lack of linkages with peers and community. Substitutes for these losses must be created to meet not only the crises and day-to-day stresses of parenting but to ensure that growth-enhancing opportunities are available to parents.

Parents generally want to be good parents, and it is not intent but insecurity, anxiety, and difficult life circumstances that interfere with effective functioning. Programs are most effective when focused not solely on teaching skills to parents to teach their infants but on creating an environment in which experiences enhance parents' self-esteem and confidence and therefore affect their behavior toward their children.

All parents are entitled to assistance from the community and society for the challenging task of parenting. Although there is a growing body of knowledge about children in the first years, the avenues for extending this information to the community are limited, and resources for parents of the very young are scarce. Supporting families to enable them to support themselves is a responsibility of society, and whatever serves our families will inevitably and vitally affect our children.

References

Anthony, E.J., and Benedek, T. *Parenthood: Its Psychology and Psychopathology.* New York: Little, Brown, 1968.

Bronfenbrenner, U. *Is Early Intervention Effective? Report on Longitudinal Evaluations of Preschool Programs. Vol. 2.* Washington, D.C.: U.S. Department of Health, Education and Welfare, 1974.

Children's Defense Fund. *America's Children and Their Families: Basic Facts.* Washington, D.C.: Children's Defense Fund, 1979.

Erikson, E. "Erikson Sees Psychological Danger in Trend of Having Fewer Children." *The New York Times,* August 4, 1979.

Gabarino, J. "A Preliminary Study of Some Ecological Correlates of Child Abuse: The Impact of Socio-Economic Stress on Mothers." *Child Development* 47 (1976): 178-185.

Gutmann, D. "Personal Transformations in the Post-Parental Period: A Cross-Cultural View." Paper presented at the annual meeting of the American Association for the Advancement of Science, Washington, D.C., February 1978.

Heffner, E. *Mothering.* New York: Doubleday, 1978.

Howard, A.E. *The American Family: Myth and Reality.* Washington, D.C.: National Association for the Education of Young Children, 1980.

Passman, R. *Current Research on Marriage, Families, and Divorce.* New York: Atcom Publishing, 1979.

Pearlin, L. "Sex Roles and Depression." In *Life Span Developmental Psychology: Normative Life Crises,* ed. N. Datan and L.H. Ginsberg. New York: Academic Press, 1975.

Rice, R. *American Family Policy.* New York: Family Service Association of America, 1977.

Ross, H., and Sawhill, I.V. *Time of Transition: The Growth of Families Headed by Women.* Washington, D.C.: Urban Institute, 1975.

Smith, C.A., and Davis, D.E. "Teaching Children Non-Sense." *Young Children* 31, no. 6 (September 1976): 438-447.

Smith, R., ed. *The Subtle Revolution.* Washington, D.C.: Urban Institute, 1979.

Diana T. Slaughter

Social policy issues affecting infants

The International Year of the Child was declared in 1980 (United States National Commission 1980). Since 1909 White House Conferences on Children and/or Families have been held, and research into childhood growth and development has been conducted over several decades. Where are we now, relative to social policies for child care, in this nation? Have we progressed, retrogressed, or remained constant in our understanding of the needs of children and families? Do we use all the available information in our decision making? Are we equally and appropriately responsive to the needs of all sectors of society? This chapter offers a critical analysis of the issues we confront as we attempt to generate infant care policies for children under age three. Establishing guidelines for such a young group of children is a relatively new experience. However, we should be able to benefit by our successes and failures from such attempts with older children.

Societal trends, related infant care issues, and social policies

Social policies for infant care will be particularly affected by three parallel societal trends involving children and families in the next decade: (1) the movement of mothers into the labor force, (2) the quest for standards for high quality infant care, given scientific research findings, and (3) the burgeoning of underclass families. Each of these trends has specific implications for infant care policies; yet thus far policies have *not* kept pace with these trends.

Movement of mothers into the labor force

Smith (1979) and others have pointed to gradual, subtle changes in the economic and social fabric of American society that call for reorganization of existing child care resources and the generation of new ones. Between 1947 and 1978, the female labor force (those women working or actively seeking work) gradually increased from 20 to 48 percent. The most pronounced increments were observed among married women and in 1979 about 55 percent were in the labor force. Projections for 1990 suggest that married women will constitute an even greater percentage of the labor force, and that, among married women, the largest increase (about 56 percent or 3.1 million) will be among working mothers with children age six or under. By 1990 about 52 million American women are expected to be in the labor force, 11 million more than in 1978. The vast majority of these women will work during their childbearing and child-rearing years (ages 25-54).

A number of reasons have been offered for these trends, and most have implications for parenting and family life styles. For example, Moore and Hofferth (1979) observe that most young women today expect both to have children and to work. As a result, decisions about employment and childbearing patterns are intertwined. Whether she works from necessity or choice, the mother's dilemma will center around the balancing of her needs with the developmental needs of her child. In addition, those born in the late Fifties and early Sixties baby boom will reach childbearing ages around 1990. Therefore, more women who can bear children will be part of the American female labor force by then.

Along with this increase in numbers of working women, there is growing acceptance of nontraditional, nonfamily roles for women. Women can now find more social and educational supports for their occupational aspirations and pursuits. Despite the rather narrow range of jobs usually available, women are finding more options and opportunities.

Many mothers in the labor force are single parents. Smith (1979) notes that 40 percent of all new marriages are now expected to end in divorce, and many children are now spending significant portions of their lives in single parent homes; Edelman (1980) estimates that one of every seven children does so. She states that the children of teenage parents of all social backgrounds are least likely to reside in self-sufficient families. Single parent families, especially those families where the lone parent is in the labor force, have special, continuing needs for child care services.

Between 1969 and 1978, the numbers of Black families headed by women increased from 29 percent to approximately 39 percent (Williams 1980). According to Hill (see Williams 1980), the rise in the number of Black families headed by women accounts for virtually all of the absolute number increases in Black families in poverty over the decade 1969-1978, despite the fact that the majority of Black families (68 percent) depend upon earnings rather than welfare.

In this same decade, White out-of-wedlock births have slightly increased while Black out-of-wedlock births have declined. However, the rates of teenage pregnancy among Black women are more than six times higher than those of White women. The figures for White women probably reflect the increasingly liberalized sexual attitudes in White America. White women no longer fear that they and their child will be stigmatized through an out-of-wedlock birth. Conversely, the figures for Black women probably reflect the continuing social problem of unemployment or underemployment of Black males. Under such conditions, Black males do not make desirable marital partners, and childbearing and childrearing functions are, necessarily and appropriately, dissociated from married life (Ladner 1971). The slight decline in Black out-of-wedlock births, probably because of opportunities for abortion and some improvement in the economic realities of Black community life (especially middle-class Black life, see Wilson 1978), is offset by the numbers of young, poor Black women who continue to be victims of earlier social and economic discriminatory attitudes and practices toward the Black community.

Until recently, if family incomes of White and Black households were contrasted, the income of the working Black woman equated the consumer potential of the single-worker White and two-worker Black households (Slaughter 1972). In 1972 Slaughter predicted that if the majority of White families became multiple-earner families, the participation of Black women in the labor force would no longer ease economic inequities between Black and White families. This prediction is now a reality (Williams 1980), as Black men do not receive wage compensation equal to that of White men. Because Black women are even more likely than White women to hold jobs with lower earnings and status than men, subsidized, high quality child care for these working women could be an especially important benefit to help offset lower wages.

Hoffman (1979) reports that 42 percent of mothers of preschoolers are employed, and more than 33 percent of mothers with children under age three. She notes, as do Moore and Hofferth (1979), that maternal employment need have no negative effects on childhood growth and development. Moore and Hofferth report that the effects of substitute care depend upon its quality, the reasons why the mother chooses to work, the balance of her satisfactions and dissatisfactions with employment, other familial support, and the individual temperament and personality of the children. Employed mothers spend about half the time with their children that full-time mothers do, about three hours per day for children under age three. However, Bronfenbrenner (1979) and Clarke-Stewart (1977) agree that quality of parenting time has more developmental importance than quantity.

Fraiberg (1977) and others do not accept this argument. Nevertheless, the most credible perspective emphasizes how little we know about the relationship between maternal employment and childhood development at this time. For example, Hoffman (1979) notes,

> But while we have learned a great deal about the needs of infants in recent years, we know very little about how maternal employment affects the infant and young child. . . . There is obviously room for more research here. . . . What is happening to the child when the mother is at work? . . . What is the quality of the mother-child interaction when the mother is with the child? (p. 861)

Of four studies Hoffman cites as investigating the effects of maternal employment on early parent-child interactions and infant behavior, two report no negative effects in the first year of life, while one reports negative findings in the second year with language development. In a third study, four-year-old children of working mothers had better social adjustment than the children of nonworking mothers, but sons had lower IQ scores. The fourth study, also of young children, indicated that mother's employment status was not related to the child's competence, but the *most* highly competent children had working mothers who were obviously cognizant of, and sensitive to, how their employment might affect their relationship with their child.

If we are to encourage *optimal parental behavior* in this society, there are social policy implications. Does the female worker receive her fair share of economic and social support? The more satisfied the female worker is with the conditions of her employment, the more beneficial her experiences are likely to prove to be for her family as a whole and her young children in particular (Hoffman 1979; Smith 1979).

At the level of societal or institutional change, Gordon (see Smith 1979) has argued that reforms are needed in both the income tax and social security systems. Presently two-earner married couples pay more taxes when compared with single earners at the same income level, even though there is evidence that they have no greater financial security because they are even more dependent on purchased goods and services, and that they have higher work-related expenses. The marriage penalty actually increases proportionately as income levels rise. Many advocate that married couples be allowed to file as single people.

Further, the social security system has not kept pace with women's increased employment. Wives who work regularly would not necessarily receive significantly more benefits than they might receive if they remained at home because under this latter condition, women are entitled to 50 percent of their spouse's income benefits. Women working part-time and/or at lower-paying positions (the vast majority of women) are most adversely affected by present policies. A gradual, phased-in over 20-to-30-years policy of equal earnings sharing between spouses is advocated to offset these difficulties.

The important point we wish to emphasize is the need for a concept of *family economy* in interpreting the impact of women's work on family life styles and, of course, childhood socialization, behavior, and development. The greater economic independence married women achieve by working will not contribute to their self-esteem unless the benefits of their labors significantly affect their short- and longer-term family economies. The vast majority of married women who work are not career building. Rather, they are striving to maintain or improve the quality of life of their families.

Hill (Williams 1980) observes that male-headed families could only keep up with inflation between 1969 and 1978 if females also worked. Family income over this time period rose by 22 percent among Black Americans, for example, when the wife worked. The comparable figure for White Americans was 5 percent. Conversely, family income relative to inflation declined for both Black (3 percent) and White (1 percent) female single parent families over the same time period. In short, most women work because they have to; whether or not they perceive the experience to be personally beneficial will determine its impact on their young children.

Explicit or implicit public and private industry policies about working women also affect women's vocational choices and life styles. Thus, decisions about childbearing and childrearing are intertwined. When both parents work, given the typical organization of work life (Monday to Friday, 35 to 40 hours a week), there is less time for leisure activities with all family members. Family rituals are, at best, confined to holidays and weekends. The family's needs and the needs of the workplace are increasingly in conflict (Laslett 1979).

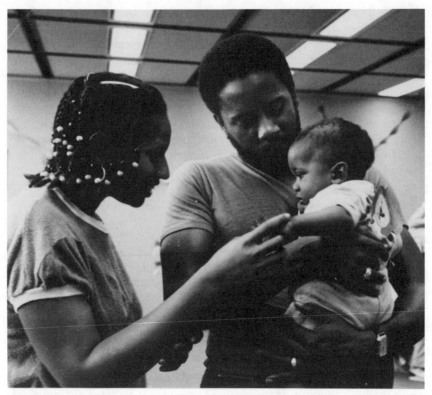

The basic needs of children of racial and ethnic minority families are frequently not met because the existence of those needs is often categorically denied.

Working women are more likely to postpone marriage and childbearing. Family planning services and sex education are available on only limited bases at present. The social supports for infant care in the first two years of life are not available to working women as needed (Hofferth 1979; Smith 1979). Most corporations do not provide for prenatal care, maternity leave, or resources for quality child care.

Importantly, to date there has been no widespread adoption of flexitime or part-time work options in business and industry, although working married women with children experience the least psychological role strain when they have a reduced number of working hours that they can plan or schedule in accordance with their needs and preferred family life styles (Smith 1979). Rather, there appears to be a general expectation that the woman who works will establish a life style that is most like that of a married man who works. Promotional decisions and salary increments are made according to how well the woman, usually without commensurate economic and social supports for working, keeps pace with men in her occupation. There is a desperate need for what Neugarten (1980) has characterized as policies that are responsive to American life styles.

In short, we need fewer policies based on age-linked expectations about individual occupational behavior and productivity. Instead, we need policies based upon family needs as parents of both sexes try to construct their life styles. These policies would link work regulations and guidelines to developmental phases in the life of the family. These new policies would also diffuse the increasing conflict between the family system and the work system.

> The moral of this . . . is that if families were provided the opportunity to make real choices about work versus family and dollars versus hours, both family adjustment and earnings would probably increase, in the short and the long run. Certainly federal and state governments can take the lead in providing good part-time jobs, and incentives might be offered to private industry to do the same. (Smith 1979, p. 155)

What if the mother of the younger child should choose not to work or, more likely in the future, to work on a part-time basis such that additional subsidies might be appropriate to the family from public sources? Keniston (1977) observes that a federally funded experiment in New Jersey from 1968 to 1972 demonstrated that an income guarantee did not discourage the men who participated from working. The welfare poor want to work. There is every indication that Americans would not abuse such an option because of a pervasive work ethic characteristic of even the most impoverished groups. Keniston states that staying at home to rear children is as socially productive as paid work outside the home. In view of our present understanding of the importance of effective early parenting to infant development, this seems to be a particularly crucial point in favor of making it possible for parents of young children to pursue any child care option that is in their own, as heads of a family, and the child's, best interests.

For both Black (McMurray in Williams 1980) and White (Hofferth 1979; Smith 1979) working parents, quality child care is the major support service most needed. This includes infant, preschool, and after-school care. At present, extended family arrangements and family day care, typically of relatively unknown quality, appear to be absorbing this deficit in available services. If parents must work, they should be able to afford care and/or public policies must support quality care. While many of the needs of infants have been discussed earlier in this volume, it is useful to highlight them again to relate them to policy implications.

Toward standards for high quality infant care

The authors in this book have almost uniformly stressed the importance of our increased appreciation of infants' contribution to the early dyadic relationships experienced in view of their special adaptive capabilities. They have emphasized the need for continuity of care, and that the nature of the care does matter in these early months. It seems that the involvement of caregivers with their infants and toddlers in reciprocal, playful interactions that are flexible and verbally stimulating provides the conditions for optimal early learning and development. Caregivers need not be restricted to natural mothers, but they must be sensitive to the developing child's social-affective and cognitive needs. In brief, recent research shows that the capabilities of infants interact with the communicative styles of their caregivers to produce distinctively human beings (Haith and Campos 1977; Kagan, Kearsley, and Zelazo 1978).

Infant care policy issues must identify the many economic and social factors which support or mitigate the creation and maintenance of the optimal human conditions that encourage caregiver responsiveness to the infant's emergent individuality. A major set of factors already identified is associated with the ways in which mothers now participate, and are expected to participate over the next decade, in the American labor force. A second set of related factors has generally to do with how this society apparently regards the social and caregiving needs of its children. Here emphasis is not so much on the shifting role demands placed upon those who are or will become parents but on the relationship between larger social institutions and the needs of the family if it is to effectively perform its nurturant and protective functions. It is useful to examine the infant social development/group day care issue as an illustrative focal point of these problems.

The vastness and diversity of this nation's investment in day care services can be seen in the amount and division of financing for day care. In 1978, about $10 billion was spent in relation to day care services. Two billion of these monies was funded by the federal government, 1½ billion by state and local governments, and 6 billion was paid by children's parents. Approximately 11 percent of publicly funded day care programs provide for the care of children under the age of three (Morgan 1977-78).

Since the numbers of young children who need group care will significantly increase by 1990, the issue is not whether group care is as good as care offered in the home by one's natural parents but what aspects of infant and day care foster the growth and development of the participating children. Research examining the effects of out-of-home care of the infant and toddler on the attachment relationship and the child's subsequent development indicates that this bond between parent and child need not be adversely affected by extended group care, even in the first year of life. However, the child's social, emotional, and cognitive development probably will proceed normally only if the group care is stable and of high quality (Bronfenbrenner 1979; Caldwell 1977; Hoffman 1979). Quality day care can have a beneficial effect on the intellectual development, as measured by IQ tests, of children from lower socioeconomic backgrounds and does not hinder the intellectual development of children from higher socioeconomic backgrounds. Because quality care is often mentioned by researchers and policy makers concerned with the care and development of young children, those aspects of this care that appear central will be compared with those highlighted by existing and proposed federal regulations concerning the care of young children. Two classes of variables affect the care of young children: ecological variables and caregiver-child interactional variables.

One of the most important *ecological* variables affecting the care of children under age three is the ratio of number of children to each available caregiver (caregiver/child ratio). The results of the National Day Care Study suggest that this ratio be 1:4 for children under age three (Ruopp et al. 1979). Under such conditions, research with low-income children indicates that there are few differences between home-reared children and children in group care situations (Caldwell 1977). The caregiver/child ratio is much more highly correlated with classroom behavior and adult-child interactions for children under age three than for older children. In infant-toddler settings, high caregiver/child ratios are associated with reduced management activities and increased interactions with children on the part of caregivers. Children display fewer instances of distress, apathy, and potentially harmful behavior toward each other (Ruopp et al. 1979).

Group size itself was found to be an important correlate of the classroom behavior of children under the age of three and of the frequency and quality of their interactions with adults. Finally, both the age compo-

sition of the children and the physical availability of one adult caregiver
to each child for a one-to-one relationship at least 10 to 15 percent of the
time seem important (Ruopp et al. 1979; Bronfenbrenner 1979; Slaughter
1980).

An extremely important *interactive* factor in quality care is the stability
and continuity of the child's human environment. In child care facilities
there should be a minimum of staff turnover, always gradually introduced. There should also be ongoing, careful, and flexible planning so
that the total environment is responsive to the individual child. An
age-appropriate plan for the continuity and development of educational
activities that encourage the child to develop social, emotional, cognitive, and physical skills should exist. The physical environment should
be structured so that the child can freely and comfortably maneuver
within it.

In regard to the caregiver and child, Bronfenbrenner has stated that
"the ability of caretakers to engage in . . . reciprocal, one-to-one interaction appears to be most effective in meeting the needs and facilitating the
development of the very young child" (Bronfenbrenner 1979, p. 202). For
high quality care, adult caregivers must be physically *and* emotionally
available to the child. They structure activities that include questioning,
praising, and elaborating upon the child's behavior. They label experiences and provide comfort during times of distress. They facilitate
rudimentary turn-taking, exchanges, and contacts with peers and other
older children. This is particularly important up to age three. Between
ages three and five it is important that caregivers establish an educational
environment that complements and extends the child's natural thrust
toward exploration, play, and mastery of the immediate physical and
social world. The responsive adult caregiver understands that the child's
emergent sense of self is predicated upon an emotionally responsive
human environment, which supports the gradual internalization of
social norms of reciprocity and exchange, and the use of this rudimentary sense of selfhood to plan and execute increasingly complex actions.

How do federal regulations and standards currently address the above
guidelines for high quality group care of infants, toddlers, and preschoolers? The answer is simple. They do not.

The proposed HEW Day Care Requirements (HEWDCR) appeared in
the Federal Register on March 19, 1980 (*Young Children* July 1980, p. 64).
These new regulations were built upon the Federal Interagency Day
Care Requirements of 1968 and then modified in 1974. The two main
goals of the HEWDCR were to protect children ages birth to 14 years in

publicly funded day care from exposure to potential harm, and to ensure that they experience conditions believed to promote their development. The regulations covered family day care homes, serving up to 6 children in a home; group day care homes, serving up to 12 children; and day care centers, serving 12 or more children.

Guidelines for services to children were stated broadly. They were intended to encompass family day care homes, group homes, and day care centers, and did not differentiate by age group. Group sizes were regulated according to children's ages, pupil enrollment, and attendance. Educational opportunities appropriate to the child's age were to be provided for every child. Adults providing such care were to have had training or demonstrated ability for working with children. Materials for educational development and creative expression were to be found in each facility; daily activities for each child were to be designed to influence positive self-concept development, and to enhance social, cognitive, and communication skills. However, the proposed HEWDCR did not offer guidelines about how environments were to be structured or specific curricula to accomplish these goals.

Neither HEWDCR nor any other existing or proposed policies addressed the fact that most young children, especially infants and toddlers, are cared for in informal family home care situations (Hoffman 1979). The HEWDCR did apply to family day care homes which were licensed to care for up to five children under age six. However, these regulations only affected day care homes that were federally funded and licensed. State licensing standards regulate the operation of private facilities, but these regulations are generally less stringent than the proposed HEWDCR. Typically, state licensing codes mandate only building, sanitation, and physical health standards.

The 1980 proposed HEWDCR technically went into effect, but congress prevented the Department of Health and Human Services from spending funds to implement or monitor them. As of June 1981, President Reagan's administration has completely abandoned HEWDCR. Any federal regulations for day care now would probably have to be totally reconstructed if there were to be a public demand to issue such regulations. Meanwhile, after over ten years of concentrated public effort, more than 3 million children under age 14 are in programs which have no national standards of child care that even minimally reflect the child development research (Class and Orton 1980; Ruopp et al. 1979; U.S. Congressional Budget Office 1978).

Burgeoning underclass families

The third trend in society that has important policy implications for infant and child care is the possible creation of what some authors (deLone 1979; Glasgow 1981) have identified as a permanent underclass. Glasgow graphically characterizes the Black underclass:

> . . . A war against poverty was launched with the view that in a few years the condition would be eradicated. However, as the sixties waned and the seventies developed, the war was assessed to be an abominable failure as social analysts, sociologists, and social workers pondered why had the poor not been eliminated, and why were there poor people in the seventies, and most disconcerting, why were there to be, and who were to be, the poor in the eighties? . . . Blacks who have consistently represented a disproportionately high percentage of the nation's poor over the past three decades, not only continue to hold this unenviable distinction, but the children and offspring of their families constitute the poor in the seventies and are the projected poor of the eighties. . . . (p. 4)

The basic needs of children of racial and ethnic minority families are frequently not met because the existence of those needs is often categorically denied. For example, until recently most Americans could financially support essential health care services for their children. However, obtaining essential health services has been a continuing problem for minorities, including Black, Chicano, and Native American, as well as Appalachian, children. Prospective mothers in these groups are least likely to receive adequate prenatal and postnatal care. Ladner (1979) and Edelman (1980) both report that infant mortality, for example, is now 70 percent higher for Blacks than for Whites.

Social indicators such as birthrate, maternal mortality rates, likelihood of living below the official poverty level, susceptibility to preventable childhood diseases like influenza and pneumonia, malnutrition, vulnerability to foster care placement, vulnerability to inferior quality schooling, vulnerability to acts of crime and violence, etc., demonstrate that Black children as a group fair less well than White children. Edelman (1977) observes that whenever a practice or policy is found to be pernicious for children, it is likely to be especially so for Black and other minority children. Certainly, for example, minority children have been most severely hurt by the fact that the nation has so long lagged on the Child Health Assessment Program (CHAP). Similarly, despite its credible history, Head Start serves less than 30 percent of the eligible children and families.

Many low-income Black and other minority children and families have the same needs for child care services that other families do. However, their needs are typically not identified as a result of a changing role or life style or of an increased awareness of the capabilities of the children as a result of sound, scientific research, but, rather, they are seen as permanent members of a societal underclass whose needs have, given their life styles, *never* been adequately served by the larger society. Policies made in the name of the broader society, until the Sixties, were exclusionary of these children and families. During the Sixties and the Seventies, as Ladner (1979) notes, many policies were designed to change rather than support the children and their families. These policies were disrespectful in that, logically, children would have been led to reject their own families and communities. Most recently, national and local policies are either neglectful of these children's basic needs (e.g., adequate health and dental care) or misleading. The unassuming, uncritical layperson, for example, is often led to believe that these people "have something [e.g., Head Start programs] I don't," as if any of the early education intervention programs ever reached a significant number of eligible and needy young children (Beller 1978; Huntington 1978). Perhaps most importantly, most of the existing policies are unsupportive of the necessary institutional changes that must be made or solicited when any new programs or policies for minority children are developed.

Toward effective infant care policies: barriers and preliminary successes

There are many barriers to effective social policies for children. Some barriers are sustained by the myths we elaborate upon and perpetuate in our own consciousness (Edelman 1977, 1980). One example is the myth that the modern family can be entirely self-sufficient. Another barrier is that many states implementing Title XX have separated the fiscal and administrative responsibilities to the obvious detriment of the children and their advocates (The Black Child Development Institute 1977). The fragmentation of services to children and families in national and local governmental structures is a major problem. A fourth barrier is the increasing public disaffection with scientific research in general, and behavioral scientists in particular. That research which is conducted is frequently not used effectively in shaping policy. Handler (1980) observed,

> Important to the future of science and technology is the fact that the public has somewhat lost confidence in the ultimate value of the scientific endeavor. It is not that they hold pure science or scientists in any less esteem. But they are less certain that scientific research will inevitably yield public benefit. . . . (p. 1093)

It is precisely when scientists have been most unscientific that the seeds of public disaffection have been sown. Many social programs, for example, were generated in the Sixties to "help disadvantaged children." Yet even now, little developmental research data, longitudinal or otherwise, exist that could be appropriately used to rationalize such a massive effort at social engineering. Now, however, we have concluded that we have not solved the problems of poverty, and we cannot rationalize social programs through empowerment by research findings. Many practitioners have, accordingly, become extremely pessimistic about research in general. Because research cannot immediately impact policy, they would argue, why support the research effort?

From our perspective it is important to keep three points in mind. First, the collection and analysis of data is, or should be, virtually the endpoint of the research process itself. The process governs *how we think about children and families*, what theoretical frameworks and models we bring to bear to the study. These frameworks and models do indeed infuse public consciousness. In part, we identified and labeled children "culturally deprived" because the extant research models and paradigms were so constructed. We impose an inappropriate class of ideas or a mosaic in our discussions of those children and their families. We always need research, therefore, to serve corrective functions; as society changes, so too must the conceptual models which we use to understand it and its members.

Second, there have been some clear instances where research has influenced policy within a relatively short time period. Importantly, these efforts all had what Bronfenbrenner (1979) has identified as one important requirement of ecological validity: the information was obtained in natural, not laboratory, settings. Three examples come to mind: (a) the pioneering work of Kennell and Klaus (Kennell, Voos, and Klaus 1978) in which hospital practices have been shown to affect early maternal-infant bonding by facilitating the development of maternal attachment to the newborn; (b) the research of the national longitudinal

Research results which have influenced policy within a relatively short time period were obtained in natural, not laboratory, settings.

consortium (Beller 1978; Bronfenbrenner 1979), which suggests that, at the least, early intervention programs served to prevent children from being labeled educationally retarded or designated for special education classes; and (c) the general impact of early childhood research over the past 15 or so years upon what we perceive to be necessary and essential to any high quality early childhood program, namely parental involvement; a clearly visible educational component; and consistent, responsive caregiving.

These results, of course, are not what many scientists promised the public and this has become one source of disgruntled, public disaffection. Many promised the public eradication of poverty, and therefore, a reduction of crime and violence in the streets (deLone 1979). These were lofty promises which we now know we could not possibly have realized, if only because we did not know enough about what it was we wished to change. Scientists have a responsibility to realistically educate the public as to what they can reasonably expect of the research process; the public has the responsibility to participate in this process as informing, contributing members of the team, if the data generated are to be grounded in objective reality.

Third, scientists have to think seriously about how, collectively speaking, they can and should affect policy. In the past, their influence has been primarily vulnerable to the opinions and predilections of leading, self-designated scientists. These individuals have been willing to use their personal prestige in their professions in support of children's causes. This approach to policy making, while better than none, is often exclusionary and has weak follow-through potential. One individual arbitrarily defines her or his constituency and is expected to mount all future efforts on behalf of its viewpoint. In the future, scientists need concerted education and training about their *collective*, cooperative professional roles in the political process. Such an approach is inherently more democratic, and also has much more follow-through potential. The establishment of the Social Policy Committee of the Society for Research in Child Development is certainly one example of a positive step in this direction, just as are the various training sites in child development and social policy currently supported by the Bush Foundation. What is at issue, of course, is how to institutionalize such fledgling efforts and how to keep them from becoming self-serving. Such groups must always primarily serve the interest of the scientific study of children, not the interests of the scientists who study children. The former is a universal and enduring issue; the latter is highly particularistic and short term.

We believe that each of the above considerations are pertinent to practitioners and researchers who begin to work toward comprehensive social policies for infants and infant care in this decade. They comprise the experience base upon which we must sketch new, more productive theoretical and research models and form more dynamic and efficient coalitions on behalf of young children. Our success depends upon the *plurality* of perspectives we can bring to the research, and programs we develop and operate, and the *integration* of these perspectives into clear directions and goals for our nation's children.

This chapter was written while the author was a Visiting Associate Professor of Afro-American Studies in the Afro-American Studies and Research Program, The University of Illinois, Champaign-Urbana. The author gratefully acknowledges the support and encouragement of the Program Director, Dr. Gerald A. McWorter. The assistance of Ms. Wendy Stephenson, formerly a student at the School of Education, Northwestern University, is appreciated.

References

Barrett, N. "Women in the Job Market: Unemployment and Work Schedules." In *The Subtle Revolution*, ed. R. Smith. Washington, D.C.: Urban Institute, 1979.

Baumrind, D. "New Directions in Socialization Research." *American Psychologist* 35, no. 7 (1980): 639-652.

Beller, E.K. "Early Intervention Programs." In *Handbook of Infant Development*, ed. J. Osofsky. New York: Wiley, 1978.

The Black Child Development Institute. "Monitoring Services to Children: Title XX." *Urban League Review* 3, no. 1 (1977): 31-36.

Bronfenbrenner, U. *The Ecology of Human Development*. Cambridge: Harvard University Press, 1979.

Caldwell, B. "Child Development and Social Policy." In *Current Issues in Child Development*, ed. M. Scott and S. Grimmett. Washington, D.C.: National Association for the Education of Young Children, 1977.

Clarke-Stewart, A. *Child Care in the Family*. New York: Academic Press, 1977.

Class, N., and Orton, R. "Day Care Regulation: The Limits of Licensing." *Young Children* 35, no. 6 (September 1980): 12-17.

deLone, R. *Small Futures*. New York: Harcourt Brace Jovanovich, 1979.

Edelman, M. "An Agenda for Children." *Urban League Review* 3, no. 1 (1977): 8-15. An elaborated version entitled "The Rights of Children in the 1980's" was also presented at Northwestern University, Evanston, Ill., on April 24, 1980.

"The Federal Day Care Regulations: More to Be Done." Public Policy Report. *Young Children* 35, no. 5 (July 1980): 64-65.

Fraiberg, S. *Every Child's Birthright*. New York: Basic Books, 1977.

Glasgow, D. *The Black Underclass*. New York: Vintage, 1981.

Haith, M., and Campos, J. "Human Infancy." *Annual Review of Psychology* 28 (1977): 251-293.

Handler, P. "Public Doubts about Science." *Science* 208, no. 4448 (1980): 1093.

Hofferth, S. "Day Care in the Next Decade: 1980-1990." *Journal of Marriage and the Family* 41 (1979): 649-658.

Hoffman, L. "Maternal Employment: 1979." *American Psychologist* 34, no. 10 (1979): 859-865.

Huntington, D. "Supportive Programs for Infants and Parents." In *Handbook of Infant Development*, ed. J. Osofsky. New York: Wiley, 1978.

Kagan, J.; Kearsley, R.; and Zelazo, P. *Infancy: Its Place in Human Development*. Cambridge, Mass.: Harvard University Press, 1978.

Kantor, R. *Work and Family in the United States: A Critical Review and Agenda for Research and Policy*. New York: Russell Sage Foundation, 1977.

Keniston, K. *All Our Children*. New York: Harcourt Brace Jovanovich, 1977.

Kennell, J.; Voos, D.; and Klaus, M. "Parent-Infant Bonding." In *Handbook of Infant Development*, ed. J. Osofsky. New York: Wiley, 1978.

Kiesler, S. "Federal Policies for Research on Children." *American Psychologist* 34, no. 10 (1979): 1009-1016.

Ladner, J. "The Black Child: An Overview." *Urban Research Review* 5, no. 3 (1979).

Ladner, J. *Tomorrow's Tomorrow: The Black Woman*. New York: Doubleday, 1971.

Laslett, B. "Production, Reproduction, and Social Change: A Theory of the Family in History." Paper presented at the meeting of the American Sociological Association, Boston, 1979.

Leik, R., and Hill, R. "What Price National Policy for Families?" *Journal of Marriage and the Family* 41 (1979): 457-459.

Moen, P. "Family Impacts of the 1975 Recession: Duration of Unemployment." *Journal of Marriage and the Family* 41 (1979): 561-572.

Moore, K., and Hofferth, S. "Women and Their Children." In *The Subtle Revolution*, ed. R. Smith. Washington, D.C.: Urban Institute, 1979.

Morgan, G. "The Trouble with Title XX: A Review of Child Care Policy." *Hearings before the 95th Congressional Subcommittee on Child and Human Development, 95th Congress, Senate*, 1977-78, Part 2, p. 1282.

National Urban League. "Some Facts about Black Youth." *Urban League Review* 3, no. 1 (1977): 37-38.

Neugarten, B., April 3, 1980: personal communication.

Nye, F.I., and McDonald, G. "Family Policy Research: Emergent Models and Some Theoretical Issues." *Journal of Marriage and the Family* 41 (1979): 473-485.

Ruopp, R.; Travers, J.; Glantz, F.; and Coelen, C. *Children at the Center: Final Report of the National Day Care Study*, Vol. 1. Cambridge, Mass.: Abt Associates, 1979.

Slaughter, D. "Becoming an Afro-American Woman." *School Review* 80, no. 2 (1972): 229-318.

Slaughter, D. "Brief: The Effects of Day Care on Early Childhood Development and Related Social Policy Implications." Invited paper presented to Congresswoman Cardiss Collins, May 1980.

Smith, R. "The Movement of Women into the Labor Force." In *The Subtle Revolution*, ed. R. Smith. Washington, D.C.: Urban Institute, 1979.

Steiner, G. *The Children's Cause*. Washington, D.C.: Brookings Institution, 1976.

United States Congressional Budget Office. *Childcare and Preschool: Options for Federal Support*. Washington, D.C.: U.S. Government Printing Office, 1978.

United States Department of Labor. *Draft: Statistics on Working Women*. Chicago: Bureau of Labor Statistics (Region V), January 21, 1980.

United States National Commission. *International Year of the Child, Report to the President.* Washington, D.C.: U.S. Government Printing Office, 1980.

"Washington Update." *Young Children* 35, no. 5 (July 1980): 66.

"Washington Update." *Young Children* 35, no. 6 (September 1980): 58.

Williams, J., ed. *The State of Black America 1980.* New York: National Urban League, 1980.

Wilson, W. *The Declining Significance of Race.* Chicago: University of Chicago Press, 1978.

Zimmerman, S.; Mattessich, P.; and Leik, R. "Legislators' Attitudes Toward Family Policy." *Journal of Marriage and the Family* 41 (1979): 507-517.

Development." *Abilities of Sexual Behavior*... (1978) 929-938...

Lewis, M. "Early Socioemotional Development and Its Relevance for Curriculum." *Merrill-Palmer Quarterly* 23, no. 4 (1977): 279-286...

Lewis, M. 1977, personal communication.

Lewis, M. and Wilson, C.D. "Infant Development in Lower-Class American Families." *Human Development* 15 (1972): 112-127.

Lambie, ?. "Predictors and Correlates of Two-Year-Old Competence in Preterm Children." Paper presented at the biennial meeting of the Society for Research in Child Development, New Orleans, March 1977.

Lozoff, B., Brittenham, G., Trause, M.A., Kennell, J.H. and Klaus, M. "The Mother-Newborn Relationship: limits of Adaptability." *Journal of Pediatrics* 91 (July 1977).

Lyberger-Ficek, S., and Sternglanz, S.H. "Innate Sex Differences in Neonatal Crying: Myth or Reality." Paper presented at the biennial meeting of the Society for Research in Child Development, Denver, April 1975.

MacNamara, J. "Cognitive Basis of Language Learning in Infants." *Psychological Review* 79, no. 1 (1972): 1-13.

Maccoby, E.E. and Jacklin, C.N. *The Psychology of Sex Differences*. Stanford, Calif.: Stanford University Press, 1974.

Matas, L., Arend, R.A. and Sroufe, L.A. "Continuity of Adaptation in the Second Year: The Relationship Between Quality of Attachment and Later Competence." *Child Development* 49 (1978): 547-556.

McCall, R.B. "Exploratory Manipulation and Play in the Human Infant." *Monographs of the Society for Research in Child Development* 39, no. 155 (1974).

McDonald, M.A., Pederson, ? and Sutherland, J.R. *Looking and Learning: Interaction with Your Baby from Birth to Age ?*. New York: Harcourt Brace Jovanovich, 1975.

McGraw, M.B. *Growth: A Study of Johnny and Jimmy*. New York: Appleton-Century, 1935.

Minde, K., Ford, L., Celhoffer, L. and Boukydis, C. "Interactions of Mother and Nurse with Premature Infants." *Canadian Medical Association Journal* 113, 1975: 741-745.

Moss, ?. "Children and York, Child-Mother Interactions with Regard to the State of the Child." *Journal of Psychology* ?, no. ? (1972): 229-258.

Moore, E. "Language and Visual Stimulation in Early Infancy." *Merrill-Palmer Quarterly* 18 (1972): 239-258.

Moerk, E. "Processes of Language Teaching and Training in the Interactions of Mother-Child Dyads." *Child Development* 47, no. 4 (December 1976): 1064-1078.

Moss, H.A. "Early Sex Differences and Mother-Infant Interaction." In *Sex Differences in Behavior*, ed. R.C. Friedman, R.M. Richart and R.L. Vande Wiele. New York: Wiley, 1974.

Ostrea, E.M., Jr. and Chavez, C.J. "Perinatal Problems (including Neonatal Withdrawal) in Maternal Drug Addiction: A Study of 230 Cases." *The Journal of Pediatrics* 94 (1979): 292-295.

Palmer, F.H. "The Effects of Early Childhood Intervention." Paper presented at the annual meeting of the American Association for the Advancement of Science, Denver, 1977. (ERIC Document no. Ed 148 842, 1978.)

Papousek, H. "Conditioned Head Rotation Reflexes in Infants in the first...

Index

Information about NAEYC

NAEYC is . . .

. . . a membership-supported organization of people committed to fostering the growth and development of children from birth through age 8. Membership is open to all who share a desire to serve and act on behalf of the needs and rights of young children.

NAEYC provides . . .

. . . educational services and resources to adults who work with and for children, including

- *Young Children, the* journal for early childhood educators
- **Books, posters, brochures, and videos** to expand professional knowledge and commitment to young children, with topics including infants, curriculum, research, discipline, teacher education, and parent involvement
- An **Annual Conference** that brings people from all over the country to share their expertise and advocate on behalf of children and families
- **Week of the Young Child** celebrations sponsored by NAEYC Affiliate Groups across the nation to call public attention to the needs and rights of children and families
- **Insurance plans** for individuals and programs
- **Public policy information** for knowledgeable advocacy efforts at all levels of government
- **The National Academy of Early Childhood Programs,** a voluntary accreditation system for high-quality programs for children
- The **Information Service,** a computerized, central source of information sharing, distribution, and collaboration

For free information about membership, publications or other NAEYC services . . .

. . . call NAEYC at 202-232-8777 or 800-424-2460 or write to NAEYC, 1834 Connecticut Avenue, N.W., Washington, DC 20009-5786.

Other NAEYC Publications

For information about these and other NAEYC publications, write for a free publications brochure.

NAEYC
1834 Connecticut Ave., N.W.
Washington, DC 20009-5786
202-232-8777   800-424-2460